HEALTH CARE FOR US ALL: GETTING MORE FOR OUR INVESTMENT

Health Care for Us All challenges the common belief that health care problems in the United States are difficult and possibly insoluble. Americans want to get more for their health care spending, including insurance coverage for everyone that is patient-centered, portable, and permanent. In addition to these two goals, they want a system that respects incentives for high-quality care, exhibits a responsible approach to the budget, and is sustainable. *Health Care for Us All* adopts these five objectives and applies an efficiency filter to identify the virtually unique framework that meets all objectives. Impediments to achieving Americans' goals can be summarized under the rubrics of too little insurance, too little income, and too little properly functioning market. The efficient remedy for each is the subject of the book. Related philosophical as well as economic issues, such as why there should be government involvement in health care, are analyzed.

Earl L. Grinols has been Distinguished Professor of Economics at the Hankamer School of Business, Baylor University, since 2004. He has previously taught at MIT, Cornell University, the University of Chicago, and the University of Illinois. Professor Grinols worked as a research economist for the Department of the Treasury and as Senior Economist for the Council of Economic Advisers. He has extensively published in the fields of finance, public finance, international economics, and macroeconomics. He is the author of three previous books, including *Gambling in America: Costs and Benefits* (2004), also published by Cambridge University Press. He has testified before Congress and numerous statehouses, and his work has been cited by leading newspapers and news outlets including *The Economist, Wall Street Journal, Los Angeles Times, Boston Globe, Financial Times, Chicago Tribune, Philadelphia Inquirer, Time, U.S. News and World Report, Washington Post,* and *New York Times.*

James W. Henderson, Ben H. Williams Professor in Economics at Baylor University, received his Ph.D. from Southern Methodist University. He has taught at Baylor in Waco, Texas, since 1981. Professor Henderson's health care research on diverse issues such as alternatives to pharmaceutical patents, cost-effectiveness of cancer screening, availability of hospital services in rural areas, hospital location decisions, and the cost-effectiveness of prenatal care appears in various places, including *Pharmacoeconomics, Health Care Financing Review, Journal of Rural Studies, Expert Review of PharmacoEconomics and Outcomes Research,* and the *Journal of Regional Science.* His current research includes examining the cost of state-level health insurance mandates. His book *Health Economics and Policy (South-Western)* is now in its fourth edition.

Health Care for Us All

Getting More for Our Investment

EARL L. GRINOLS
Baylor University

JAMES W. HENDERSON
Baylor University

CAMBRIDGE
UNIVERSITY PRESS

CAMBRIDGE UNIVERSITY PRESS
Cambridge, New York, Melbourne, Madrid, Cape Town, Singapore, São Paulo, Delhi

Cambridge University Press
32 Avenue of the Americas, New York, NY 10013–2473, USA

www.cambridge.org
Information on this title: www.cambridge.org/9780521738255

First published 2009

Printed in the United States of America

A catalog record for this publication is available from the British Library.

Library of Congress Cataloging in Publication data

Health care for us all : getting more for our investment / Earl L. Grinols . . . [et al.].
p. cm.
Includes bibliographical references and index.
ISBN 978-0-521-44566-5 (hardback) – ISBN 978-0-521-73825-5 (pbk.)
1. Medical economics – United States. 2. Medical care – United States – Evaluation. 3. Health
services administration – United States. I. Grinols, Earl L., 1951– II. Title.

RA410.53.H4165   2009
362.1068–dc22   2008045749

ISBN 978-0-521-44566-5 hardback
ISBN 978-0-521-73825-5 paperback

For Shelly, Chris, Kimberly, Tom, Lindsay, Josh, and Daniel,
and Luke, Lisa, and Jesse

Help, or at least, do no harm.

Hippocrates (460–377 B.C.)

Contents

List of Tables

List of Figures

Preface

We wrote this book for two reasons. The first is that well-meaning but uninformed proposals to reform the health care system can harm people – *really hurt* those who trust the government experts and politicians to do their public job of selecting health care policy that prevents predictably harmful consequences as conscientiously and as well as they, not in government, do their private ones. People have died because their diseases became untreatable while they waited to be seen by their government health care plan. Others face financial ruin because they encountered medical catastrophes without adequate insurance. People deserve better. Openness, respect, and deference to the individual and the household must be evident in the social institutions and structures involving health care. Professed good intentions are not enough: health care arrangements must be uniformly compassionate, consistently effective, persistently efficient, and financially sound. Creating a system that tends naturally and organically in that direction does not happen by accident. It must be inculcated with sound principles and nurtured by their thoughtful application, coupled with the avoidance of bad principles, before so large and vital a sector as health care can be further affected by political action.

The second reason is that – contrary to widespread belief – it is eminently possible to implement a health care framework for the United States that meets the fivefold requirements of universal access, patient-centered personally responsive portable coverage, respect for incentives for high-quality care, fail-safe cost containment by government of its injections into the health care sector, and sustainability – and to do so efficiently. For the most part, the answers to Americans' health care concerns have been available for a long time. We have tried to be adept in illustrating for the first time the appropriate design of the entire system using components that minds smarter than ours have made available. At the same time, the endeavor is not entirely a simple project of assembling pre-made parts; we also address features that have not received widespread attention, yet are the key to success.

If the answers to America's health care issues are already known in principle, why have they not been acted upon? We think the answer is that the health care debate has been dominated by two groups that are unable to hear each other. Group A consists of academics, health care experts, and economists who have provided suggestion after suggestion in article after article, in testimony after testimony, of what should be done. Some of the finest minds in the nation and world, including Mark Pauly, Peter Zweifel, Alan Enthoven, Patricia Danzon, Regina Herzlinger, John Goodman, Jonathan Gruber, and David Cutler, have clearly illustrated how health care and health care insurance should operate.

Group B consists of individuals who lack the background and tools to make knowledgeable decisions about health care alternatives. Emperor Diocletian is remembered for noticing that wherever the Roman legions marched, the prices of food rose. He determined to put a stop to exploitation of the army, declaring by edict that prices should not rise and there was to be cheapness. He thought that he had taken a necessary and laudable action. How much about supply and demand did he really know?

Many proponents of health care reform from legal disciplines, from medicine, from various nooks and crannies of government, and from the not-for-profit sector have admirable intentions, but they do not understand what they are being told. Like Diocletian, they wish to decree that there be plenty. They do not see why the goodness of their intentions cannot cut through the hazards and obstacles that impede the poor from receiving the health care desired for them. Not truly comprehending the fatal defects in their plans, they ascribe the opposition to their proposals to meanness and selfishness of the opposing political party, the "rich," or various other scapegoats. The resulting public discussions of health care are often characterized by political posturing and so are unproductive – void of learning and the necessary discourse required to move to workable solutions. In this environment, even those who understand the issues are unable to achieve consensus to make forward progress.

A third group, Group C, consists of laypersons in all walks of life who, rightly, want their elected officials to do what they are elected to do: consult the experts, think through the issues, and select the wisest course of action. Our goal is to produce a book that draws the three groups together by explaining in as compelling a way as we can why Group A says what it says, addresses Group B's difficulty in understanding what it hears, and explains what efficiency says about the way health care and health care insurance should be reformed.

How do we propose to move the groups together and fix health care, without creating new problems in the attempt to solve the old? The answer is found in *identifying the precise goals, applying principles that most effectively lead to those goals,* and *being aware of policy triage.*

It is not necessary to re-invent the wheel when very good wheels addressing the purpose already exist. Engineers have known for years that innovations in one field or application get used over and over as the solution to problems in other fields and applications. The repetition of problems and solutions, repeated patterns of technical evolution, and the re-use of existing innovations caused them to think about "how to solve the problem of how to solve problems." *TIPS* is the acronym for "Theory of Inventive Problem Solving."[1] According to the TIPS process, once the essential elements of a problem are identified and isolated, available solutions should be accessed and applied to the solution in the new context. We follow the TIPS principle in this book by applying standard economic solutions – what we call "off-the-shelf" parts – to the objectives laid out in Chapter 2, "Goals," and fill in the gaps with our own chinking and mortar. This protects us from misguided and often overly complicated policy solutions that derive from incremental adjustments to the very structures that do not work now.

Policy triage is another important consideration. On the battlefield, initial medical care is made more effective by giving priority to lifesaving measures. A similar understanding applies to health care policy. In health care there are problems that result from various false structures now in place. Health care policy should not be directed to these problems because they will disappear when the underlying structures causing them are replaced. A second group consists of problems in health care that, while unfortunate, may be intrinsic and not susceptible to policy. Health care policy should not be directed to them either. The problems to which health care policy can and must give priority relate only to features that determine system-wide incentives and behavior. The health care sector (we hesitate to say "market" for reasons discussed in Chapter 10, "Preserving Prices") needs rationalization (in this book we use the term to refer to removal of unreasonable and counterproductive features) and correction to allow it to function as a market. These issues are the battlefield wounded to whom medical attention is

---

[1] Developed in the former USSR beginning in 1946 and now being practiced throughout the world (Mann, 2002), *TRIZ* is the acronym for the same phrase in Russian, where the concept originated. http://www.trizjournal.com/whatistriz_org.htm [accessed 9 January 2007].

devoted. One implication of policy triage is that the reader will not see in this book countless institutionalized details regarding the current (failed) health care market (non-market is a better description). Much of American health care is the result of years of misguided government intervention and tax policy.[2] Fixing the system does not consist of making adjustments to failed structures, but of replacing them with sound ones.

Recall the man who came upon his friend one night diligently searching underneath a street lamp and asked, "What are you looking for?" "My wallet," the friend replied. "Where did you lose it?" he asked. "Over there," the friend said. "Then why are you looking for it here when you lost it over there?" the man asked. "Because I can see better here."

The story is amusing because we know how easy it is to fall into the comfortable trap of pursuing an easy-to-see, though fruitless, remedy when common sense says something else is needed. Health care is like that. Consider 1885 and the desire to improve transportation. The internal combustion engine was already invented, long known to experts, but not widely understood at large. The "experts" would not be serving the needs of progress in transportation if they had devoted themselves to describing the details of leather harnesses and whips, and changes to buggy and horse-drawn wagons that might make marginal improvements. Devising ways to deal with three ruts in dirt roads caused by horse-drawn conveyances may have sounded helpful but, in fact, would represent time poorly spent. No matter how voluminous their treatises or how knowledgeable these experts might be, their knowledge was about to become irrelevant when the way of life that horse and carriage represented was replaced with a more effective mode of transport. In this book we want to reference the fundamentals to see what they imply: the goal is to discover the best way to meet a given list of objectives that we all agree on and, in so doing, to get the most from our investment.

Conclusion

It was tempting to produce a longer treatise filled with theoretical innovations and novel insights. Ignoring whether we would have been capable of the needed profundity, our time and the reader's can be better spent because the main task for the United States is ensuring that everyone has access to needed health care through health care insurance. It turns out that this requires little profundity and is easily accomplished by moving to the

---

[2] Goodman (2007) traces a number of ways that government policy perversely encourages people to make socially undesirable decisions with respect to health care.

fore a few economic principles that accomplish the objective efficiently and lead to a virtually unique framework. *Health Care for Us All* is not intended to be a lengthy review of institutional details, but the description of a sustainable, cost-effective response to the health care dilemma of the uninsured. We have provided only material that we considered necessary to that objective.

In the 1930s Baylor University Hospital instituted a program for Dallas area schoolteachers that provided specific inpatient services for a set monthly premium. The idea was conceptually sound, grew with time, and became the basis of Blue Cross insurance. Today we need a "New Baylor Plan" that has the potential for the success and longevity of the first. We name the plan described in this book the "Targeted Intervention Plan" but speak only for ourselves and implicate no others in the book's content.

The Executive Summary and Chapter 12, "Summary," detail the elements of the Targeted Intervention Plan in short, direct fashion for those who wish to see the end from the beginning. The rest of the book justifies how we got there.

Acknowledgments

Without implicating them in our errors and deficiencies, we would like to acknowledge gratefully the valuable input and suggestions that we received from the following individuals who took time from busy schedules to read the manuscript, discuss, or otherwise provide support and guidance:

John Anderson, Senior Economist, Council of Economic Advisers
Mrs. G. C. Bradstreet, Tampa–St. Petersburg, Florida
Michael Fulmer, Department of Economics, Southern Methodist University
Scott H. Garner, FACHE, Administrative Director, Baylor Master of Business Administration Healthcare Administration
John C. Goodman, President of National Center for Policy Analysis
Anne Grinols, Assistant Dean, Baylor Hankamer School of Business
Bob Helms, Resident Scholar, American Enterprise Institute
Office of Senator Kay Bailey Hutchison
Tom Kelly, Department of Economics, Baylor University
Camille Miller, President and CEO of Texas Health Insitute
David Mustard, Associate Professor of Economics, University of Georgia
Rachel E. Reichard, Aon Corporation
Greg Scandlen, President, Consumers for Health Care Choices
Grace-Marie Turner, President, Galen Institute, Member of Federal Medicaid Commission

We especially thank our editor, Scott Parris, for his input and support of this project.

Portions of *Health Care for Us All* make use of previously published material: Chapter 3: Earl L. Grinols, "The Intervention Principle," *Review of International Economics*, 14, 2, May 2006, 226–247, used with permission; Chapter 11: Earl L. Grinols and James Henderson, "Replace Pharmaceutical Patents Now," *PharmacoEconomics*, 25, 5, 2007, 355–363. (This article has been reproduced with permission from Wolters Kluwer Health Adis. Copyright Adis Data Information BV 2007. All rights reserved.)

Executive Summary of the Targeted Intervention Plan

Universal health care implies that everyone have health insurance and enough income to buy it. The intervention and incentive symmetry principles determine the efficient way to extend coverage. Patient-centered care and respect for the patient require that the patient be the center of the financial arrangements for health care. Health care is a private good, except for relatively limited public health aspects (e.g., epidemics and spread of disease). Standard welfare economics applied to economies with private and public goods[1] suggests that healthy markets are the efficient mechanism for distributing private goods. Health care markets and health insurance markets have correctible problems that are part of the fix. Next, incentive compatibility for efficient income transfers so all can afford insurance suggests the need to distinguish between the capable and incapable needy. A modification of the Earned Income Tax Credit has desirable features for income transfers. With individuals all having enough income to buy health insurance, and being efficiently incentivized to do so, there remains only the issue of government budget management and framework sustainability. These are delivered by a provider revenue tax and the fact that consumers buy their insurance on an actuarially fair basis and buy their health care at competitive prices. These arrangements are indefinitely sustainable and treat all individuals fairly and alike. For most consumers, who surveys show are happy with their insurance and health care arrangements, nothing changes. The framework merely intervenes at the minimal number of points to accomplish all of its selected objectives efficiently.

---

[1] We use the terms "private good" and "public good" in their technical sense. A "private good" provides benefits only to the one consuming. Consumption of a private good by one individual prevents it from being consumed by another. "Public goods" provide benefits to everyone, because public goods can be simultaneously consumed by many. National defense is a public good because the service of "safety" provided to one can be consumed by many at the same time.

1. Every American voluntarily buys adequate, basic health insurance.
2. Everyone can afford insurance and everyone receives an economic benefit for its purchase.
3. Government defines the basic policy. Risk groups are defined by age, sex, and geographic location.
4. Participants can change health plans at any time.
5. Health insurance policies:

    (a) Are priced on the basis of actuarial fairness and competition.
    (b) Cover insurance events plus the risk of reclassification into a higher risk status.
    (c) Guarantee renewability at the same price for all in one's risk group.

6. Government budget outlays are predictable and sustainable and contain no unlimited entitlements or uncontrolled net expenditures.
7. Pro-competitive policies reform the health care and health insurance markets, including the following:

    (a) Incentives for high-quality care are present.
    (b) Health care providers post prices.
    (c) Prices for identical service must be offered by a health care provider on the identical terms it offers to all buyers.
    (d) Insurers have freedom to underwrite and compete in insurance markets.
    (e) Insurance users are protected from unfair practices.

8. Those with satisfactory insurance through place of employment or self-purchase may continue current arrangements. Medicare, Medicaid, and State Children's Health Insurance Programs may be replaced by the program if desired.

The Targeted Intervention Plan takes an efficiency perspective. Efficiency means selecting methods to accomplish a given objective at least cost, or, equivalently, with the highest possible citizen well-being. An efficient outcome is one for which it is impossible to improve one individual's well-being without harming another's. Efficiency rules out certain ways of doing things and accepts others.

I. **Universal Coverage.** Individuals who buy health insurance meeting the minimum standard are rewarded in the form of lower prices for their non-health-insurance purchases.

- The price advantage conferred by health insurance is an efficient inducement to buy insurance. This means that other means to the same objective have higher social costs (or, at best, the same costs).
- Using the incentive symmetry principle (see Section 3.2, Principle 2: Incentive Symmetry), there are different ways that an efficient incentive to buy insurance can be implemented. We find attractive the one that requires no program budget outlays to support the price differential and impacts *only* those who do not buy insurance. See discussion of the *Subsidy Version* in Section 8.1, The Plan. Because no one needs to pay any tax related to the program, the price differential can be made as high as needed. When it accomplishes its objective, it is a self-erasing intervention that collects no revenue and necessitates no budget outlays.
- It is wastefully inefficient to subsidize everyone's health insurance purchases – creating tax deadweight loss and distortions – just to affect a few who do not now buy coverage.[2] Were everyone's insurance purchase to be subsidized as in a refundable tax credit (contrary to the proposal here), it would no longer be possible in future periods to distinguish those who would buy insurance without government help from others. In the Targeted Intervention Plan, the incentivized non-compliers self-identify.
- If efficiently inducing the uninsured to buy health insurance is dropped as an objective, then the price-differential-incentive intervention described here can also be dropped.

II. Income Support. To address equity issues, everyone will have enough income to buy health insurance, made available in a separate, efficient, and incentive-compatible way.

- Many of the perceived "problems" of health care are not health care problems, but problems of too little income that can be better addressed through dedicated income programs. Separate problems require separate solutions.
- Income of the capable needy is augmented by an amount that, combined with their other income, is sufficient for them to buy health insurance. A modification of the Earned Income Tax Credit is consistent with proper work incentives.

---

[2] There must be special reasons for government to take money not needed for government functions and give it to others. Government charity creates false incentives (see Section 5.3, Summary on Public Provision of Private Goods and Charity). However, if one posits that everyone must have health insurance, then the most efficient means to enable people to have enough income to do so must be used.

- The incapable needy are not susceptible to work incentives and so may be provided direct income aid.

III. **Market Rationalization.** Key changes to the way health care is bought and sold and to the way health insurance is bought and sold are critical. It is not possible to expand health insurance coverage beneficially if the insurance market and health care sectors are not also adequately reformed. Imposing expensive, unaffordable insurance through a badly designed plan and unreformed market can be worse than no plan at all (see Appendix B, "Badly Done Insurance Programs Can be Worse Than No Insurance").

   Enhanced competition means that insurance will be patient centered and personal. Other proposed changes make it portable and permanent (see Section 8.1, The Plan).

- The Basic Health Insurance Policy
   - **Freedom to Underwrite.** A national framework for health insurance cannot depend for its success on insurance companies acting against their own interests. Entry and exit are critical to market contestability and competition. Underwriting freedom allows competition to improve service, deal effectively with moral hazard, and lower administrative overhead costs.
   - **The Base Policy.** The base insurance policy coverages must be allowed to vary by age and sex to keep prices low and fair. The base policy is sold by an insurance company to all members of the same risk class (age, sex, location) at the same price, eliminating adverse selection issues for base insurance.
   - **Guraranteed Renewability.** Guaranteed renewability at standard rates is enforced for all health insurance policies. A national re-insurance mechanism (see the discussion of guaranteed renewability in Section 7.2, Time and the Uninsurable, and Section 8.1, The Plan) allows individuals to change providers consistently with guaranteed renewability.
   - **Homogeneous Risk Pooling, Actuarially Fairly Based Premiums.** Homogeneous risk pooling and actuarially fairly based premiums are good insurance tenets. Competition keeps prices to the lowest feasible.
   - **No Utilization Gatekeeping.** No gatekeeping is a freedom-of-choice provision. If insured individuals wish to purchase a covered service and are willing to pay the required co-pay or co-insurance rate, then they may decide to do so. This rationalization will cause

the base insurance policies to be devised with moral hazard kept foremost in mind.

– **Source Tax Neutrality.** Tax neutrality implies that individual purchase of health insurance is kept on a tax basis comparable to insurance offered through place of employment.

– **Affordability Safeguards.** The base health insurance product is kept affordable several ways. The mandated base coverage (insurance meeting the minimum standard introduced in Section I, Universal Coverage, of this summary) incorporates only features that are premium-reducing (such as selected preventive care) and needed. Pre-paid (routine) care is excluded from the base policy (unless such care is premium-reducing). Unwanted, unneeded, and purely elective benefits are excluded from the base policy. When individuals are appropriately insured in homogeneous risk pools (rated by age and sex), the problems of making insurance more expensive than it is worth to the insured largely disappears. For example, requiring 20-year-olds to pay for colonoscopies and heart bypasses of the elderly could easily make their policies too expensive relative to what they are worth because they are paying for procedures that they rarely use and do not benefit from. However, even if colonoscopies are included in basic plans for all age groups, they will become significant in pricing only for those in the older risk pools. Those in older pools, however, want such coverage because they use it with higher frequency.

– **Insurance Connector.** An "insurance connector" (see Section 9.2 for discussion of the Massachusetts connector) serves an efficiency function by facilitating information flows.

– **Other.** Price transparency, freedom of sourcing by the insured (see Section 8.1, The Plan, Step 4), and insurance portability by the insured (supported by a re-insurance mechanism; see discussion of Section 8.1, Table 8.1) are other safeguards to effective insurance (see Section 7.2, Essential Insurance).

• Health Care
Efficiency-creating, pro-competitive rationalizations are desirable. We list here only two that taken by themselves would transform health care competition.

– **Price Transparency.** In a rationalized market, providers have the freedom to set prices however and in whatever manner they choose. However, their prices must be transparent and posted.

— **Most Favored Customer Pricing.** Providers must charge one customer on the same terms that they charge to their most favored customer. The effect of a most favored customer clause in health care will be that concessionary prices negotiated in the market for one buyer will be made available to all buyers on the same terms. Competition and most favored customer pricing will result in prices near marginal cost, as a rational market should have. Because government has ability to impose prices that the marketplace does not, Medicare and Medicaid prices would need to be treated differently.

IV. Sustainability and Government Budget Control

- **Provider Revenue Tax.** A provider revenue tax is essential to access cost-shifting dollars already in the health care system and re-direct them to a more efficient means of covering the "top-off costs" (see Chapter 1, Introduction, and Glossary and Definitions) of universal coverage.

- **Budget Control.** Government support enters the health care and health insurance sectors through income transfers, A. If B is *removed* from the health care sector and is a program choice, then government net expenditure, $(A - B)$, is a program choice. Since B subtracts from the sectoral revenue stream, it must be implemented as a revenue tax on health care providers and insurers.

- **Sustainability.** When government provides income support in an amount that covers top-off costs, it fully pays for the additional health care usage of the newly covered population. With everyone paying actuarially fair prices for health insurance and the health care sector receiving revenues sufficient to cover its costs of health care provision, the program does not depend for its success on agents acting against their own interests. Moreover, by separating efficient inducement to buy health insurance from income support, the program sits on its own base (see Section 3.3, Principle 3, Every Pot Sits on Its Own Base), does not governmentalize (see Section 3.5, Principle 5, No Governmentalizing), and is not a Ponzi scheme (see Section 3.6, Principle 6, No Ponzi Schemes). Such a program is indefinitely sustainable (see Section 2.5, Goal 5, Sustainability).

PART I

GOALS AND WORKING PRINCIPLES

ONE

Introduction

I do not believe in a fate that falls on men however they act; but I do believe in a fate that falls on them unless they act.

G. K. Chesterton, English author (1874–1936)

Summary: *Many despair of solving the health care crisis in America, currently defined by the presence of large numbers of uninsured, large numbers of indigent and other limited-pay and no-pay users, rising costs, questionable quality, and budgetary challenges exacerbated by an aging baby boom generation. The problems are real, but the despair is unfounded.*

Working from the requirements that Americans say they want their health care system to satisfy and applying economic principles to meet these stated objectives identify a unique framework within which options for implementation can be selected. The key to a self-sustaining program is respecting the relevant principles and intervening at the minimal set of system points required to accomplish the objectives.

There is growing recognition that the time is at hand for serious action on American health care policy. Even though 8 out of 10 Americans are happy with their own medical care experiences,[1] approximately the same percentage are concerned that the U.S. health care system is not functioning as it should for others and requires serious attention. At the time of writing, the Census Bureau estimates that 15.8 percent of Americans are without health insurance at any point.[2] Because almost 60 percent of all uninsured were employed in full-time or part-time jobs, it is a fair approximation to say that over 75 percent of the uninsured have some labor force connection – through their own employment or that of a family member.

While the public hopes that its leaders will take prudent steps to overhaul the system, they fear that bad decisions, partial measures, and political

---

[1] Blendon, et al., 2006.

[2] Out of a total population of 297.437 million, 46,995 million were reported to be uninsured at some point during the year. See U.S. Census Bureau, 2007.

3

agendas might make matters worse. In addition to the problems themselves, the planning failures of the early 1990s are still on the minds of many. Government is engaged with many problems, of which health care is only one. Most legislators know that the solution to health care cannot be the creation of an unending, untenable, and unsustainable budgetary burden: the public purse cannot solve the problem of health care; health care must solve the problem of the public purse. There is need for guidance and a workable course of action. Health care providers, the public, and government need to find consensus in a framework that is sustainable and implementable.

We have been taught that solving the health care problem in the United States is difficult. It is not. Health care issues are neither complicated nor, on the whole, hard to understand. It is possible to guarantee that everyone's health is insured with good coverage, provided in a sustainable way that reduces costs relative to the present, does not require large government budget participation, and imposes minimal limitations on the freedom of choice – for consumers and providers alike – without needing particularly vast sums of money.

The first step to finding the most desirable framework for activity is to identify the specific goals we want achieved, understand why collective action is needed, identify the agent of action (some or all of markets, voluntary private organizations, or government), and establish a road map to the desired destination. Packing for the journey will follow after we know where we are going.

The foundational assumption of this book, and of our work as economists, is that people know what is in their own best interest. This is not a statement of faith about perfect omniscience, but rather the understanding that the large majority of people, most of the time, know best what they want, and for virtually all those who do not, that circumstance is temporary. This suggests that while many people have dwelled on various aspects of the health care system as the source of our problems – employer-provided insurance that causes holders to lose coverage at just the time they may be losing their jobs comes to mind – we should cut away from secondary issues and go to the heart of the matter: *many people have no health insurance, and some of them truly cannot afford it.* The first is an insurance problem and the second is an income problem. Those who confuse the two run the risk of solving neither, or at best solving neither well. Our goal is to create incentives that will induce everyone to purchase insurance, will enable that purchase for those who truly need enabling, and will not provide aid to anyone else. Solutions to the two problems should not be inappropriately comingled.

We view the Targeted Intervention Plan (TIP) as a framework. As with the steel frame of a skyscraper, once a framework is erected that is compatible with the type of building being constructed, finishing choices can be made to suit the preferences of the users. As noted in the Preface, the intellectual content of the TIP owes much to the work of others. From them we have learned why there are a right way and many wrong ways to implement collective action in health care. In the remainder of this chapter we summarize the dimensions of the problem. Our message is an optimistic one.

Insurance status varies greatly by groups as shown in Table 1.1. For example, almost 30 percent of all 18- to 24-year-olds are uninsured, along with almost 27 percent of the 25- to 34-year-olds. Among native-born whites (non-Hispanic) the percentage is only 10.8. In contrast, 34.1 percent of

Table 1.1. *Individuals without Health Insurance by Characteristics, 2006*

Group	Uninsured (000)	Percentage of group that is uninsured	Group uninsured as percentage of total
All persons	46,995	15.8	100.0
Nativity			
Not a citizen	10,231	45.0	21.8
Naturalized citizen	2,384	16.4	5.1
Native citizen	34,380	13.2	73.2
Race			
Hispanic origin	15,296	34.1	32.5
Black	7,652	20.5	16.3
Asian and Pacific Islander	2,045	15.5	4.4
White, Non-Hispanic	21,162	10.8	45.0
Age			
Under 18 years	8,661	11.7	18.4
18 to 24 years	8,323	29.3	17.7
25 to 34 years	10,713	26.9	22.8
35 to 44 years	8,018	18.8	17.1
45 to 64 years	10,738	14.2	22.8
65 years and over	541	1.5	1.2
Income			
Less than $25,000	13,933	24.9	29.6
$25,000 to $49,999	15,319	21.1	32.6
$50,000 to $74,999	8,459	14.4	18.0
Over $75,000	9,283	8.5	19.8

Source: U.S. Census Bureau, 2006.

those of Hispanic origin have no insurance. Among non-citizen Hispanics the uninsured level is even higher, at 45.0 percent. And almost two-thirds of all illegal immigrants lack health insurance.[3] Finally, it is not accurate to assume that only the poor are uninsured. Almost 38 percent of the total uninsured have household incomes that exceed $50,000 per year.

In truth, the number of uninsured may be significantly smaller than 47 million, perhaps less than half that number,[4] depending on which survey and data source you use. Regardless, the precise numbers change from year to year, and our purpose is to show what they imply. We intentionally have rounded up some of the numbers, addressing the worst case to be on the safe side in presenting our optimistic message.

The most persistent finding in studies of the composition of the uninsured population is that its membership is constantly changing. Those uninsured today are not the same group that was uninsured last year. Being uninsured is a temporary phenomenon for most people. Robert Bennefield estimated that one-half of all spells without insurance last less than 5.3 months.[5] Similarly, Craig Copeland estimated that approximately two-thirds of the uninsured population are re-insured within less than one year.[6] But while being without insurance is a temporary phenomenon for most, there is a persistent group that remains chronically uninsured.[7]

Uninsured individuals nevertheless use health care resources, though they use fewer resources than individuals with full coverage use. The average uninsured spends on health care roughly half of what the average American spends. For example, one reason the uninsured, as a group, tend to use less health care is that they include a larger proportion of younger people than the population at large. Approximately 14.5 percent of American gross domestic product (GDP) is devoted to *personal* health care expenditures that would be expected to rise were uninsured individuals to become insured.[8] Were uninsured individuals to become insured, their use

---

[3] Derose, Escarce, and Lurie, 2007.

[4] The number of uninsured may be 21–31 million rather than the higher numbers often reported. See Congressional Budget Office, 2003.

[5] Bennefield, 1998.

[6] Copeland, 1998.

[7] Short and Graefe, 2003, estimated that this group numbers approximately 10 million, or about 3 percent of the U.S. population.

[8] In 2004 total personal health care expenditures were $1,696.896 billion, or 14.521 percent of GDP (GDP = $11,685.9 billion, Table B-1, *Economic Report of the President*, February 2008). Including expenditures for research, structures and equipment, and public health activity, which are not personal expenditures, raises the total to $1,877.622 billion, or 16.07 percent of GDP ("National Health Expenditures," in *Health Guide USA*, http://healthguideusa.org/NationalCosts.htm).

of health care resources would rise by approximately one-half.[9] As a percentage of income, the extra cost of full insurance coverage to the nation – what we call in this book T, the "top-off cost" – is therefore less than $0.0058 \times GDP$, or 58 one-hundredths of 1 percent of GDP.[10] This calculation is consistent with increased usage of medical care by each uninsured person of 25 percent of typical full usage.[11] Even if the figure 0.58 percent is imperfect, adjusting it to the extreme limit in which usage would rise by 50 percent of typical usage means that T is barely more than 1 percent (1.16 percent) of income.

What does this mean for extending coverage? First, not all of this amount would have to be provided by public dollars, because many uninsured can afford to pay for their own coverage. Some uninsured are temporarily between jobs and can afford transition coverage. Others in transition do not know that they are effectively covered by medical insurance for two months[12] and mistakenly report that they are uninsured during this period. Many uninsured earn incomes above $75,000 annually. Kate Bundorf and Mark Pauly conclude after careful consideration that at least 28 percent, and perhaps as many as 71 percent, of the uninsured can afford coverage.[13]

Treat Disease, Not Symptoms. Sometimes when a system fails at one point, everything else about it appears to need attention. Scarlet fever is caused by the Group A Streptococcus bacterium. It often is accompanied in an infected child by a reddened sore throat, fever above 101 degrees

---

[9] Marquis and Long, 1994/95, estimate that the uninsured increase their health care spending by 50 percent when they get insurance. Estimates of one-third have also been reported. In the most recent study of which we are aware at time of publication, Hadley, Holahan, Coughlin, and Miller, 2008, Exhibit 5, simulate increases of 38.4 percent and 117.6 percent for part-year uninsured and full-year uninsured. Since the uninsured consist of both groups, their figure for increased spending would be 69.9 percent.

[10] $0.5 \times 0.5[(Health\ expenditure/Uninsured\ capita)/(Health\ expenditure/Capita)]$
$\times 0.16\ [Uninsured\ capita/Capita] \times 0.14521\ GDP$
$= 0.0058\ GDP$

[11] $0.5 \times 0.5 = 0.25$ in footnote 10.

[12] The Consolidated Omnibus Budget Reconciliation Act (COBRA) of 1986 provides that an ex-employee may pay the former employer the cost of insurance and stay on the company's medical insurance plan. The election is made within 60 days of job termination by delivering the appropriate payment for insurance to the employer. Various provisions of COBRA effectively extend this period to two months with retroactive election, even when medical events have occurred within 60 days after employment.

[13] Bundorf and Pauly, 2006.

Fahrenheit (38.3 degrees Celsius), swollen glands in the neck, chills, body aches, loss of appetite, nausea, and vomiting. Tonsils and the back of the throat may be covered with a whitish coating, and the tongue may have a whitish or yellowish coating that later in the infection turns red, when its surface begins to peel. In fact, all symptoms will disappear when the root cause bacterium is killed – a simple process using modern antibiotics.

Second, making corrections to other aspects of the health care market– "rationalizing" the market – has the potential to produce savings approaching 2 percent of national income.[14] Economists would classify these as "moral hazard" gains (see the Glossary and Definitions and Chapter 7, "Insurance"). Market rationalization will also lead to lower-cost health insurance for many of those now uninsured. If the market is rationalized at the same time changes are made so that everyone is covered by insurance, the change in total spending on health care to the nation can be zero or negative.

The modest top-off costs perhaps explain a certain disappointment that many show about the failure to take action regarding health care insurance coverage. On the other hand, it is easy (and tempting) to write shortsighted legislation that instead of providing only essential – usually temporary and partial – aid to a fraction of the population offers inessential permanent full coverage to nearly everyone. This, of course, is not providing top-off costs, but much more.

Figure 1.1 graphically displays the health care market. The horizontal axis measures the size of the insured and uninsured populations. The vertical axis measures cost of care: the arrow to the right shows the true

---

[14] Traditional "major medical insurance" consisted of a list of covered services, a deductible, a co-insurance amount, and an out-of-pocket limit. Individuals with traditional insurance had an incentive not to solicit health care that was worth less to them than what they paid for it. Modern insurance contains features that are not true insurance, but rather are pre-paid care (see Section 7.2, "Essential Insurance"), which reduces users' personal out-of-pocket costs to zero. Overuse of medical services is wasteful. Studies of the effect of returning to traditional insurance products suggest that savings on the order of 5–15 percent of current expenditure levels are possible (RAND, 2005). Milton Friedman (Friedman, 1991) earlier had estimated that just two changes – moving to higher deductibles and eliminating the tax preference for employer-provided insurance – would lower national medical spending by 5 percent of GDP. Since national income devoted to personal health care expenditures is currently 14.5 percent of GDP, savings are potentially $0.15 \times 0.145 = 0.0217$, or 2.17 percent of GDP. Actual savings would be smaller because some plans already incorporate the beneficial effects discussed here.

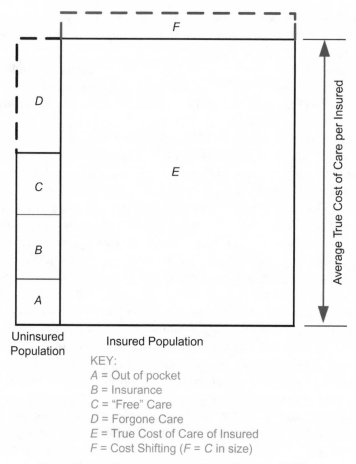

Figure 1.1. Pre-Program Costs and Embedded Cost Shifting

cost of care for an average insured individual. Area *E*, therefore, measures the health care costs of the insured population. The insured are currently charged for more than the true cost of their care because they are paying cost-shifting dollars (area *F* above area *E*) tacked onto the care they get. This money covers care given to the indigent, limited-pay, and no-pay consumers.

The size of the population of uninsured is displayed on the left of the diagram by the horizontal distance from the lower left corner. Areas *A* through *D* explain how the uninsured cover their care. Area *A* is usage by the uninsured paid through out-of-pocket expenditures by the uninsured, and area *B* represents care paid by insurance payments (Recall that roughly half of the uninsured are uninsured for only part of the year)[15] and area C is "free care" that is paid for by cost shifting. Area C, therefore, equals area F in size. Area D is forgone care.

Figure 1.1 is not drawn to scale. Were it more detailed, we would separate the uninsured into full-year uninsured and part-year uninsured, and we would separate insured into the Medicare/Medicaid population and the privately insured population.

Returning to the figure, area D represents the "top-off costs" or forgone care of the uninsured. We draw area D as if the uninsured after becoming insured use the identical level of care per person as the insured do. As noted, they likely would use less because they are a statistically different population mix than the insured group, which includes Medicare and elderly patients.

The calculation of top-off costs T indicates that area D is roughly 1/2 to possibly slightly more than 1 percent of GDP. How is area D paid for in a well-designed framework? First, include incentives that cause the retention or enlargement of areas A and B because the uninsured include large numbers of people who can afford to purchase insurance and cover more of their own care. Second, include mechanisms that collect the money contained in area F and translate it into the program budget so that current cost-shifting dollars support the purchase of insurance by the fraction of the population that needs such aid. With the right framework, top-off costs will be all that is needed in addition to what the public is already paying. The TIP meets these requirements.

Figure 1.2 displays post-program finances. Both groups now have insurance and, as users and buyers of health care services, are indistinguishable to providers. The payment for care is also the same for both groups, meaning that everyone now pays for the true cost of his or her care plus a small uniform premium shown as area H. (More information about the rationale for the arrangements and its benefits is provided in Chapter 8, The Targeted Intervention Plan, and Appendix D, Plan Workability.) Rather than the sick paying cost-shifting dollars as in Figure 1.1, in the post-program world, the public cost of the program is spread proportionately to everyone.[16] The effective cost of care to the newly insured is not really area $A + G$ because a portion of area G is program aid for insurance purchase.

The program budget is met via a revenue tax that is nominally levied on all health care suppliers and providers. However, we hasten to note that because providers and insurers are free to set their prices, they naturally

---

[15] Hadley and Holahan, 2003, say 41 percent.

[16] Note that insurance premiums reflect insurance benefit outlays and thus each individual who buys insurance – that is, everyone – contributes to area H.

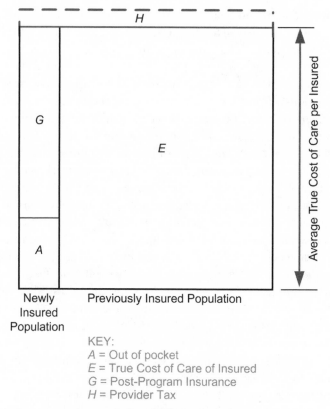

Figure 1.2. Post-Program Costs and Financing

pass on costs to consumers, who are the real payers in the form of higher prices. While we do not expect any tax to be popular a revenue tax is not an arbitrary choice and must be understood in context. The reasons are described in more detail in Chapter 8, "The Targeted Intervention Plan." However, we provide a few here, not least of which is that a revenue tax (1) treats all health care users (i.e., everyone) the same with respect to the elements of the program; (2) is appropriate because health care providers and insurers are recipients of public dollars through their sales to public aid recipients; (3) is needed to access cost-shifting dollars already in the system; and (4) is required to give government the ability to execute prior control over its net expenditures assigned to the program.

The goal is to pay for top-off costs in a fair manner; various details can be implementation choices. For example, should insurers be included in the base? To answer, presume care of $100 in equilibrium where a levy of

$3 is applied to providers and so insurance outlays for the care are $103. If insurers also pay a levy of $3, consumers pay premiums of $106. If instead, providers pay no tax, the same outcome is reached if insurers pay a levy of $6 with consumers paying premiums of $106 – exactly as before. Care is unchanged and final cost to consumers is unchanged. Other equivalent arrangements are possible. Because all consumers are the ultimate payers, it is immaterial whether the base is stated to include providers only, insurers only, or both. The taxes have a real impact, but it is the same regardless of how the base is stated. The choice of base is accounting labeling only and not substantive. In particular, the tax is not a tax on sick people because everyone has insurance whose premiums reflect payments to providers.

At what point the tax is levied is a policy implementation choice. We choose to levy it at the same rate on insurers and providers. Area H in Figure 1.2 represents the 3–4 percent provider revenue tax. Some of area H is already being paid as cost-shifting dollars in the pre-program world, so the net burden of the program consists of the top-off costs discussed earlier. If market rationalization occurs at the same time – as called for in the Targeted Intervention Plan – the arrow on the right will shrink as health care expenditures fall. The actual impact of extending coverage on total health care expenditures will therefore be smaller.

A program along these lines is feasible and unburdensome if implemented in a way that is consistent with the schematics in Figures 1.1 and 1.2. Indeed, Chapter 9, "Forestalling Free Riders," explains that a similar program has been at work for years in Switzerland. If instead, however, arrangements are selected that result in 100 percent coverage being given to the uninsured group and, furthermore, some of the previously insured become program beneficiaries, the cost of area $A + G$ plus an undetermined part of area E becomes the program obligation. This point bears emphasis. David Cutler and Jonathan Gruber (2006), for example, estimate that for every dollar of Medicaid expansion in the 1990s, private coverage was reduced by 50 to 75 cents. In other words, because of the way the expansion was implemented, providing for those without coverage cost *two to three times* the cost attributable to those originally without coverage.

This phenomenon is called "crowding out" because the public program supplanted or "crowded out" private coverage. In poorly crafted programs with substantial crowding out, the issue becomes politicized and economics is less able to predict what the program will be and its ultimate costs. On one extreme are those who fear that *any* collective action by politicians to federalize or governmentalize health care will result in eventual nationalization of 15–16 percent of the American economy. Combined with the 31 percent of national income that is already spent by federal, state, and local government, this would imply that a much larger percentage of the economy would be government administered. Every dollar run through a government program costs the economy more than a dollar because its budget must be raised in taxes.[17] A badly designed program can be worse than no program at all. This possibility is discussed in more detail in Appendix B, Badly Done Insurance Programs Can Be Worse than No Insurance.

Mushrooming Costs. In recent years, federal taxes have been 16.5–18.5 percent of GDP. Few Americans realize that the bottom 55 percent of income tax filers contribute in total less than 1 percent of income taxes paid. (This is 0.08 percent of GDP.) In comparison, the 5 percent of highest-income filers contribute 59 percent.[18]

If a government program to provide health care to all uninsured is to be paid by taxes on the rich and if the rich are the top 1 percent of filers, then the proposal requires raising the taxes of this group by 66 percent![19] If the rich are taken to mean anyone earning $50,000 or more, then the proposal requires raising the taxes of this group 26 percent.[20] Defining the rich to fall between these two extremes produces tax increases in between. Tax increases of this magnitude are substantial, and many would question their fairness.

Fortunately, it is possible for everyone to be covered by health insurance and incur net program costs equal to top-off costs alone.

One obvious political idea that might be proposed is to tax one group – these can be called "the rich" – to pay for government provision of health care to another group – called "the poor." The problem with this approach is that the cost of providing health care to the uninsured is no longer the "top-off" costs just described. Assuming that medical usage for individuals who become fully insured in a government-provided free program rises to 80–100 percent of the current national average per insured person means that instead of a program costing 0.5 percent of GDP as discussed earlier,

---

[17] See the discussion in Section 4.3, Deadweight Loss of Taxation.

[18] Joint Economic Committee, 2001. 2001 GDP = $10,128 billion.

[19] Working from the appropriate fractions of GDP, $(3.535 + 2.32)/3.535 = 1.66$.

[20] In 2001 income tax filers reporting income of $50,000 or higher were 36.2 percent of filers. This group paid taxes equal to 95.8 percent of all income taxes collected, or 8.96 percent of GDP. $(8.96 + 2.32)/8.96 = 1.26$.

we are talking about costs four to five times higher.[21] Any slippage or error in the program design that allows members of the already-insured group to drop their coverage and obtain coverage through the program would imply yet greater program costs.

HOW TO READ THIS BOOK

Reforming the U.S. health care system is not an insurmountable challenge. Approaches to improving health care access that address countless symptoms rather than their causes will not work, but others that are careful to deploy a small, but fundamental, list of economic principles will. Applying them requires a radical departure from current band-aid approaches that treat symptoms. We begin with two goals: (1) moving to universal health insurance coverage in an efficient fair manner coupled with (2) restoring the efficient use of resources in the health care sector. The guiding principle is efficiency with lack-of-income issues (equity) addressed in a transparent and separate manner.

In Chapter 2, "Goals," we describe the requirements that most Americans desire from their health care system. We explain in Chapter 3, "Principles," the relevant rules that ensure the efficient and equitable use of scarce resources. Choosing the goals, knowing the requirements, and following the principles lead inevitably to a framework for reform that we outline in Chapter 8, "The Targeted Intervention Plan."

Chapters 4, "Markets, VPOs, Government"; 5, "Education, Charity, and the American Ethical Base"; 6, "Why Government in Health Care?"; and 7, "Insurance," provide the necessary grounding and background material. This material is required because the logical foundations for a government presence in health care must be consistent with the economic (efficiency) approach that we adopt and are not available in the existing literature, to our knowledge. The message of these chapters is the following:

Chapter 4: Efficiency considerations apply to assign group activity to markets, voluntary private organizations, or government. This chapter is a guided tour of welfare economics to set the stage for the efficiency foundation that underlies the book's treatment of health care: that is, who is the efficient agent to *do* health care?

---

[21] If 80–100 percent of the usage of an already-insured is program provided to every currently uninsured individual, the program cost is four to five times greater. For example, offering 100 percent of coverage of an average insured would imply $1 \times 0.16 \times 0.145 = 2.32$ percent of GDP cost. Our calculations in the box "Mushrooming Costs" work out the implications of this for the public tax burden.

Chapter 5: Today education and charity are prominent government activities, which we examine for potential lessons to apply to health care.
Both end as cautionary tales, education because the arrangements now
in place were never theoretically grounded nor particularly tied to efficiency, and charity, because it is an individual obligation for which
government can have an efficiency-based facilitating role but does not
offer an example to follow for health care.

Chapter 6: This chapter is the first application of efficiency to the question
of the government role in health care. We learn that government has
an interest, and we learn on what basis it may contribute consistently
with the efficiency considerations of Chapter 4.

Chapter 7: This chapter tours the economics of insurance. In it we learn
why insurance objectives and charity objectives should be separated,
all program basic insurance should be sold on an actuarially fair basis,
and charity issues should be handled as a separate matter in accor-
dance with efficiency dictates. The insurance lessons are applied in the
national health care framework of Chapter 8.

Chapter 8, "The Targeted Intervention Plan," walks through the logic
(efficiency and Chapter 3 principles) that results in the "Targeted
Intervention Plan." With a few exceptions that are described in the
chapter, the implied framework is made up of familiar components.
Elements that can be left as implementation choices are noted. The
plan is summarized in the Executive Summary and in Chapter 12.

Finally, Chapter 9, "Forestalling Free Riders," Chapter 10, "Preserving
Prices," and Chapter 11, "Inducing Innovation," deal with critical special
topics. For example, Chapter 11, which appeared as a journal article,[22] deals
with the important question of how to solve the dilemma that insured purchase of prescription drugs enhances the market power of patent holders
and leads to problematic and burdensome price increases. The studies covered in Chapter 2, "Goals," show that 60 percent of consumers currently use
prescription drugs, and that prescription drug coverage is a key factor that
consumers use to compare health plans. In fact, three out of four consumers
say coverage for prescription drugs would influence their choice of a health
plan.[23] This chapter can be viewed as a direct application of the intervention
principle of Section 3.1, Principle 1, The Intervention Principle.

---

[22] Grinols and Henderson, 2007.
[23] See Deloitte, 2008.

The Contents allow readers to move more directly to material of interest to them. We reserved supplementary material and some technical material for the appendixes. This is for the usual reason that we did not want to impede the readability and flow of the main content, but also because we feel it is our duty to justify the form that the "Targeted Intervention Plan" takes. The rules dictate the outcome. We view ourselves merely as applying the rules that have independent existence.

In the political realm, America's founders were passionate in their belief that households and families could be trusted to know their own interests, that representative government was superior to monarchy, and that the natural selfishness and rapaciousness of human nature expressed in political leaders required carefully crafted checks and balances to countervail these tendencies. Many of the best and the brightest of their time did not see the point. Was not European monarchy the model? Had not this served the world tolerably well? Were not the promoters of the untried American *novus ordo seclorum* (new order of the ages) too brash? Even in the American colonies, the large majority were unsure whether they wanted to support something so radical. Others, however, insisted that a significant change was needed to implement new principles.

We take comfort in the fact that the founders of our country were proved right by history. Because their assessment of the problems and the political principles they brought to bear were sound, they won over the doubters and set a course that has been the single greatest political engine for good that the world has ever witnessed. The health care sector and people's health are being badly treated by current approaches; a radical departure to apply sound principles is the answer.

TWO

Goals

I am not among those who fear the people. They, and not the rich, are our dependence for continued freedom.
Thomas Jefferson, Monticello, 12 July 1816

Summary: Left free to pursue their own interests, people naturally establish markets, voluntary private organizations, and enough government to accomplish collectively what they cannot do alone. Government of the people respects the people's wishes to receive health care from whom they want, when they want, and how they want, subject to the usual constraints of commerce. The starting point is to understand what people want.

Arelene had fallen in a Florida parking lot, fracturing her femur in three places and requiring surgery to reconstruct the knee. Having traveled by plane and wheelchair to recuperate in her daughter's home in another state, she complained of harsh leg pain the next day. Her daughter took her to the local overcrowded emergency room, where she was made to wait. Three hours passed. Her daughter and son-in-law took turns imploring the admitting nurse that she be seen. Finally, her daughter remonstrated, "My mother is 81 years old, has just had major surgery on her knee, taken a long plane journey, and complains of severe leg pain in her lower leg. If she has a blood clot that causes her to have a stroke or die, do you want this to happen on your watch?" This produced action, examination by a physician, and ultimately prescription for blood thinner.

But why was the emergency room so crowded and the wait so long? One reason was Mabel. In the examining room, Arelene and her daughter could hear the conversation in the next curtain-separated booth. "Hello, Mabel," the doctor said. "What is it this time?" Though Mabel complained of various undefined pains, the doctor said that she was fine after dutifully examining her. When he said that he was calling her son to pick her up and take her home, she became unpleasant, vociferous, and loud in stating that she wanted to be admitted to the hospital for the weekend.

In another example of delay, 14-year-old Matthew's mother took him to the emergency room with a fever and puffy knee. Three hours passed, after which his condition was discovered to be so critical that his parents were told, "Now is the time to tell your son you love him," before the doctors whisked him by helicopter to a hospital better equipped for critical care.[1] He was infected with a deadly methicillin-resistant *Staphylococcus aureus*. Would more delay have cost him his life?

Anyone who has spent time in America's emergency rooms knows them to be generally overcrowded and often filled with individuals without insurance who inappropriately use them as access points for non-emergency care. It may seem compassionate to treat them there, often without consideration of their ability to pay for the care they receive, but when emergency room personnel are delayed in responding to true emergencies, there are consequences that no one wants.

Artificially overcrowded emergency rooms are a consequence of income deficiencies and imbalance in the purchase of health insurance.[2] The first step to restoring balance is to sort out what the issues are and to distill our wants and needs to the irreducible core of necessaries, which, once achieved, will satisfy Americans' health care needs.

A review of Americans' expectations for health care shows how similar we really are. Appendix A, "Top Ten Goals for the American Health Care System," presents an unscientific "top ten" list of health system goals compiled from the public statements of individuals, organizations, and government. We want everyone covered by health insurance; we want to choose whom we go to for care; we want to receive high-quality care that takes advantage of the latest advances; we want our care to be responsive to our desires; we want to pay a fair price for what we get; we want transparency in accessing health care information. If we want to know the price of a service, we want to find it without undue difficulty.

If we are a provider, such as a doctor or hospital, we want access to the patient's file electronically if that is fastest and best. We want to be able to practice the best medicine we know without hindrance or red tape, and we want to charge for our work and set our own prices. Users and providers

---

[1] Drexler, 2006.

[2] Among the causes of increased waiting time in emergency deparments – up to 150 percent increase for acute myocardial infarctions (heart attack, the leading cause of death in the United States) – are emergency department closures, increase in total emergency department visits, and increasing uninsurance. See Wilper, et al. 2008, p. 92. Emergency department closures and increased emergency department visits are themselves influenced by the use of emergency departments as routine access points.

alike want health care to be continuous, not episodic or sporadic, and they want preventive care.

In this chapter, we use the results of policy triage to refine and shorten the wish list. The Preface introduced the concept of policy triage to remind us that features that self-correct when underlying structures are fixed are not the proper subject of policy. The same applies to wants that may be resistant to useful influence. For example, certain elements of health care are intrinsically expensive. It makes little economic sense to attempt by policy to reduce cost below the natural level for those elements. Establishing a functioning and competitive health care market corrects a multitude of failures when it comes to achieving many of the desired objectives.

We easily can reduce the list to five. Appendix A elaborates more on the way that the five requirements result from policy triage.

2.1. Goal 1: Universal Coverage

The first goal is providing universal coverage. This need not mean that everyone receives free health care or that insurance provides first-dollar coverage. It does mean that no American will be put at jeopardy of life, limb, or financial catastrophe due to the inability to receive medical treatment or to pay for it. This is a widely discussed and broadly-supported objective.

To seek health insurance for everyone means that there must be some *minimum* standard of coverage identified. Defining the minimum standard of coverage is a policy implementation choice. There are considerations, such as not making the coverage too broad or burdensome, that are critical to keeping insurance affordable. See Chapter 8 for more discussion. The minimum may vary with age so that young adults just entering the labor force and the poor of any age can afford to buy coverage. If some individuals want more than the minimum insurance coverage, it may be purchased voluntarily as a supplement. Properly administered health insurance should not

> **No American will be put at jeopardy of life, limb, or financial catastrophe due to the inability to receive medical treatment or to pay for it.**

require the poor and the young to pay for coverage they do not need and do not want, or require them to subsidize the coverage of older, wealthier, and often sicker consumers. See Chapter 7 and Chapter 10 for a discussion of proper structuring of health insurance and distinctions among insurance, charity (alms), and pre-paid care.

If universal health insurance is a policy objective, it follows that there is an obligation to provide help to selected individuals who are incapable, permanently or temporarily, of purchasing health insurance coverage for themselves. Various ways including cash transfers, artificially lower prices, minimum wage, and Earned Income Tax Credit are often invoked to aid the poor. Some are economically sound, some are not. Too little income is a separate problem from failure to buy insurance and should be treated separately. Chapter 8, "The Targeted Intervention Plan," discusses this aspect of the TIP framework in more detail.

Many would argue that it is in society's interest to have health insurance in order to protect the rest of society from having to pay for the medical expenses of those who select not to buy insurance but later require expensive medical care for which they cannot pay. The question addressed in this book is what means to achieving health insurance for all is the most efficient. Public provision of health care may or may not follow from efficiency.

Chapter 6 explains that health insurance is predominantly a private good. Like socks or salad dressing, its benefits accrue to the person receiving it. Health insurance is not a public good in the technical sense, like national defense, whose provision offers simultaneous benefits to many people, requiring that it be financed by broad-based taxation. (See the Public Goods discussion of Section 4.3 or the Glossary and Definitions for a discussion and definition of public goods.) Publicly provided *public* goods are justified on standard economic principles. Publicly provided *private* goods such as health insurance are not. There is, therefore, justification needed for presuming to use government to guarantee in some fashion that everyone has health insurance. After all, government does not ensure that everyone owns personal automobiles even though transportation is essential and reliable public transport is unavailable in many U.S. cities. Chapter 6 makes this case on grounds that are consistent with limited government in the context of competitive markets and voluntary private organizations. Most advanced countries have some form of organized health care system in place, and there appears to be broad-based support for health care to be among the functions government oversees in some way. The form of oversight remains to be described.

> **Publicly provided *public* goods are justified on standard economic principles. Publicly provided *private* goods such as health insurance are not.**

2.2. Goal 2: Patient-Centered Coverage

Patient-centered, personal, portable, and permanent coverage means that the care recipients – we who ultimately pay the costs of medical care – are respected as the central component in the health care process. We want our health care to be based on features that are tailored to us as the patients. While a 73-year-old widowed retiree should have the option to buy in vitro fertilization coverage for her health plan if she wants it, as should the 22-year-old bride, neither should be required to buy it.

How does an economy ensure that sellers treat the consumer well? Certain features are more conducive to a patient-centered focus than others. A clinic that is supported by tax dollars has less incentive to be patient centered because the most critical ingredient to its continued operation – its income – is not directly tied to the patient. Businesses that know that customers can hurt their bottom line by doing business elsewhere have a stronger incentive to be friendly and concerned about their customers' satisfaction. Providers and physicians who believe that they work for the patient will behave differently than those who believe they work for the network or bureaucracy. As one part of treating the patient with respect and dignity, health care coverage must provide equal access for covered care. That is, the method for achieving universal access should not distinguish one patient from another nor lead to different quality in covered treatment.

> Providers and physicians who believe that they work for the patient will behave differently than ones who believe they work for the network or bureaucracy.

Finally, Americans want their coverage to be permanent, meaning continuous over their lifetime, and portable. In the present "system," workers who lose coverage when they change employers often must change physicians and other providers. Worse yet, workers who lose jobs sometimes lose coverage altogether.

2.3. Goal 3: Respect for Incentives for High-Quality Care

In Germany, one of the best appellations for a dentist is that he "was trained in the United States."[3] Statistics on the development and use of technology,

---

[3] Information from Dr. Gregory Leman, the American managing director for the Cabot-Huels joint venture plant in Rheinfelden, Germany.

diagnostic imaging machines, and other advanced tools show a strong advantage for the United States over many foreign nations.[4]

Americans understand that voluntary interactions – a market – create incentives for continued innovation to maintain the lead in medical science. Health care providers – hospitals, pharmaceutical manufacturers, physicians, durable goods suppliers, insurance companies – therefore, should be free to compete, charge fee for service, set their price structures as they see fit, and provide services to clients as they choose. Purchasers of health care, on the other hand, should be free to contract with whomever they want for whatever services they want on the basis of ability to compare prices, quality, location, and other factors. Incentives for innovation and improvement must remain strong. This means that a group, a provider, or a patient that undertakes cost-saving innovation and change should benefit from his or her own initiative. Properly functioning markets generate quality and efficiency because doing so is in the interest of sellers. An organizational change, technical innovation, or financial innovation that improves efficiency in the present system should remain efficiency-creating in the new one.

> **Incentives for innovation and improvement must remain strong.**

> **Quality of Care.** American medicine has much to be admired and preserved. Although it is sometimes (incorrectly) reported that Americans spend more for care but get less, consider the following.
>
> Arduino Verdecchia and colleagues (2007) provide international comparisons of age-adjusted five-year survival rates for different types of cancer. Using data from European and U.S. cancer registries, they find that the United States has the highest survival rates. For all malignancies U.S. men have a 66.3 percent survival rate five years after diagnosis and women have a survival rate of 62.9 percent, whereas the European average is 47.3 for men and 55.8 for women. When cancer is diagnosed earlier there is a better chance that it can be controlled. Higher U.S. five-year survival rates may result from earlier screening. For specific cancers where early screening leads to longer life expectancies the United States does even better. The five-year survival rate for prostate cancer is 99.3 percent in the United States but only 77.5 percent in Europe. For breast cancer the rates are 90.1 percent (U.S.) versus 79.0 percent (Europe).[5]

---

[4] OECD, 2006.
[5] Verdecchia, Francisci, Brenner, Gatta, Micheli, Mangone, Kunkler, and the EUROCARE-4 Working Group, 2007.

Perceptions are often driven by failure to compare like with like. The United States fares poorly relative to developed nations in the oft-quoted statistics on infant mortality. However, the United States counts *perinatal* fatalities in the infant mortality rate whereas European nations consider them late fetal deaths and thus do not include them in the calculation. In 2004 the U.S. infant mortality rate was 6.9 deaths per 1,000 live births, compared to 4.2, 3.9, 5.1, 5.3, and 2.8 in Switzerland, France, the United Kingdom, Canada, and Japan. However, if we compare perinatal mortality rates (which include late fetal deaths in the calculation), the picture looks quite different. In 2001 the U.S. perinatal mortality rate was 6.9, compared to 8.0, 6.9 , 6.7, 6.3, 3.6.[6]

Last, there are adjustments for factors unrelated to medical care delivery that many would suggest are needed, such as for obesity,[7] racial mix, and other causes of death, to be able to compare like with like.[8]

The advantages of voluntary interactions notwithstanding, markets can be aided by government in setting standards and legislating to guard against fraud and abuse. Government can also facilitate information flows that aid market function, just as food labeling legislation aids obtaining better information about the foods we buy.

Supporting voluntary interactions raises questions. If people are free to choose individually, should government exhibit favoritism toward one group's choices over another? For example, should policies favor rural over urban residents? Unless favoritism represents a deliberate formal national intention to encourage more people to live in rural areas, the various higher costs of living in rural areas are a natural feature that does not, of itself, require government action. Stated another way, if charity toward

---

[6] OECD, 2007.

[7] American lifestyle choices also complicate the evaluation of U.S. medical care. The obesity rate in the United States, generally caused by factors other than delivery of medical care, greatly surpasses those in the rest of the developed world – twenty-five times higher than in Japan and five times higher than France. (WHO Global InfoBase, 2007, online http://www.who.int/infobase/report.aspx)

[8] External causes of death, including motor vehicle accidents, homicide, suicide, and accidents of all types – generally caused by factors other than delivery of medical care – have a significant impact on the life expectancy of Americans. Lemaire, 2005, estimates that in 2000 the U.S. life expectancy of 76.9 years would have been 1.2 years higher without these external causes. That same year the population-weighted average life expectancy of the 33 richest counties in the world was 79.2 years. Thus, over one-half of the gap between the United States and the other developed counties is explained by this one adjustment, even before others are considered (Lemaire, 2005).

an individual is the objective, the charity should not be offered in a manner to create an unintended incentive to prefer one location of residence over another.

2.4. Goal 4: Cost Containment

Cost containment, accountability, and control for the government program constitute the fourth requirement that consumers want. In state after state, Medicaid, Medicare, and other expenditures have mushroomed to the point where they strain the capacity of states to act. The results of special interest lobbying, including by businesses that serve the medical market, often add to the burden. Political promises, constrained only by the need for revenue, drive many states' decision making. In recent years Kentucky, New Hampshire, Pennsylvania, Wisconsin, Maine, and many other states have considered legalizing slot machine gambling for the purpose of enhancing state revenues. California is not alone in dipping in and out of the news because of budget woes. Health care cannot be solved by the attempt to transfer the financial burden from one level of government to another. An acceptable health care framework, therefore, will allow the state to *decide* how much money it will place into the health care sector as the outcome of a reasoned legislative choice, not as the result of compulsion.

2.5. Goal 5: Sustainability

Sustainability suggests the ability to "endure without giving way or yielding," to "keep going," as well as the ability to support indefinitely the means and funds for such continuing operation. Americans want good health care on a sustainable basis that treats all future generations equally well. Many plans might provide the health care; some might survive for five years, a decade, even a generation. However, indefinite sustainability is possible. There is no need to settle for less.

> **Indefinite sustainability is possible. There is no need to settle for less.**

Table 2.1 summarizes what has been said. Any health care system that succeeds in providing these five requirements accomplishes for Americans what they want for their health care. Success in meeting these objectives leads to success in providing the quality and sustainability with a patient-centered heart that accompanies a caring health care sector. In subsequent chapters we explain why an approach that begins from what is wanted – and then adopts fea-

Table 2.1. *What Americans Want in Health Care*

Objective	Summary
Universal coverage and access	No American will be put at jeopardy of life, limb, or financial catastrophe through inability to receive medical treatment or to pay for it.
Patient-centered, personal, portable, permanent coverage	The care recipient is respected as the central component in the health care process.
Respect for incentives for high-quality care	The market is the best way to serve the customer diligently with concern, dignity, and respect. Voluntary interactions mediated by competition and the market create incentives for continued innovation to maintain the lead in medical science and to restrain costs to the greatest extent possible.
Cost containment, accountability, and control for the government budget	The health care framework must allow the government to *decide* how much money it will devote to its budget for the health care sector as the outcome of a reasoned choice based on data, not as the result of compulsion. Dollar amounts must be able to be set in advance on the basis of informed judgment and enforced with certainty over the budget cycle.
Sustainability	The program must have the ability to support indefinitely the means and funds for continued operation, treating all individuals and generations equally well.

tures that accomplish these objectives – provides a nearly unique blueprint for American health care. This approach produces a system that will work well not just for the next year or ten years, but indefinitely. Principles that can do this are what we seek.

THREE

Principles

Good intentions may do as much harm as malevolence if they lack understanding.
                    Albert Camus, *The Plague*, 1947

How often have I said to you that when you have eliminated the impossible, whatever remains, however improbable, must be the truth?
                    Sherlock Holmes, *The Sign of the Four*, 1890

Summary: Good intentions are insufficient to guarantee good outcomes unless good principles are applied. Knowing what to avoid is often as important as knowing what to do. This chapter introduces six principles from public finance theory and welfare economics that must be followed if the fivefold objectives of Chapter 2 are to be met.

This chapter identifies and elaborates principles to follow in establishing a health care system based on efficient use of resources where everyone is treated equitably. These are tools for later use that keep political actions on track to achieve efficiency and sustainability. Several involve warnings about pitfalls to avoid, what *not* to do in any public program concerning health care.

> Avoiding bad ideas is a good idea.

If enough bad ideas are eliminated, Sherlock Holmes would say, those that remain must be good ideas. In any case, avoiding bad ideas is a good idea.

Excitement results from being the architect of a program designed for doing good or solving a problem. The "program" could be one as simple as "Take from *A* and give it to *B*." At this level of sophistication it is easy to imagine many such programs that could work for some time. The former Soviet Union showed that even a poorly designed social system may last years before its unsound foundations cause it to fail.

Some systems may even limp along indefinitely at a fraction of their full potential.[1] To design a program that can function well and do so indefinitely, however, is our goal.

Sustainable public programs are defined by the ability to meet their design objectives efficiently for an indefinite period, treating all generations the same. Short-term thinking may be appealing, but it is not in the interest of a parasite to kill its host; it is not in the interest of a farmer to "kill the goose that laid the golden egg"; and it is not in the country's interest to plan an unsustainable health care program when one will be needed indefinitely. Sustainable endeavors require the understanding and use of a certain amount of science, whether hard science, social science, or both.

> Sustainable public programs are defined by the ability to meet their design objectives efficiently for an indefinite period, treating all generations equitably.

3.1. Principle 1: The Intervention Principle

The Intervention Principle: A rule summarizing the most efficient way to accomplish a desired change to an economy when selecting among alternate options. Efficient interventions provide the greatest well-being to citizens consistent with accomplishing the desired outcome, or, equivalently, accomplish the desired outcome in a manner that causes the least loss of well-being to citizens.

The central issue in policy economics is to find the most efficient way to intervene in an economic system to accomplish a desired objective that is not being accomplished through laissez faire. Economists have studied this question extensively, resulting in the intervention principle.[2] The *intervention principle* states that the most efficient way to accomplish a desired objective in a wide range of circumstances is to identify the margin to be

---

[1] The economist Eva Ehrlich documented the different successes of countries and systems, including the harmful consequences of socialist government planning. Pairings of countries that once had equal prospects showed different outcomes based on their social system. The degree of differences possible is surprising. For example, East and West Germany had identical people stock, language, culture, and standard of living prior to World War II, when both were organized as market economies, but by 1980 government-planned East Germany had less than two-thirds the GDP per capita of its market-oriented West German counterpart. Ehrlich, 1985.

[2] This section borrows from Grinols, 2006.

influenced and impose a tax or subsidy narrowly at that margin at the minimal level needed to accomplish the objective. For example, if the federal government wants all uninsured individuals living east of the Mississippi River to purchase health insurance, it should subsidize insurance purchase for individuals living east of the Mississippi who do not currently purchase it.[3] The intervention should apply only to insurance purchase, only to households east of the Mississippi, only to those households who do not now purchase it, and at the minimum level to achieve the objective.

In the early 1970s America faced its first oil crisis, caused by an embargo of Middle East oil producers. Many citizens and political leaders called for less dependence on foreign oil. Various options were suggested, including a tax on gasoline at the pump (reducing consumption of gasoline), subsidies to domestic oil production (increasing domestic oil production), and a tariff on imported oil (reducing import levels). Was our goal to reduce gasoline consumption, increase domestic production, decrease domestic production, reduce imports, or accomplish something else altogether? In reality, the different policy options led to different outcomes. Some suggested that "independence" meant using foreign oil first, and thereby conserving domestic stocks. The overall objective of "limiting dependence on foreign oil" was too vague to provide much direction. Worse, achieving one objective in the least cost manner was incompatible with achieving others at least cost. The lesson is that the path to success involves carefully choosing the appropriate goals and selecting policies that accomplish them at least cost to citizens.

The intervention principle is helpful in identifying flawed options as well as finding appropriate ones. If the goal is to induce individuals to leave welfare rolls for payrolls, for example, then a subsidy to child day care is a policy that has been suggested that will encourage the shift to paid work if child care costs are a prominent barrier to work for parents on welfare. But in this case, the proposed intervention involves subsidizing child day care, which is a complementary good to the desired objective. Would subsidizing this complementary good, or another complementary good, or a cleverly chosen group of complementary goods be preferable to a narrowly directed employment subsidy such as a variant of the Earned Income Tax Credit? The intervention principle says not. See Appendix C, "Incentive Symmetry and Intervention Principle," for a more formal statement and explanation of the intervention principle.

---

[3] Note that *affordability* is a non-technical term, that, in any case, we do not need. At a price close or equal to zero everyone can "afford" to buy.

3.2. Principle 2: Incentive Symmetry

Incentive Symmetry: The understanding that economic incentives operating through tax-created price differentials may equivalently be created using a subsidy applied to different parts of the economic system, and vice versa.

Few are aware that the United States has never taxed its exports because the Constitution contains a clause prohibiting such duties. "Section 9 – Limits on Congress" states,

No Tax or Duty shall be laid on Articles exported from any State.

A related ban prohibits states from taxing the exports of other states.[4] While their intentions were good, the writers apparently did not consider that the effect of a duty on exports of any good could be accomplished by placing a duty on imports of all other goods. Both actions lead to the identical economic outcome. By using import duties, which are legal, the prohibition on export duties can be totally nullified!

Why should we care about this apparent curiosity if our interest is health care policy? The answer is that the incentive symmetry principle applies to the domestic economy as well. Taxes and subsidies are different sides of the same coin. Having the ability to use a carrot or a stick, or some combination, provides flexibility. Consider bail, an arrangement instituted as a guarantee of an arrested person's appearance for trial. The objective – provide an incentive to appear for trial – could be met by a subsidy to be given an arrested person who appears for trial. Instead of a subsidy, however, the judicial system employs an equivalent incentive: the arrested individual *avoids a tax on the alternate activity (in this case, failing to appear for trial)* by posting bond, which is returned only upon appearance for trial.

We present the general incentive symmetry result first, and then talk about its importance for health care. For those who care to delve further, Appendix C provides a detailed analytical statement and proof of incentive symmetry. One way to see the principle is to look at prices for two activities (p_x, p_y). Prices create the incentives that guide our economic choices.

For simplicity, assume that $p_x = p_y = 1$ initially. If X is subsidized 25 percent, prices become $(0.75p_x, p_y)$. Relative attractiveness of the activities

---

[4] "Section 10 – Powers Prohibited of States" reads, "No State shall, without the Consent of the Congress, lay any Imposts or Duties on Imports or Exports, except what may be absolutely necessary for executing its inspection Laws: and the net Produce of all Duties and Imposts, laid by any State on Imports or Exports, shall be for the Use of the Treasury of the United States; and all such Laws shall be subject to the Revision and Control of the Congress."

is no longer one to one, but $3/4$. *However, the same incentive is achieved with the ratio of prices equal to $3/4$ by taxing Y to establish prices $(p_x, (4/3)p_y)$.* In the words of Sancho Panza in the musical *Man of La Mancha*, "Whether the stone hits the pitcher or the pitcher hits the stone, it's going to be bad for the pitcher": Whether one subsidizes X or taxes Y, it is going to be good for X and bad for Y.

Why is the incentive symmetry principle so important to avoiding the rocks and shoals that might otherwise scuttle our health care plans? Our goal is to have everyone who does not now buy health insurance do so. It is difficult to provide a subsidy just to those who do not now buy insurance, however. In fact, well-known subsidy proposals that have been made for health insurance purchase involve providing a refundable tax credit to *every* American, a much more extensive and costly program than the intervention principle calls for.

> Our goal is to have everyone who does not now buy health insurance do so.

Consider what your reaction would be if you were told that to induce arrestees to appear for trial, *everyone* was to be given a subsidy conditional on appropriate behavior with respect to appearing for trial. That is, those not arrested receive the subsidy, and, if someone is arrested, he or she receives the subsidy only if he or she appears for trial. Most would consider such a program bizarre or even absurd because it draws in the entire American population just to deal with a small number of arrestees, not to mention that it *pays* arrestees to appear for trial. This is why we apply the called-for intervention in the symmetric form. By bonding arrestees only, we tax *only those arrestees who fail to show up for trial* – exactly what the intervention principle calls for.

Beyond the objection that it fails the intervention principle, providing a government subsidy to everyone's health insurance purchase makes it impossible by observation thereafter to distinguish those who would have bought insurance without government help and those who would not. It also carries the negative implication that we have assigned to government the responsibility to buy health insurance for citizens. If such a subsidy is approved on D-Day, on D-Day + 1 a politician will rise to the podium to argue that the amount is inadequate to enable the poor to purchase health insurance. Because we cannot afford to give everyone free health insurance – costs would rise well above the percentage increases in income taxes described in Chapter 1 – only selected people would be given the higher subsidy while others would be made to pay the higher taxes without receiving added benefits. The simple desire to provide an incentive for individuals to buy health insurance would quickly morph into something quite different.

Using incentive symmetry, there is an alternative, economically equivalent approach that avoids all of the stated risks. In a manner similar to the bonding example, the identical incentive is created by taxing purchases of everything other than health insurance through a value-added tax and rebating it if the individual has health insurance: only those who do not buy insurance are affected and everybody buys his or her own insurance. As in the case of bonding arrestees, the intervention principle is satisfied and the program remains efficient.

It is also important to keep the insurance-purchase objective separate from the too-little-income issue. When selected individuals cannot afford health insurance, financial assistance may be provided as a separate matter. The Earned Income Tax Credit, for example, has the right kinds of incentives associated with it. This issue will be taken up in more detail in Chapter 8.

To summarize this section, public programs should not "do acupuncture with a fork," drawing in unwanted elements that create enormous programs of immense scope and cost. We acknowledge that no political arrangement is foolproof. As much as possible, however, as many tools against political abuse and inefficiency should be accessed and applied at the outset. Incentive symmetry is one.

3.3. Principle 3: Every Pot Sits on Its Own Base

Every Pot Sits on Its Own Base: Pots that sit on their own base are internally stable and do not need propping up with external support. A public program that sits on its own base is likewise incentive-compatible for participants and does not need external support. The pot-base analogy derives from the recognition that public programs destroy their own effectiveness when they intermingle goals, fail to use independent tools to accomplish independent objectives, and force some or all participants to act against their own interests. Typically, pots do not sit on their own base because charity transfers are embedded into programs designed for other purposes. Charity is better accomplished separately and transparently.

We have tried to give this principle a memorable title because, in many ways, it is the least considered yet most important. The expression "Every Pot Sits on Its Own Base" means that social insurance programs should be self-funded by the revenues of beneficiaries who are like one another

> Social insurance
> programs should be
> self-funded by the
> revenues of
> beneficiaries who are
> like one another with
> regard to the
> program and
> indistinguishable
> from one another
> with respect to it.

with regard to the program and indistinguishable from one another with respect to it. Had Social Security been structured as a forced savings plan with the savings invested in real assets and the earnings returned to the savers, it would sit on its own base. If the program in question is *intended* to be a charity transfer program, of course, then it need not sit on its own base.[5] However, charity transfer programs should be done separately and transparently.[6]

If revenues from beneficiaries do not support the program, it does not sit on its own base. Further, if a subset of program beneficiaries who are not self-funding can be identified *ex ante*, the program does not sit on its own base. Programs that do not sit on their own bases confound charity transfer objectives with social insurance objectives. Lack of income is a separate problem from lack of insurance and can be treated more effectively by explicitly using the previous two principles. The requirement that every pot sit on its own base is not an injunction against charity or alms. It is an injunction to treat distinct problems distinctly rather than let one solution interfere with the other.

Many insurance claimants obviously collect more than they pay in premiums but, as discussed in Chapter 7, cannot be identified in advance. Hence insurance with homogeneous risk pools satisfies the principle. Because so many government programs that deal with social insurance issues involve hidden charity elements, this is usually a point of sensitivity. Outside infusions of cash when charity is a required feature must be conveyed transparently and efficiently, and doing so virtually always means separately to the individual and not through the social insurance program.

Why should pots sit on their own bases? Because tipping pots create unintended consequences and harmful incentives. A program that relies for its success on agents working against their own interests faces severe challenges. It is not in your economic interest to pay for something that you do not receive, and it is not in your interest to refuse or conserve something for which you pay nothing. Likely you will try

---

[5] Charity transfer programs where the giving and receiving are voluntary "sit on their own base" with respect to the requirement that no agent operates against his or her own interest.
[6] Efficiency implies that income transfers are superior to embedded concessions, preferential prices, and the like.

to avoid paying something for nothing. Likewise, the recipient of something for nothing is saddled with wrong incentives and acts in ways that work counter to program effectiveness.

> **It is not in your economic interest to pay for something that you do not receive, and it is not in your interest to refuse or conserve something for which you pay nothing.**

The most common way the every-pot-on-its-own-base requirement is violated is through providing an individual or group an embedded price advantage when the hidden transfers could be given more economically in another way. Why would politicians choose inferior methods? One naive answer might be that they do not know better, but this has little credibility when so much expert advice is available. The natural desire to hide transfer and charity elements of social programs causes these elements to be embedded in wastefully costly ways.[7]

Two examples show the extent to which government hides its actions, the success that it can have in confusing its real functioning, and the incentive misalignment consequences. The American position in the Uruguay Round of trade negotiations was that farmers should be able to export their crops without market interference and that farmers could be given the same amount of help as under the present system in separate income transfers. Near the end of an agricultural conference where these views were presented, a gentleman from the rear of the room rose to speak his thoughts, which were on this order: "I am probably the only person in this room who has plowed a field or walked a furrow. Farming is hard work. Those like me are not getting rich on it, and now you are talking about doing away with our farm subsidies."

One of the speakers replied, "No, you do not understand. What we are talking about will give you the same income from the government that you now receive, but it will not be tied to prices or crops you sell and thus impose unnecessary costs on those in the market." Surprised, the farmer replied, "You mean I would get money from the government equal to what I am getting now, but I wouldn't have to farm for it?" "*Exactly!*" the speaker said. The farmer's response was slower: "But that would be *welfare!*"[8] If this farmer did not understand the welfare nature of the

---

[7] See Chapter 4 for a discussion of social costs in the form of deadweight loss.

[8] Related to the authors by a U.S. government agricultural expert who attended the conference.

subsidy program that he was part of, why should we expect the non-farmer to be different?

The issue is not charity to farmers or income insurance for them. The issue is that the same amount of charity can be given without collateral damage. Separating charity from the mechanism of favored prices meant that farmers could get the same charity they had before, and taxpayers pay less. Everyone would win. As it is, because of wrong incentives, agricultural supports are well known to lead to wasted produce and distorted land values; they go predominantly to the largest farmers and do little or nothing to save the family farm (a sometimes-stated objective), which must compete with ever more efficient corporate farms regardless of price supports.

The second example is federal sugar policy. The program benefits a small number of producers in the United States. But rather than being designed to write checks to these producers, it instead limits imports of sugar from the rest of the world to create an inflated domestic price. During the program, U.S. retail price of refined sugar has been over five times the world price of refined sugar.[9] The objection to providing charity to sugar producers through inferior means (favored prices) is that we could bestow the same support on sugar producers as we do now but cost the country $986 million less annually.[10] This would fund annual gifts of nearly $7 to every member of the workforce. The program is easy to ridicule – "artificially induced oversupply of domestic sugar has forced the U.S. government to store sugar or in some cases to have sugar fields plowed under"[11] – yet has persisted for many years through many attempts to eliminate it. Not surprisingly, the campaign contributions of the sugar lobby to political parties number in the millions of dollars.

In crafting a health care plan that achieves the two goals of universal insurance coverage and income to those who need it, we do not want to create programs like these.

The every-pot-on-its-own-base rule tends to be violated in situations when politicians want to hide the fact of (and size of) their transfers by building them into the program. Another common motivation is that legislators benefit from being seen responding to a problem, but not from being associated with placing the burden of their response on others. An example makes this point. Some states require insurance companies to accept all applicants at standard rates regardless of their health status

---

[9] Groombridge, 2001.

[10] According to the U.S. International Trade Commission, abolishing the program would result in $986 million in welfare gain to the U.S. economy. Ibid., p. 3.

[11] Ibid., p. 5.

(referred to as guaranteed issue). My incentive, therefore, is to wait until just before I need care, and then apply for insurance. Insurance providers must take this fact into consideration when setting premiums. The result is that when a healthy young woman we know applied for health insurance just after college graduation, her policy in Massachusetts cost over $340 per month for a plan that would have cost less than one-third that amount in her home state. The legislature placed the burden of its decision on the young and healthy, many of whom are just starting out with low-paying jobs, because it was more politically palatable than requiring a tax to transfer money to those needing help in buying health insurance coverage. Many young people decide not to be insured rather than pay unfairly inflated rates. Had the young woman in question not received help from her father, she might have made the same choice.

THREE PITFALL-AVOIDANCE PRINCIPLES

It is a sobering thought that we entrust our leaders with monumentally vital decisions, including issues such as health care, about which they may not have the training to differentiate among competing ideas. The skills that allow one to be elected and to remain in public office may be quite different from the skills needed to support specific proficiencies and qualify as a judge of economic matters in general, and health care in particular.

Imagine a group of 100 of your peers. Presume that you are all professionals. Some you know well, some very little. Further imagine that all 100 of you routinely buy an inexpensive lunch, averaging $7.50 each day. In the workday equivalent of a year (48 weeks) you spend $1,800. One of you, "the political leader," decides to formalize the lunch activity and establish a lunch program. If adopted, the plan provides each of you with a free lunch on 99 days out of 100. In return, on the 100th day you will buy lunch for the entire group. He argues that this will cost no more because, as things are now, you buy 100 lunches and with the lunch plan you will do the same. Besides, by pooling, the group can ensure that no one goes without lunch on any given day.

Most readers will immediately see the error in the plan. Has it not changed the incentives for every member of the group? If everyone's lunch is free 99 percent of the time, on the day that you buy lunch for everyone do you really expect plan members to limit their spending to $7.50? Instead they are likely to spend noticeably more, maybe $12–$15. If everyone is now spending $12–$15 for lunch each day, do you not suppose that the only way for you to get your money's worth is to buy a bigger daily lunch yourself?

Exactly. Spending has risen 60 to 100 percent plus the cost at the higher level of the free lunches given by the group to the few who have been going without. There are also overhead expenses associated with administering everyone's lunch through the program. In health insurance, for example, overhead can raise the cost of $100 of care to $106 for handling charges alone, plus another 5-8 percent for ordinary business return. We leave the math to you: How much will you now spend on lunch each year as part of the proposed system? (Answer: A number over $4,000 is possible.)

What seems reasonable to the leader is not realistic because of the effect the plan has on *incentives* for larger lunches. Economists are trained to think in terms of incentives – but most people are not. Moreover, if the political leader wants to promise "free" lunches, how can he explain that his program will cost over $4,000 for something that his listeners' current actions reveal they want to spend only $1,800 on?

Examples of public programs whose pre-program estimated budgets were exceeded many times over by post-program reality are not hard to find. Medicare is one. It is pointless to blame these kinds of outcomes on bad leadership or misguided elected officials. Politicians, just like the rest of us, merely respond to *their incentives* in predictable and expected ways. The checks and balances built into American government have worked tolerably well only because our founders had a justified distrust of *any* government and *anyone* in government.

Good government requires avoiding bad choices to which the nature of public life and public servants is susceptible. Innate pitfalls unleash system-wide incentives whose natural outcome, while unintended, can be calamitous. The remaining three principles discussed in this chapter, therefore, focus on avoidable mistakes. Where possible we make reference to the wisdom of Nobel Prize–winning economists and other notable thinkers who have established the foundations on which these warnings rest. Knowing what to avoid and what to embrace puts us in the position of knowing what to do.

3.4. Principle 4: No Polittroughing

"Polittroughing": a shortening of the phrase "politician public troughing." Intransitive verb. A form of political abuse whereby a politician creates or promises to create programs that benefit some constituents who "feed from the public trough" and to pay for them through taxes on other constituents. The purpose of polittroughing is to buy votes and political support. Polittroughers seek power and continued time in public office.

George Bernard Shaw (1856–1950) is remembered for remarking that "a government that robs Peter to pay Paul can always depend on the support of Paul." Any number of government actions or programs could be examined to find the influence of polittroughing. Because we are interested in health care, however, a brief look at the Medicare program is an obvious choice. When the U.S. Government Accountability Office (GAO) reported, "Our current financial condition is worse than is widely understood. Our current fiscal path is both imprudent and unsustainable,"[12] as it did in 2007, it should capture our full attention. The most prominent feature of the "major fiscal exposures" (unfunded liabilities) cited by the GAO was Medicare, accounting for $32,300 billion of the $50,500 billion total (Social Security and public debt account for most of the rest). In other words, $255,842 of unfunded Medicare "exposure" is owed to the program *per full-time worker*.[13] The GAO also noted that median household income is $46,326.[14] The issue is whether the typical family will be able to "pay off" a debt that is five to eight times the size of its income, in addition to meeting its other obligations, before reaching retirement age and expecting to collect Medicare benefits.

With this as background, we can ask, How was Medicare planned and how did it arrive at its current state? From the outset, supporters of the program were determined that its beneficiaries would not have to pay for their benefits. According to the 1969 history commissioned by the Social Security Administration, a White House–aided project "involved an effort to mobilize elderly people themselves in behalf of Medicare. . . . Starting with a nucleus of union retiree organizations"[15] to form a confederation of senior-citizen groups to stimulate political action. Many interactions and congressional committee debates showed sponsors' intentions: "Reportedly, the administration was unwilling to accept the terms of the [Ways and Means] committee members involved – that those elderly persons already retired be required to contribute premiums in order to qualify for benefits."[16] Culminating a struggle that lasted over a decade, Medicare's passage in 1965 did not end the debate over government-run health care: it only intensified it. During these debates Robert Ball, an official with the Department of Health, Education, and Welfare, observed, "Those

---

[12] U.S. GAO, 2007a.
[13] U.S. Government Accountability Office, 2007b, reports total burden per full-time worker of $400,000.
[14] U.S. GAO, 2007b.
[15] Corning, 1969.
[16] Ibid.

who advocated Medicare wanted something more. . .. This was to be the entering wedge. . ."[17]

It may be argued that while the initial generation of beneficiaries was not expected to pay for the government benefits they received, workers from 1965 onward would be expected to pay for their benefits in their payroll taxes. The subsequent history of Medicare is uniformly one of expansion and enlargement. An entire working career can be fitted between 1965 and the present, yet the program is less financially sound today, suggesting that more benefits were promised than paid for. In 1964 Medicare spending was projected to be $12 billion in 1990; in reality spending topped $110 billion that year, over 800 percent more.

The largest expansion since passage of the original Medicare legislation for which polittroughing charges also can be made took place after financial problems were well known. Instead of addressing the problems, Congress made them worse by creating an outpatient drug benefit in 2003. The present discounted value of Part D's unfunded liability is $7,900 billion.[18] The Bush administration backed the legislation, named H.R. 1 to emphasize its importance: "Republicans believed that they could buy off the senior vote as well as convince Americans that they were compassionate, in order to maintain the White House and their Congressional majority."[19] Many saw this as nothing more than an attempt to prop up sagging public opinion – particularly among senior voters – by promises of increased benefits to this group at the expense of another (the unaware young).[20]

Politicians of all ideological stripes fall victim to this tendency. In the 2008 presidential campaign, candidate Hillary Clinton proposed a plan that would give a matching $1,000 to individuals to invest in their 401(k) plans.[21] "American Retirement Accounts" would be available only to those making less than $100,000 per year and be funded from higher estate taxes on the estimated 7,000 estates in the United States worth more than

---

[17] Quoted in Helms, 1999.

[18] U.S. Government Accountability Office, 2007b.

[19] Schiller, 2004.

[20] The unfortunate partial consequences of a well-known social movement offer a second case in point. James Meredith, the first black student at the University of Mississippi, civil rights activist, and scholar, argued that the original participatory goals of the civil rights movement were abandoned and replaced by "a host of federal programs and giveaways," by "liberals looking to buy power." He went on to link this strategy to other harmful consequences. Meredith, 1997.

[21] "For families making up to $60,000 a year, the government will match dollar for dollar the first $1,000 you save. For families making between $60,000 and $100,000, the plan will provide a 50 percent match on the first $1,000 of savings." Hillary for President Press Release, 2007.

$7 million.[22] Promoted as a way to increase retirement savings and ensure a dignified retirement for all participants, the $20–$25 billion program cost would also seem to be a good political move because countless more voters earn less than $100,000 per year than expect to have estates worth more than $7 million.

These examples should not cause us to think that no political decisions are made for right reasons. Nor is polittroughing a newly invented phenomenon: the political maneuver of ingratiating yourself to your political supporters by giving them benefits from the public purse began in ancient times. Moreover, private seekers of public giveaways that benefit them in their businesses or in their private persons welcome and encourage polittroughing.[23]

Critics of the excesses of capitalism are quick to point to overweening greed and love of money as motivations for the evils they wish to fight, forgetting that gold is not all that glitters. Without denying the motivating influence of money, the desire for power and public position is often a stronger motivator.

In the nineteenth century, Alexis de Tocqueville wrote that communities "are composed of certain elements that are common to them at all times and under all circumstances."[24] These groups are the wealthy (in de Tocqueville's time the aristocracy), those in easy circumstances (middle class), and "those who have little or no property and who subsist by the work that they perform" for others. If those with little income or property control politics, "the tendency of the expenditures will be to increase" because,

> as the great majority of those who create the laws have no taxable property, all the money that is spent for the community appears to be spent to their advantage, at no cost of their own.

More surprising is that the wealthy also "will not be sparing of the public funds" because for them taxes only diminish "superfluities" and "are, in fact, little felt" in reducing their lifestyle. Devices such as fostering a dependency on government and polittroughing are agreeable means for the wealthy to satisfy their desire for political office. According to de Tocqueville,[25]

---

[22] Bombardieri, 2007.
[23] The well-used phrase "bread and circuses" traces back to early Rome. "Bread and circuses" is now regarded as describing short-sighted policies that do not address actual problems, but only serve as distractions.
[24] Alexis de Tocqueville, 1835.
[25] Ibid.

content with their lot, power and renown are the only objects for which they strive; placed far above the obscure crowd, they do not always clearly perceive how the well-being of the mass of the people will redound to their own grandeur.

> **Power and renown are the only objects for which they strive.**

Thus, politicians who want power and the masses for whom "all the money that is spent for the community appears to be spent to their advantage, at no cost of their own" form a perfect pairing for polittroughing transactions that can, ironically, be damaging to the interests of all. Promising a lunch club may *sound* good for the masses, but actually is opposed to their good. A similar statement applies to polittroughing generated in response to business lobbying interests.

Polittroughing methods and the class warfare they create were also concerns expressed by the U.S. Supreme Court in its opinion dealing with the income tax (*Pollock v. Farmers' Loan and Trust Company*). The court explained:[26]

Whenever a distinction is made in the burdens a law imposes or in the benefits it confers on any citizens by reason of their birth, or wealth, or religion, it is class legislation, and leads inevitably to oppression and abuses, and to general unrest and disturbance in society. . . . The objectionable legislation reappears in the act under consideration. . . . It will be but the stepping-stone to others, larger and more sweeping, till our political contests will become a war of the poor against the rich; a war constantly growing in intensity and bitterness.

"If the court sanctions the power of discriminating taxation, and nullifies the uniformity mandate of the Constitution," as said by one who has been all his life a student of our institutions, "it will mark the hour when the sure decadence of our present government will commence."

The Supreme Court did not predict an immediate consequence, only that a process "will commence." Political theory is unsuited to predict how long such a process might take. Scientific and social revolutions progress as one generation that adopts a new mode of thinking – this can be for good or for ill – replaces another. Several generations may be required before full effects are felt – long enough for the living memory of the older generations to pass fully and a new generation to come to power. Unrestrained by principles that are no longer remembered, the new political leaders take self-interested action based on the rationale that it is morally just for one group only, the rich, to pay taxes for programs on which all vote. The Supreme Court explained its logic:

[26] Pollock v. Farmers' Loan and Trust Company, 1895.

If the purely arbitrary limitation of $4,000 in the present law can be sustained, none having less than that amount of income being assessed or taxed for the support of the government, the limitation of future Congresses may be fixed at a much larger sum, at five or ten or twenty thousand dollars, parties possessing an income of that amount alone being bound to bear the burdens of government. . . . A majority may fix the limitation at such rate as will not include any of their own number.

One might argue that we are not far today from the Supreme Court's prediction. In 2001, the bottom 43 percent of income tax filers paid no federal income tax. As noted in Chapter 2, the bottom 55 percent of filers paid only 8/10 of one percent (0.8 percent) of the income taxes paid.[27]

Much more could be gathered to support the argument that polittroughing is the natural outcome of the political process. De Tocqueville's message is mirrored in numerous statements including those of such well known economists as Knut Wicksell, Nobel laureate James M. Buchanan, and others. In Buchanan's view, "If you want to improve politics, improve the rules, improve the structure. Don't expect politicians to behave differently. They behave according to their interests."[28] If the majority pays no taxes, the operative incentives collapse to one: provide the majority benefits paid for by the minority.[29]

We conclude thus: With respect to health care, is it unrealistic to believe that federal intervention, however slight, will become the object of political abuse by program supporters for their personal interests if the arrangements of the program are not set in advance, as much as is possible, to prevent polittroughing? If the answer is no, it behooves us to establish a firm foundation with ample safeguards for a new health care plan.

3.5. Principle 5: No Governmentalizing

"Governmentalizing": Conversion of an action better handled by individuals, markets, or the voluntary private sector into a government function, often with worse or harmful results.

Polittroughing can involve the abuse of otherwise legitimate government programs. Governmentalization is the expansion of government into areas that are better left to markets, individuals, or voluntary private organizations. Governmentalizing exposes programs to the dual threat of less

---

[27] Joint Committee on Taxation, 2001. For low-income filers, the Earned Income Tax Credit causes net taxes paid to be negative.

[28] Buchanan, 1995.

[29] "A politician who's seeking office or seeking to remain in office. . . wants to go back to a constituency and tell them that. . . he's brought them program benefits." Ibid.

effective outcomes and the excesses of polittroughing. The Nobel economist Milton Friedman enunciated a principle that we summarize as follows: Write down the objectives of a public program. Write down the opposite of the objectives. The public program very often will more closely accomplish the opposite of its intended objectives. The tendency to accomplish the opposite has been discussed and explained by a number of economists over the years. In the second half of the twentieth century, the debate over central planning was a debate about government. Friedman writes:[30]

> Which if any of the great "reforms" of past decades has achieved its objectives? Have the good intentions of the proponents of these reforms been realized?...Is it an accident that so many of the governmental reforms of recent decades have gone awry, that the bright hopes have turned to ashes? Is it simply because the programs are faulty in detail?
>
> I believe the answers are clear. Few, if any, of the great reforms accomplished their intended objectives, despite good intentions. It is no accident that they have gone awry; they were flawed from their inception. The central defect of these measures is that they seek through government to force people to act against their own immediate interests in order to promote a supposedly general interest.... This is the major reason why the measures have so often had the opposite of their intended effects.

Economist Gary Becker, also a Nobel recipient, discusses the Americans with Disabilities Act.[31] "The Americans with Disabilities Act (ADA) of 1990 was supposed to end discrimination against disabled workers." Instead, "employment of disabled workers fell rather than rose,... Truly disabled workers might be better off if the ADA were scrapped altogether." The reason: "Many companies apparently avoid hiring job applicants whom they believe would prove litigious under the ADA."[32]

California wanted in recent years to ensure that women received a greater share of the joint estate in divorce settlements. A law requiring that women should be paid no less than half the estate was passed. The result: Women were harmed by the law and eventually came to oppose it. Why? Requiring the divorce settlement to provide them with half of the assets often required that the couple's house be sold. Previously, the wife was allowed to live in the home while the husband found shelter elsewhere. Intended to improve the welfare of divorced women, the law did the reverse.

Producing additional examples, which is possible, might still be interpreted wrongly unless one sees that the examples are not meant to point out

---

[30] Milton Friedman, 1962, pp. 197–200.
[31] Becker, 1999.
[32] Ibid.

the failings of a particular place, person, or time but instead say something about the act of intervention itself. In 1840, Fredric Bastiat explained:[33]

In the economics sphere an act, a habit, an institution, a law produces not only one effect, but a series of effects. Of these effects, the first alone is immediate; it appears simultaneously with its cause; it is seen. The other effects emerge only subsequently; they are not seen; we are fortunate if we foresee them.

There is only one difference between a bad economist and a good one: the bad economist confines himself to the visible effect; the good economist takes into account both the effect that can be seen and those effects that must be foreseen.

Yet this difference is tremendous; for it almost always happens that when the immediate consequence is favorable, the later consequences are disastrous, and vice versa. Whence, it follows that the bad economist pursues a small present good that will be followed by a great evil to come, while the good economist pursues a great good to come, at the risk of a small present evil.

The quality of government decision making is dependent in the long run on the information available to the decision maker, which can never be as complete as the relevant information known to the public. Commenting over 150 years later on Bastiat's observations, yet another Nobel economist, Friederich Hayek, said that individuals must be able to "make full use of the particular circumstances of which only they know" that provide benefits to them and others.[34] On some probabilistic basis, therefore, government actions are unavoidably restrictions.

Bastiat, Becker, Buchanan, and Friedman are not saying that government is necessarily inept; certainly they do not say that it has no role. Rather, a scientific understanding of private information, incentives, and the way politicians must function implies that when government

> When government goes beyond identifiable bounds, disappointing results should be expected.

goes beyond identifiable bounds, disappointing results should be expected to follow. In Buchanan's words, people could see "that political programs were failing. Public choice came along and was there to provide them an explanation – an understanding – of why politics was failing as it extended beyond certain margins."[35]

Recognizing that certain government-limiting margins exist is a justly celebrated major advance in modern understanding. It is hard to find something unless you look for it.

[33] Bastiat, 1995.
[34] Hayek, 1995.
[35] Buchanan, 1995.

3.6. Principle 6: No Ponzi Schemes

Ponzi scheme: A financial arrangement that is characterized by participants' being paid returns from the contributions of those who come later, and actual economic undertaking or investment is token or nonexistent. Ponzi schemes are named for Charles Ponzi, who deceived thousands of New England residents in the 1920s with such a method.

Virtually universal agreement exists on the need to avoid Ponzi schemes in public programs. If some particular favorite government program, which may be the subject of much polittroughing and the hoped-for source of personal political or economic gain, is revealed to be a Ponzi scheme, then avoiding it should be non-controversial. A program cannot be a Ponzi scheme if it is to survive in a financially sound and stable way for all generations to benefit from equally. As pointed out in Chapter 2, and touched on again in this chapter, sustainability is one of the core requirements of a national health care plan.

Ponzi schemes and their pyramid scheme variants require a proper ratio of money taken in from new recruits relative to the payouts of earlier participants to continue operation. The tendency for the promoters of Ponzi schemes is to promise payouts beyond what can be maintained in a steady-state equilibrium. Thus, ever increasing exactions in the form of increased number of new recruits and increasing amounts taken from each one characterize the history of Ponzi schemes. According to the Securities and Exchange Commission "at some point the schemes get too big, the promoter cannot raise enough money from new investors to pay earlier investors, and many people lose their money."[36] If the Ponzi scheme is private and new participants cannot be forced to enter, the scheme collapses. If the Ponzi scheme is public, collapse is avoided by some or all of (1) forcing new investors into the plan, (2) treating new investors less well than early investors, (3) harming some new investors by their association with the program, or (4) reducing previously promised benefits to old investors. The natural progression is that early adopters are handsomely paid, but as the scheme progresses, larger and larger numbers of new investors must be recruited to keep the scheme going. At first this is possible, but eventually not.

The most obvious example of a government program set up like a Ponzi scheme is Social Security. Social Security began as a modest program that many had no idea would grow into the enormous social institution that it

---

[36] See U.S. Securities and Exchange Commission, 2007.

actually became. Social Security and later Medicaid and Medicare started small but quickly became the object of enlargement by congresses eager to earn votes from the elderly and support from companies that profited from the programs. One of the resulting confusions about Social Security has been whether it is a forced savings plan, an insurance plan, or a government welfare plan. Because the amount of charity embedded in the money given to earlier generations of Social Security recipients is unsustainable by almost all accounts, it is unlikely that future generations will receive similar windfalls.

The insecurity of Social Security has not gone unnoticed, as the following collection of opinions from experts, including a Nobel economist, and the media attest.

Just like Ponzi's plan, Social Security does not make any real investments – it just takes money from later "investors," or taxpayers, to pay benefits to earlier, now retired, taxpayers. Like Ponzi, Social Security will not be able to recruit new "investors" fast enough to continue paying promised benefits to previous investors. Because each year there are fewer young workers relative to the number of retirees, Social Security will eventually collapse, just like Ponzi's scheme.[37]

Social Security is a Ponzi scheme headed for collapse. It is a pay-as-you-go program. Taxes from working Americans go directly into the pockets of retired Americans. (There's a tiny bit left over for a so-called "trust fund," which will soon be depleted.) Initial retirees scored big, as early winners who are bait for any Ponzi. The very first recipient, Ida May Fuller, paid in $44 and collected benefits of $20,934.[38]

The assurance that workers will receive benefits when they retire does not depend on the particular tax used to finance the benefits or on any "trust fund." It depends solely on the expectation that future Congresses will honor promises made by earlier Congresses – what supporters call "a compact between the generations" and opponents call a Ponzi scheme.[39]

In its present form, Social Security is a ticking bomb. By taxing a large part of a worker's income and promising "security," the system reduces the worker's ability and incentive to save and hinders long-term growth. Although the program was initially designed to invest funds for retirement, it was changed to a pay-as-you-go system in 1939.... Like all Ponzi schemes, the Social Security system is coming under increasing strain. What will actually happen, and is already happening, is that the government will welsh on its promises.[40]

According to polls, more members of Generation X believe in UFOs than do in Social Security.... Gen-Xers seem more willing than older folks to grasp the essential truth about Social Security, which is that it is a Ponzi scheme.[41]

---

[37] Cato Institute, 2005.
[38] Glassman, 2005.
[39] Friedman, 1999.
[40] Genetski, 1993.
[41] Kinsley, 1996.

Why would we select something as controversial to highlight as Social Security? The point is this: if Social Security – as widely beloved, with as much attention and support as it has received over the years – cannot continue on a basis that is equally generous to later generations as it was to the first, then what hope is there that *any* public program based on Ponzi principles can be sustainable?

Summary

A health care system could be constructed that ignores the principles of this chapter. But why would we want to? The intervention principle guides us to the efficient tool to induce insurance purchase. Incentive symmetry is a public finance tool that allows us better to target incentives. The every-pot-on-its-own-base principle implies that the base insurance should be bought and sold on an actuarially fair basis and that charity should be separately and transparently provided. Polittroughing describes a political threat that public programs can recognize and guard against. Governmentalization recognizes that efficiency requires that collective actions be assigned to the appropriate type of agent chosen from markets, voluntary private organizations, and government. Ponzi schemes are unsustainable. Requiring that public programs not be Ponzi schemes is a necessary condition for sustainability. Applying these principles points us toward specific health care arrangements that are efficient and equitable, and able to sustain themselves for all generations.

PART II

BACKGROUND ECONOMICS AND ETHICS

FOUR

Markets, VPOs, Government

I think the tendency when anyone thinks of a policy is that either individuals should do it for themselves or the state should do it. I'm struck by the fact that there are a number of situations where the policy expert doesn't understand that there are other institutions. There are many cases where these other institutions are probably superior, because the state has constraints on its actions, even the ideal state, leaving aside corruption and things like that.

Kenneth Arrow, Nobel Economist, 2006

Summary: The debate is not between government and markets, but rather about the proper division of collective action among the available institutions of collective action. Markets, voluntary private organizations (VPOs), and government each work best in some arenas and less than best in others. Their range of potential operations overlap. Thus, it is important to be aware that there is a proper division and assignment of responsibilities in the affairs of men, which "taken at the flood," in the words of the poet, "leads on to fortune. Omitted, all the voyage of their life is bound in shallows and in miseries. On such a full sea are we now afloat. And we must take the current when it serves, or lose our ventures" (Shakespeare).

Man is characterized by the fact that we are a cooperative species. Cooperators tend to succeed more often than non-cooperators because they create win-win encounters. Two can do more than twice one, and many working together can do exponentially more. Even as simple a task as making the bed takes less than half the time when two work together. Economists like Cornell's Robert Frank have spent their careers exploring issues of cooperation such as the following: How do cooperators identify one another?[1] How do norms that punish non-cooperation

> **Cooperators tend to succeed more often than non-cooperators because they create win-win encounters.**

---

[1] See, for example, Robert Frank, 2004.

enhance social outcomes? Do certain types of education change cooperative behavior? Conflict also characterizes our interactions with one another,
but cooperation is important for explaining societal advancement, whereas
conflict leads to decline. As individuals, we are certainly better off living in
society compared to isolation.

Seeing the world from the vantage of individual versus collective action
provides a natural perspective to wonder, When is collective action better
and what type of collective action is best? Most people can identify those
activities for which individual action is appropriate. I do not need a committee to oversee my tying my shoes or buying my lunch. I do need others
to be involved, however, in providing a nearby restaurant or the road on
which to drive to it. In this chapter, therefore, we explore the rationales
that select among private markets, voluntary private organizations (VPOs),
and government as the vehicle of collective action.[2] All three are coordi-
nating devices that harness the efforts and energies of multiple people to
accomplish something that each acting alone could not.

> **When VPOs, government, or the market is wrongly applied to tasks, it can cause significant, predictable, and avoidable social losses and harm.**

This chapter is necessary because many
people do not realize that markets, VPOs,
and government frequently overlap in their
ability to accomplish objectives, but the
quantity and quality of the outcomes are
not indifferent to the agent. When VPOs,
government, or the market is wrongly
applied to tasks, it can cause significant,
predictable, and avoidable social losses and
harm. Selecting among institutions of collective action is not a matter of personal
preference; it is a matter of what works and what does not. Recall the theme,
reiterated in Chapter 3, that good intentions do not prevent ignorantly
structured plans from hurting people.

Many interpret the last half of the twentieth century as a testing period
across many economies and countries. It took the better part of 50 years to
reach the conclusion that even though government is a planning mechanism, so are markets, and the outcome of government central planning is
not as successful as market outcomes over a broad range of activities. At the

---

[2] While the term may be self-explanatory, it is important to note that the legal structure often
recognizes *VPOs* in special ways. Thus, not-for-profit organizations of all kinds, charitable
foundations, educational institutions, giving organizations like the United Way, and the
Red Cross are examples of VPOs.

same time, markets must be kept in check by the presence of competition, which frequently requires government. Firms can make profits to the benefit of their customers, but they can just as easily make profit at their expense. When you buy a carton of milk you must be reasonably sure that it contains what it says it does on the label, not some disease-laden white-colored liquid.

Ultimately, we want to know what activities to assign to government, to VPOs, and to markets because we want what is best for the provision of health care.

4.1. Voluntary Private Organizations

Voluntary private organizations, as their name implies, are the result of like-minded individuals willingly banding together to achieve common economic purposes. Examples might include the American Cancer Society, a group formed to provide funding for research on a class of diseases, or the United Way, a charity organization that facilitates the giving function. Another might be the Harvard Coop of Cambridge, Massachusetts, a buyers' cooperative where the surplus of the group is distributed to members according to the extent of their participation, measured by the value of goods bought through the cooperative. A sellers' cooperative is also possible, as in the case of Wisconsin dairy farmers who sell their milk to the cooperative, which in turn sells the milk to other buyers. Farmers receive a share of the cooperative end-of-year surplus according to their participation as measured by amount of milk sold to the cooperative. A business firm is a capital cooperative, where the surplus of the firm is distributed according to participation measured by shares of capital supplied (stock owned) to the economic endeavor.

Not-for-profit organizations are the most commonly considered voluntary private organization, perhaps because they receive the special sanction of law in recognition of their religious, charitable, educational, scientific, fraternal, literary, or research objectives. Not-for-profit organizations operate under different legal rules in view of the presumed value to society of their activities. For example, not-for-profits do not pay taxes, can receive tax-deductible donations, cannot distribute profits, and are governed by one-member, one-vote boards of directors, among other differences. The legal distinctions between not-for-profit and for-profit organizations constitute a demanding study in itself.

Many people presume that not-for-profit organizations are more "virtuous" or high-minded than for-profits precisely because they are not motivated by profit. On reflection, however, the case is not so clear cut: the lack of tax liability can be interpreted to mean that not-for-profits do not contribute to the common good by paying their share of taxes; the lack of a board elected by shareholders can mean that they are not accountable for good behavior and efficient operation; and the inability to distribute profits may mean that the surplus is instead applied to extravagances for the executive directors and board members, rather than for the worthy objectives stated in the organization's bylaws or constitution.

A better, economic-based interpretation is that usually one type of circumstance or objective can fruitfully be matched to a particular structure for best outcomes. The study of VPOs has taken up such questions, in terms of both describing their many types and functions, as well as explaining the reason for the forms that they take.[3] Why does a buyers' cooperative arise in some circumstances, a sellers' cooperative in another, a charitable form in a third, and a capital cooperative in a fourth? The explanation seems to be that the forms that survive in some way lower the societal costs of accomplishing the desired collective action, and do so better than other forms. Two examples suffice: Consider that the threat to dairy farmers in a Wisconsin county is that the buyer of their milk might take advantage of them. The county is not likely to support many buyers – hence monopsony is a real risk – and the costs to an individual seller of finding the best buyer and price are high relative to pooling their efforts. A sellers' cooperative solves both problems: the cooperative is operated by the dairies themselves so its price will not abuse them, and the pooling of their selling allows the cooperative to prevent duplication and more efficiently sell the county's milk. Fine arts councils are another structure that may serve a surprising purpose. Take the case of opera. To survive, in many cities opera would need to charge some patrons far more than the price per ticket that low-end buyers are willing to pay. By significantly funding the opera through a not-for-profit, large donors are more willing to give because they get a tax break, recognition, and the personal satisfaction of being a benefactor. If they were just charged more for their ticket because they appeared to be wealthy and able to

> The explanation seems to be that the forms that survive in some way lower the societal costs of accomplishing the desired collective action, and so do better than other forms.

---

[3] See Henry Hansmann, 1996, for an economic theory of enterprise forms.

afford it, their primary sentiment might be one of resentment. Changing the structural form allows opera to survive supported by a not-for-profit VPO.

The lesson from this literature is that VPOs arise in response to the need for collective action and survive because they are often *the best way* to get collective "things" done. Instead of focusing attention on their legal structure, which is an artifact of legislation taken in response to their evident social value, the most important thing to be said about VPOs is that they arise spontaneously to meet a collective need.

4.2. Markets

In a market, the individual takes an action because he or she *wants* to. If a transaction is not in his or her interest, it can be refused. Sellers pursue profit because maximizing profit raises their income, and spending more income allows them to maximize their well-being. Buyers, of course, selfishly purchase what is good for them as well. Markets are not the result of planning in the way that a VPO is the result of the planning of a group of individuals but nevertheless are the outcome of separate actions planned by buyers and sellers. No one "makes" a market; the market "makes" itself.

When travelers arrive in a large city like Dallas or Chicago, they do not need to have planned every detail of the food they will eat. They know that a market exists there for food, and they will be able to buy what they want. Planning for their food needs occurs; it is just done by the market.

Markets have had more written about them than could be contained in many books. Readers scanning this section may fear that we are about to launch into an attempt to describe their virtues and wonders. As much as we would like to, it is impossible to match – and certainly impossible to exceed – the quality of what has already been written about the desirable features of collective action accomplished through markets.[4] For non-economist readers, however, there must be some "guided tour" of relevant results to form the basis of comparison when the time arrives to discuss health care and how to accomplish economic objectives in the health care sector.

Economics as a separate discipline is widely regarded as beginning with the publication of the Scottish author Adam Smith's *An Inquiry into the Nature and Causes of the Wealth of Nations* in 1776. Smith's main message was that a nation's wealth lay in the industriousness and abilities of its people, not in other notions popular at his time. Smith's justly famous "invisible hand" passage explains that because the amount of social good created

---

[4] Those interested in more on the virtues of markets may want to begin by reading Friedman's *Capitalism and Freedom*, 1962.

in society is measured by the "exchangeable value" of everything produced, and this, in turn, is made as large as possible by individuals, the action of all such entities operating independently makes the total social good as great as possible. This was the first enunciation of the role of markets as engines of social good for the creation and provision of private goods.

As every individual, therefore, endeavours as much as he can both to employ his capital in the support of domestic industry, and so to direct that industry that its produce may be of the greatest value; every individual necessarily labours to render the annual revenue of the society as great as he can. He generally, indeed, neither intends to promote the public interest, nor knows how much he is promoting it... by directing that industry in such a manner as its produce may be of the greatest value, he intends only his own gain, and he is in this, as in many other cases, led by an invisible hand to promote an end which was no part of his intention. Nor is it always the worse for the society that it was no part of it. By pursuing his own interest he frequently promotes that of the society more effectually than when he really intends to promote it. I have never known much good done by those who affected to trade for the public good.[5]

> **The remarkable insight of Adam Smith was that uncoordinated promotion of self-interest was socially good, and that expression of compassion by those who "affected to trade for the public good" was not effective and often inimical to the social good.**

The remarkable insight of Adam Smith was that uncoordinated promotion of self-interest was socially good, and that expression of compassion by those who "affected to trade for the public good" was not effective and often inimical to the social good. It took economists nearly 175 years to formalize Smith's doctrine in a precise enough way that it could be stated as a mathematical theorem. In the intervening years, more has been learned about the nature of markets. Competitive markets, of which Smith was speaking, are described by four related characteristics.[6]

1. *Standardized Product.* A product that is standardized is "commoditized" in business parlance, meaning that buyers in a competitive market are familiar with the product and can compare like with like when shopping various suppliers. Products sold by one supplier are perfect substitutes for those sold by any other.

---

[5] Adam Smith, 1776b.
[6] These are discussed in more detail in Grinols, 1994, pp. 263–268.

2. *Price Taking.* Closely related to the requirement that the product be susceptible to comparison across suppliers is the requirement that sellers do not have the ability to act strategically in controlling the market price at which they sell. Price taking usually results from the ability of a firm's buyers to access products from competitors easily.
3. *Contestability.* A competitive market is contestable, meaning that firms can enter and exit easily in response to profit incentives. There is competition *for* the market as well as competition *in* the market.
4. *Perfect Information.* Buyers know the price, description, and availability of products. They are able to acquire the information necessary for making their choices. Likewise, firms can acquire the information they need to make production and selling decisions.

Markets operate in the context of "an economy." An economy is a collection of citizens, physical endowments of resources they control, and their available technology (know-how) to use resources in production. In a competitive economy, firms choose their actions to maximize profits taking prices as given, households make their purchases and sales to maximize personal satisfaction (utility) taking prices as given, and markets clear in equilibrium, meaning that quantity demanded equals quantity supplied in each market.

We are nearly ready to state Smith's theorem in a modern way but need one additional concept. How do we identify a healthy economy? To answer this question we turn to work originating with Vilfredo Pareto, an Italian economist of the late 1800s and early 1900s, who said that an economy is *efficient* if it is impossible to reorganize it to increase one individual's utility without harming another's. Equivalently, an economy is Pareto efficient if any reorganization of it harms someone

> If you can do things differently in a way that helps someone and hurts no one, then doing things differently is better.

or leaves everyone indifferent. If you can do things differently in a way that helps someone and hurts no one, then doing things differently is better.

Pareto efficiency identifies situations as *inefficient* when a change could be made that harms no one but helps one or more. Much of the field of welfare economics is devoted to describing tests for an economy to see whether it is Pareto efficient or Pareto inefficient. For example, assume that you have an economy. If persons 1 and 2 can be found in it for which the first would be willing to trade one apple for one orange, and the second would be willing to trade at any different rate, then it is possible to reorganize (allow them to conduct certain trades with one another) and make both better off and harm no one. Economists call the willingness-to-trade ratio for two goods x and y the *marginal rate of substitution of x for y* ($MRS_{x,y}$). In essence, $MRS_{x,y}^1$ is person 1's personalized value of good x. $MRS_{x,y}^1 > MRS_{x,y}^2$ implies that person 1 values good x more highly than person 2 and should acquire x from person 2 in trade. Thus eBay, by linking buyers and sellers who value the things being traded differently, creates greater utility for the nation by facilitating such trades in the same way that neighborhood garage sales do. Pareto efficiency, or often just "efficiency," is the measure of success for an economy that we want.

First and Second Fundamental Theorems of Welfare Economics (FTWE)

The first fundamental theorem of welfare economics, appearing in several forms in the 1950s, was proved in *Theory of Value* (1959) by Gerard Debreu, who later received the Nobel Prize in economics for his work. We state here in a non-technical way the content of the theorems.

First Fundamental Theorem of Welfare Economics (FTWE): A competitive equilibrium is Pareto efficient.

The first FTWE can be fully understood only in conjunction with the second, equally important theorem.

Second Fundamental Theorem of Welfare Economics: Any Pareto efficient arrangement of an economy replicates the circumstances of a competitive equilibrium for the economy with appropriate assignment of ownerships.

In other words, if firms are maximizing profits by what they make and sell, households are maximizing their utility by what they sell (e.g., labor) and buy, and markets clear, the resulting outcome is efficient.

The theorems are beautiful in their simplicity. The precision of the theorems in their mathematical form (not shown) has sometimes obscured their meaning and led to misunderstanding. An economy owned by a single despot certainly would not operate in the interests of its citizens because the despot would act as a monopolist against them. To rule out this and other situations, the theorems deal with the four market characteristics of competition and require that they apply, which, strictly speaking, they cannot with complete force. For example, taken to the extreme, the characteristic that products be standardized would require that products be *exactly* identical across suppliers. Contestability of markets requires costless entry and exit, and entry or exit costs can never be literally zero. Also, information is never perfect. In other words, the act of stating with precision the circumstances in which the theorems hold produces conditions that can be approached only as a limiting or ideal case. How should this be interpreted?

It is said that if you are a hammer, everything looks like a nail. By unintentionally fixing attention on the characteristics required for the theorems to hold, a whole generation of economists was taught to believe that the theorems described inapplicable idealizations, overlooking the fact that the first and second fundamental theorems of welfare economics reveal in a precise way that efficiency is an independent property of economies. Whether one speaks of a market economy or a centrally planned one, whether the economy is one of the pharaohs or of feudal lords, whether it exists in a hunter-gatherer society or an agricultural one, and whether markets and prices are present or not, efficiency in any economy *is the same thing as* a competitive market equilibrium. Competitive markets are not the means to an end; they are the same thing as the end. To achieve a social state that is efficient, you want to achieve a social state that is a competitive market equilibrium because the two are identical. This understanding eliminates the sterile debate over whether markets or government or voluntary private organizations are "better." Rather, the issue is what governments, markets, and VPOs need to do to cause the economy to look as close to a competitive market equilibrium as possible, because we want efficiency. Each form of collective action has a role. Improperly assigning those roles is what causes problems.

As already noted, the twentieth century from the time of the Bolshevik Revolution onward is interpreted by many historians and others as a grand global experiment in which communism, Nazism, socialism, central planning, and market-based democratic systems vied for supremacy as the means to organize society.

The decay of the Soviet experiment should come as no surprise. Wherever the comparisons have been made between free and closed societies – West Germany and East Germany, Austria and Czechoslovakia, Malaysia and Vietnam – it is the democratic countries that are prosperous and responsive to the needs of their people. And one of the simple but overwhelming facts of our time is this: of all the millions of refugees we have seen in the modern world, their flight is always away from, not toward the Communist world.[7]

What the twentieth century taught was that government failure and system failure in non-market structures are just as important a consideration as market failure. Friedrich Hayek's *The Road to Serfdom* is a justly

---

[7] Ronald Reagan, 1982.

celebrated review and analysis of the consequences of government planning in parts of the economy where markets and the decentralized planning associated with them work better. John Jewkes's *Ordeal by Planning* and *New Ordeal by Planning* document the standard traps that central planners fall into. These include "the craving for a new world," "oversimplification of the economic problem," "consumption as a crime," "fear of the price system," "contempt for the distributor," and "obscurity of language."[8] Every generation produces yet again a group of reformers who long for a better world. Their goal is to form through their re-arrangement of society a new order that will improve on the arrangements that free interaction of economic agents produces, which are markets. The bottom line is that few economists today believe that central planning demonstrated its superiority over markets. The vast majority believe the reverse is true.

VPOs, Markets, Government in FTWE Framework

Connecting market equilibria to efficiency offers a useful template against which VPOs, markets, and government can be measured. Efficiency requires the equivalent of competitive markets, defined by a set of conditions that can be identified. Those conditions that must be present before others can follow result in an inventory of requirements for Pareto efficiency: national defense, law and order, contract enforcement, provision for equipping, competition, provision for public goods and externalities, and provision

> Efficiency requires the equivalent of competitive markets, defined by a set of conditions that can be identified.

for the incapable needy. Many items on the list point to the need for collective action that clearly will not be met by voluntary private organizations or markets. We elaborate on each briefly before moving to an expanded discussion of the implied role of government in this and the next chapter.

1. **National defense.** Little need be said to justify protection of a nation's citizens against violence and physical harm from outsiders. The Constitution begins with the words "We the people of the United States, in order to form a more perfect union, establish justice, insure domestic tranquility, provide for the common defense, promote the general welfare, and secure the blessings of liberty to ourselves and our posterity, do ordain and establish this Constitution for the United States

---

[8] Jewkes, 1968, pp. 97–120.

of America." The first and second fundamental theorems of welfare economics presume that the buyers and sellers they describe are *secure* in their persons.

2. **Law and order.** Without social order and enforcement of law, peaceful dealings are impossible: we would be hostage to victimization by the misfits, brigands, wrongdoers, fraudsters, and criminals who inevitably are born into every generation.

3. **Contract enforcement.** Rules of interaction oil the machinery of commerce. They govern ownership of property, agreements, contracts, and the other conventions that facilitate exchange among honest people.

4. **Provision for equipping.** The first and second fundamental theorems of welfare economics presume agents (families and households) that are able by virtue of their abilities, asset ownership, and intentions to make their way in the economy. This presumption is notably violated in the case of children and adolescents, who must acquire education, reach majority, and acquire skills sufficiently valuable to allow them to provide for themselves. At a minimum, every agent owns his or her own labor time, the sale or use of which should be valuable enough to sustain existence. Equipping the next generation to provide for themselves is consistent with the first and second fundamental theorems of economics because the theorems presume families and households are able to sustain themselves in equilibrium.

5. **Competition.** An efficient economy is an economy whose configuration replicates a competitive market equilibrium. It is consistent with the first and second FTWE that competition is present and invalid forms of competition are absent.

6. **Provision for public goods and externalities.** Many goods and services are private in nature, but others are public, a distinction that has close ties to the concept of externalities, defined as follows:

An externality is an effect that a firm or household's choices have on other firms or households that does not operate through market prices. A helpful effect is referred to as a positive externality; a harmful effect is referred to as a negative externality. A firm whose production process pollutes the air creates a negative externality. It is the nature of externalities – because the positive or negative effects apply to others – that the agent causing them does not consider them properly when making the decisions that cause the externality.[9]

---

[9] Grinols, 2004 pp. 198–199.

Private provision of private goods (markets) and public provision of public goods are generally regarded as appropriate and consistent with the first and second FTWE where public goods are present. This is explained further in the public goods discussion of Section 4.3, "Government."

7. **Provision for the incapable needy.** There are individuals who for various reasons never reach the state of being able to provide for themselves. It is consistent with the first and second FTWE that these individuals be recognized in social arrangements overseen by government as a matter of social insurance. We will elaborate on this conclusion in Chapter 5.

4.3. Government

We now have an efficiency framework – the requirements of well-being for families and households – to determine the scope of operation for VPOs, markets, and government. Political thinkers, particularly John Locke and the other philosophers consulted by the framers of the Constitution, studied social contract theory and human nature to refine the format that their government would take for best results. They were primarily concerned about issues of liberty, corruption, and excesses of power. Concepts of man in the hypothetical state of nature, the role of social compacts, and the need for means to regulate the interactions of humans as they live in proximity to one another and as they function in government form a body of political theory that still has relevance today. John Adams, who wrote the Massachusetts constitution, was instrumental in framing the U.S. Constitution, and later served as second president, spent a great deal of his intellectual life in the study of republican government. The Nobel laureate James M. Buchanan and others have advanced the science of government,[10] but in many ways the work of Adams's generation is still relevant and among the best available.

National defense, law and order, and contract enforcement issues are government tasks that have been so recognized for centuries. The remaining identified tasks – provision for equipping, maintenance of competition, provision for public goods and externalities, and provision for the incapable needy – are more modern concerns. How do we synthesize and incorporate the recent insights – most established within living memory – of economics?

---

[10] The Library of Economics and Liberty maintained by the Liberty Fund has compiled a fully searchable version of Buchanan's works. See Liberty Fund, 2008.

The goal is to recognize the essential contributions of government in achieving the highest feasible production of well-being for "the people."

We would like to reserve discussion of provision for equipping and provision for the incapable needy for Chapters 5 and 6. That leaves competition, provision for public goods, and externalities to cover here.

Competitive Markets and Externalities

We described competition in Section 4.2 as the mechanism – a policeman of sorts – that keeps firms maximizing profit *in* the public interest instead of *at the expense of* the public interest. Most of us recognize the need for some kind of oversight to ensure that competition is present. The trust-busting days of the 1890s and the presidency of Theodore Roosevelt inaugurated the modern era of pro-competitive government involvement.

The absence of competitive markets also plays a large role in the contributions of the Nobel economist Robert Coase. Coase was the first to understand the significance of the fact that the existence of an externality implies the absence of an associated market in the externality, and the absence of a market is the result of inappropriate or missing property rights.[11]

For example, in the classic honeybee-apple orchard externality (honeybees provide beneficial pollination to neighboring fields), the number of bee hives placed in fields near a neighbor's apple orchard will be too low if there is no market in pollination services. One can imagine the difficulties that hive owners could have in trying to collect for the pollination that their bees performed by chance in neighboring fields. Some of the constraints could be technological, some legal. However, if there is a market in pollination services – as indeed there is in the real world – the externality problem disappears. Pollination services are bought and sold as other commodities are, and the placement of hives in the orchards during pollination season delivers the service. Coase made other important contributions by pointing out that agents who can costlessly bargain with one another have an incentive to act in ways that

> Coase was the first to understand the significance of the fact that the existence of an externality implies the absence of an associated market in the externality, and the absence of a market is the result of inappropriate or missing property rights.

---

[11] Coase, 1966.

will appropriately solve the externality issues among them. If the beekeeper and orchard owner can costlessly talk, they will work out between them the best way to get the most honey and apples. To do otherwise is for them to leave money on the table.

> The principle that applies is that social arrangements should be such that the agent that has the ability to take the best corrective action to deal with the externality should also have the incentive to do so.

In the absence of costless interaction among agents, however, the way government sets the rules of ownership and rules about who is liable for externality-caused damages creates incentives that govern agent behavior and matter to the achievement of efficiency. The principle that applies is that social arrangements should be such that the agent who has the ability to take the best corrective action to deal with the externality should also have the incentive to do so. The implication of Coase and others is that government may have a role by selecting as appropriate from the following list of responses:

1. First line of defense. Do nothing. It may be that the perceived problems are self-correcting. For example, monopolies sometimes result from temporary conditions that market forces will eliminate. Andrew Carnegie wrote, "There are only two conditions other than patents which render it possible to maintain a monopoly. These are when the parties absolutely control the raw material out of which the article is produced, or control territory into which rivals can enter only with extreme difficulty."[12] Technological knowledge needed to produce the commodity or its substitute can be considered a form of input. Thus cable television experienced competition from dish satellite only when technological advances made the latter available. When the issue is externality, it may be that private parties involved have the incentives and ability to solve the problem without direct government action.

2. Second line of defense. Property rights. Presuming that the first line of defense is insufficient, establish property rights and the necessary conditions for markets so that competition results and, if externalities are present, they are internalized.

3. Third line of defense. Per-unit taxes. Presuming the first two defenses are unavailable, set taxes so that a firm or household sees in its decisions

---

[12] Carnegie, 1962.

the proper social costs and values. If my production of widgets imposes costs of $10 on society for each unit I produce, then I should be taxed $10 per unit so that I take account of these effects. The analysis of Robert Coase reminds us that the arrangements should be selected so that the agent that has the best ability to deal with the externality should also have the incentive to do so.

4. Fourth line of defense. Direct regulation. This is always available to government. However, acquiring enough information to be able to tell industry what it should do satisfactorily is frequently a difficult-to-impossible task.

5. Fifth line of defense. Nationalize the activity. Running the enterprise or industry as a government division is an option that is always available. The practical objections and difficulties in succeeding have generally been prohibitive, however.

Public Goods

Most economists agree that public goods should be publicly provided and private goods should be privately provided. This may seem obvious but requires understanding of the standard definitions of public and private goods. Public provision of private goods mixes assignments and creates problematic incentives.

Rivals are two individuals vying for something that only one can have. Rival goods are goods that can be consumed by only one individual. Private goods are rival. On the other hand, pure public goods are defined by the fact that they can be consumed by many people without diminishing the ability of others to consume the same good. Public goods are non-rival. A sunny-side-up cooked egg is a private good because when you eat it for breakfast, no one else can have the same egg. A radio broadcast is a public good because additional listeners do not diminish anyone's ability to pick up the same signal and listen. Public goods exhibit externalities because one person's

> Most economists agree that public goods should be publicly provided and private goods should be privately provided.

> Public goods are defined by the fact that they can be consumed by many people without diminishing the ability of others to consume the same goods.

provision of a public good creates benefits that accrue to others in the ability to consume the same good. The same is not true for private goods.

Club goods are intermediate cases where congestion begins to play a part in diminishing others' ability to consume the good. A movie theater, once it reaches capacity, cannot offer more individuals the same showing without diminishment of patrons' enjoyment and ability to watch.

Pure public goods, those for which congestion or diminishment does not apply, are typically distinguished from private goods by two other characteristics: nonexcludability and demand revelation problems. The physical production of public goods is done in the normal way: a firm makes the public good from raw materials and inputs of labor and capital. Production costs the firm money that must be made up by sales of the good. If potential buyers cannot be excluded from consuming the good without paying, the firm has no way to prevent losses. For example, presume that the rest of the nation buys national defense; then everyone else's security becomes yours too, whether you contribute to its provision or not.

The benefits of private goods are fully received and paid for by the persons who buy them in private markets, which, if competitive, lead to Pareto efficiency (first FTWE). The same is not true for a public good. Our abbreviated discussion of the issues of public goods in conjunction with the fundamental theorems of welfare economics explains why private goods, rival in nature, are generally best privately provided by markets, and public goods, with spillover effects, are generally best publicly provided by government. With respect to health care we note that scheduled surgery in operating room 5 on Friday at 9 A.M. is a rival good. With the exception of a few things such as the oft-noted public benefit of vaccinations to prevent the spread of epidemic diseases, health care is a private good.

What considerations apply to providing pure public goods? Ideally we would want to know what the benefits to consumers of the good are, and, presuming that we know how much each person benefits, we would have each pay for the benefits he or she gets. This mimics the way markets work for private goods: Paying $4.50 for your sunny-side-up egg breakfast demonstrates that you get at least $4.50 of benefits from eating it. No one else pays for your egg because no one else benefits from eating it.

Presuming traffic density below congestion levels, interstate freeways are a non-rival and, therefore, public good. Charging tolls to those who use them is proper because the tolls are user fees that reflect the amount of driving and benefits that each driver receives. Trucks pay more because they damage the roads more and receive a higher level of service than do cars. Drivers whose benefits from using the interstate fall short of the required tolls will exclude themselves (as is appropriate) and decide to use other roads. Meanwhile, technological advances such as the introduction of EZ-Pass cards and similar devices can greatly diminish the inconvenience of toll paying.

We already apply similar principles in other situations. If you live in New York City, should you pay for the operation and upkeep of a city park in Indianapolis? Our current system says no. The park is paid for by the people who benefit from it (those who live in the city of Indianapolis). In an ideal world, Indianapolis taxes would reflect the exact degree of benefits received from the park, but technological demands of this principle are too great in the current world to make a perfectly precise match between benefits and payments. An approximation is the best we can do.

Paying for public goods in proportion to the benefits received from them is a feature of Lindahl equilibria – essentially the equivalent of competitive equilibria for economies where public goods are present – which can be shown to reach an efficient outcome for an economy.[13] In a Lindahl equilibrium, a public good G conveys benefits to individuals $i = 1, 2, \ldots, m$ and each individual i pays amount p_i per unit of the good equal to the benefit he or she received from it. The total price paid for the public good is the sum of individual payments, $p_G = p_1 + p_2 + \ldots + p_m$. Because prices to the individual reflect benefits received by that individual, all willingly choose the same level of public good G, which is the amount provided. Lindahl equilibria are Pareto efficient and fair: all pay for the public good in proportion to value they receive.

Lindahl equilibria offer a guide to policy. The practical implementation problem is that for many kinds of public goods – unlike freeway use – it is impossible to know the truth about how much someone benefits. Let us say your passion is bird watching, and you are retired coastal dweller and can choose when your capital gains are taken and taxed as income. To sharpen the example, presume that you usually pay no taxes. You are asked how valuable it would be for the government to establish a bird sanctuary on the opposite coast. It might someday be a destination for your hobby, but consider: if you were required to pay taxes in proportion to your response, you might alter your response. Alternatively, if you can state your opinion about building the sanctuary without having to pay taxes toward it, then you have an incentive to overstate the sanctuary's importance to you.

Economists have carefully considered the problem of eliciting truthful revelation about the value to citizens of public goods and concluded that

---

[13] Lindahl equilibria are named for the Scandinavian economist Erik Lindahl, who formalized equilibria involving public goods in the early twentieth century. See Lindahl, 1958.

no perfect mechanism exists for general cases. Nonexcludability and demand revelation issues mean that public goods that cannot be well financed
by user fees must be financed by taxes. Nevertheless, taxes levied should
try to reflect benefits received. Knowing how much public good to provide
is another problem for which demand revelation problems exist. Deciding
simply by voting suffers the obvious incentive problems associated with de
Tocqueville's observation in Chapter 3 for those who pay no taxes that "all
the money that is spent for the community appears to be spent to their advantage, at no cost of their own."

Deadweight Loss of Taxation

If taxes, instead of perfect user fees, are used to pay for public goods, we need
to know something about their harmful side effects. For this we compare
two diagrams, the first showing the effects of a monopoly and the second
the effects of a tax. Figure 4.1 displays a downward sloping market demand
curve on the left half of the diagram. The marginal cost of providing an additional unit of the good is $MC = \$1$. Because it is the only supplier, the
monopolist has the ability to select for itself the best price-quantity point
on the demand curve. Generations of students have learned the rule that
identifies point a as the profit maximizing choice. All of that does not matter to us, however. What matters is that the resulting price p_0 charged by
the monopolist at point a exceeds MC. In the diagram p_0 is 10 times MC.
If prescription drugs are the product, a single pill that costs $1 to make is
sold for $10. As we discuss in Chapter 11, if buyers instead had a prescrip-
tion plan with a 10 percent co-insurance rate, then the monopolist would
charge up to $100 for the $1 pill! Even though the pharmaceutical company

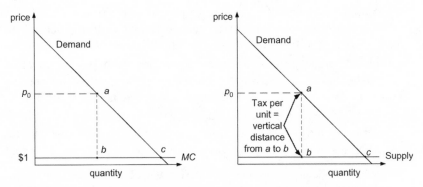

Figure 4.1. Monopoly Loss and Tax Deadweight Loss

could make the pill available for a small fraction of what it actually charges, the firm refuses to do so in order to maximize its profit. This is the reason economists and consumers love to hate monopoly. If we compare the outcome that would occur were the product competitively supplied at price $1, the monopoly causes much harm.

The right-hand side of Figure 4.1 shows the same demand curve with horizontal market supply curve at price $1. Equilibrium occurs at point c, where price is $1 and quantity demanded equals quantity supplied. If this commodity is taxed, however, by an amount per unit $p_0 - 1$, the equilibrium price-quantity pair moves to point a. The effect of this tax, therefore, is identical to the harm caused by the monopoly! The same reasons to hate monopoly apply to the effects of a tax. Consumers cannot get the product at the price they are willing to pay because part of their payment has to go to the tax collector. The damage done to the private sector from taxes, shown in Figure 4.1, is the same kind of damage caused by monopoly and is called *tax deadweight loss*. The damage is the lost value to consumers that disappears from the system because of the tax. Another characterization of deadweight loss is that it is the amount of damage done to taxpayers that exceeds the amount collected in taxes.

The best estimate of the magnitude of tax deadweight loss for the American economy is that between $1.25 and $1.77 is lost to the private sector for every additional dollar of tax collected. The average of the two bounds is $1.51. Using this number, $0.51 represents the additional harm done to taxpayers in order for the government to collect $1 in taxes.[14] In other words, expanding government to provide "free" medical care would cost 51 percent of the tax income to collect the taxes, an additional amount that benefits no one. Any program run through government carries a significant tax deadweight loss overhead. Zycher reports that 2005 Medicare outlays are really higher by $162.1 billion if the assumed excess burden is 50 percent.[15] This translates into $1,110 in annual loss due to extra cost per worker.[16]

As a general rule, because of tax deadweight loss, it is better, if possible, to accomplish group action through voluntary private organizations or markets than to use government and taxes.

4.4. Implications for Efficient Intervention in Health

A major theme in this book is that there are often many ways to accomplish a given objective. We are interested in having all individuals purchase health

[14] See Ballard et al., 1985; Feldstein, 1999; and Gruber and Saez, 2002.
[15] Zycher, 2007, p. 15.
[16] The 2007 civilian employment was 146.0 million.

insurance that meets a minimum standard of coverage. Choosing the *best* way to intervene is the task of government and government policy. The intervention identified by the intervention principle ("Principle 1") described in Section 3.1 also creates social costs. By selecting the right intervention and limiting its scope (e.g., not subsidizing everyone's health insurance but influencing only the purchases of a selected group), we accomplish our objectives in the most efficient manner.

Voluntary private organizations, markets, and government are institutions established to bring about group action. Advances in the study of economics reveal that an efficient economy – one for which more satisfaction cannot be produced without harming someone – is synonymous with the outcome of a competitive market equilibrium. This does not mean that economies must be market economies to be efficient, but it does mean that efficiency looks like a market outcome. The first and second fundamental theorems of welfare economics, which state the connection between efficiency and market outcomes, provide a valuable framework for evaluating the contribution of market exchange, VPOs, and government. This chapter identified in the portion of Section 4.2 titled VPOs, Markets, Government in FTWE Framework seven circumstances needed for efficiency. Of these seven, the following five point to legitimate functions of government because markets and VPOs cannot perform them effectively:

1. National defense
2. Law and order
3. Contract enforcement
5. Competition (that is, establishing and preserving conditions for competition)
6. Provision for public goods and externalities, including appropriate response to externalities.

In addition, we are mindful that consideration in some form will need to be made for the incapable needy. Functions 4 and 7, provision for equipping and provision for the incapable needy, are treated in Chapter 6 in light of the investigations in Chapter 5.

FIVE

Education, Charity, and the American
Ethical Base

While the people should patriotically and cheerfully support their Government, its functions do not include the support of the people.
President Grover Cleveland, 1893

[The candidate] denies the right of any government to take from any man by means of taxation any money not needed for government expenses or to tax one man to enrich another.
Presidential Candidate William Jennings Bryan, 1896

Ask not what your country can do for you, ask what you can do for your country.
President John Kennedy, 1961

Summary: *The issue is public provision of private goods. Education and government charity are prominent examples. What can be legitimately said? Most of us would agree that individuals have a duty of personal charity. The right amount of charity is the amount fully informed individuals would choose to give when properly balancing the needs of their families and those who depend on them against the needs of others – information that government can never fully know. Frequently, government knows the needs of recipients less well than the private sector and is able to exert less accountability than private sector agents of charity.*

Historically, the American ethical base has posited that government welcomes, encourages, and facilitates charity but is not its proper agent. Consistently with the efficiency approach of Chapter 4, there may be exceptions for special circumstances when technological impediments to private sector action, such as capital and information constraints, are central to preventing knowledge of, or – in the case of widespread disasters – quick enough response to life-threatening events and circumstances. Disaster relief may sometimes require infrequently used standing capital infrastructure (e.g., military helicopters or coast guard vessels) that only government can maintain efficiently, perhaps as part of its national defense operations.

Facilitating charity (not being its direct agent), such as aiding information flows about needs, certifying integrity in the use of private funds for charity, and so on, is justifiable for government when markets and VPOs are incapable of performing these functions.

This chapter investigates two issues that are relevant by virtue of what they imply about medical care: education (public provision of private goods) and charity (provision for the needy). Many Americans have come to believe that government should protect them from the normal vicissitudes of life. If they have not been prudent and bought insurance, if they have not saved, if they have not taken other usual precautions, or even if they have, they believe that government should be the spender of last resort for their needs. The public question that this belief moves to the forefront is not whether help, aid, and compassion are appropriate or needed. The public issue is whether this is a *government* function or one better handled directly by other collective forms, individuals, and VPOs. For example, many hospitals were originally formed as charitable ventures and run as private philanthropic organizations. The Baylor University Medical Center at Dallas is a good example, as is the Mayo Clinic in Rochester, Minnesota. By the reasoning of many Americans, these could have been justified as and run as government functions. Is this true?

> The public question that this belief moves to the forefront is not whether help, aid, and compassion are appropriate or needed. The public issue is whether this is a *government* function or one better handled directly by other collective forms, individuals, and VPOs.

Hurricane Katrina, which struck New Orleans in 2005, was a natural disaster that many had predicted would eventually occur. It nevertheless found the city unprepared and the levees protecting the city inadequate, even though events revealed that decades had elapsed without protective action despite warnings of pending disaster. Levees are public goods; property insurance is a private good. We need not wonder whether action in a particular case was primarily the responsibility of the individual, the city, the state, or the federal government because the answer in each case depends on whether the benefits from such action accrue primarily to the individual; to citizens of the city, of the state, or of the nation; and whether the benefits exceed the costs to the party contemplating action.

Charity is different. A charitable action is action taken by one agent for the benefit of another. Some Americans – as a whole, compassionate by nature – believe that their responsibility to act in compassion is fulfilled by their support for government programs. Sometimes this support is verbal only. To approve of government providing housing for the poor out of sympathy, however, implies approval for the principle that government take from one person not to pay necessary government expenses, but to enrich another. Is sympathy the appropriate principle to use in this case? Katrina swept away the property of rich and poor alike. Does sympathy not apply to the expensive vacation beach houses of the wealthy?

The Fifth Amendment to the Constitution says, "nor shall private property be taken for public use, without just compensation." Compensation must be given for real estate taken for public use. What compensation is given to taxpayers for property taken when it goes not to public use but to another citizen? Is not "just compensation" for taking a dollar the paying back of a dollar? These are questions that speak to the heart of public provision of private goods and whether government is the proper agent of such provision. Specifically, what incentives do institutionalized taking and giving create, and do they lead to worse outcomes than if other methods were employed? We cover this question because it is only a step away from asking about government's taking from group B to fund a health care program whose benefits go to group A.

Other than a few selected issues such as the ability to read to follow road signs or citizen-patriot participation in the army (e.g., as opposed to a separated warrior class), education is a private good. Before turning to health care, also a private good,[1] we investigate the logic of public provision of education, and, following that, public provision of charity.

5.1. Lessons from Education

Many Americans consider that universal public education is a modern success story. A natural conclusion might be that it would provide the intellectual template for grounding the public provision of health care. Education is free, universal, and publicly provided at a minimum standard (high school). It is a socially guaranteed provision of human capital, granting the recipient the ability, combined with personal effort, to earn a living. One would suspect that the arguments supporting the method of provision have strong justification and support in the available literature. Such is

---

[1] We have already noted public health issues such as immunizations or safe drinking water that do have public goods aspects. Health care services provided to individuals that benefit them only, however, are not public goods.

not the case. The necessary grounding was never done. In fact, one of the clearest lessons may be that a massive social institution can begin, grow, attain maturity, and continue to expand regardless of whether it has been proven to be the best solution to a problem. We do not make the case that public education is a social bad. We make the case that the method we have settled on to provide it has never been justified or proven to be socially best. Possibly it is *not* best, yet it continues, by many accounts resistant to outside influence and slow to change. Consequently, it is a cautionary tale for health care.

The history of public education is extremely interesting: Education as a public endeavor began gradually and – through the incremental workings of self-interest, monopoly, and political vesting – grew into an impregnable social edifice. The workings of special interests and the incentives created by publicly provided private goods explain much of the observed history. None of this denies the value of education or denies that there are those who benefit tremendously from publicly provided education. But, as many have noted, parents pay for the education their children receive in a public or private system; the payments are simply changed in character and timing between lifelong taxes and direct fees and tuition.

As education once was, health care currently is primarily privately provided in the United States. There is no all-inclusive system of tax-supported state and national hospitals, physicians are not state employees, and the medical unions are not currently lobbying for greater control. As the case was for education in the mid-1800s, there is a growing number of voices that urge state control, even that the state take on the entire burden to relieve the citizen of any responsibility.

The "Case" for Publicly Provided Private Education

The early thinkers and writers in Great Britain and the United States recognized the importance of education and contributed their share of lavish praise eulogizing its virtues and values. Few, however, advocated nationalization of the education function or the necessity of state provision for its full expense. Adam Smith wrote in *The Wealth of Nations,*

The expense of the institutions for education and religious instruction, is likewise, no doubt, beneficial to the whole society, and may, therefore, without injustice, be defrayed by the general contribution of the whole society. This expense, however, might perhaps with equal propriety, and even with some advantage, be defrayed altogether by those who receive the immediate benefit of such education and instruction, or by the voluntary contribution of those who think they have occasion for either the one or the other.

When the institutions or public works which are beneficial to the whole society, either cannot be maintained altogether, or are not maintained altogether by the contribution of such particular members of the society as are most immediately benefited by them, the deficiency must in most cases be made up by the general contribution of the whole society. The general revenue of the society, over and above defraying the expense of defending the society, and of supporting the dignity of the chief magistrate, must make up for the deficiency of many particular branches of revenue.[2]

Smith, therefore, made the connection that the paying party should be the party that receives the benefits without knowing exactly what the division would be. He suspected that education might be "beneficial to the whole society" so "without injustice" society might contribute but allowed for the possibility that it "be defrayed altogether by those who receive the immediate benefit." He envisioned the possibility that the state might supply partial support, but he did not suggest that it provide free education at public support, nor contemplate that it would operate the education function itself. John Stuart Mill clearly distinguished between the state's intervening to see that education occurs and providing it directly. He believed that the state did better to leave it to parents to obtain the education where and how they pleased and "content itself with helping to pay the school fees of the poorer classes of children, and defraying the entire school expenses of those who have no one else to pay for them."[3] In *On Liberty* he refers to the value to society of educated opinion deriving from private sources of education:

The objections which are urged with reason against State education, do not apply to the enforcement of education by the State, but to the State's taking upon itself to direct that education, which is a totally different thing. That the whole or any large part of the education of the people should be in State hands, I go as far as any one in deprecating. All that has been said of the importance of individuality of character, and diversity in opinions and modes of conduct involves, as of the same unspeakable importance, diversity of education. A general State education is a mere contrivance for moulding people to be exactly like one another; and as the mould in which it casts them is that which pleases the predominant power in the government.[4]

Other writers through time, of course, also noted the distinction between the use of education directed to the purpose of broadening the student's awareness and thinking ability versus its use for molding thought to a

---

[2] Smith, 1776b.
[3] Mill, 1896.
[4] Ibid.

preconceived norm. John Lott has made this case forcefully.[5] Many dis-
agreements relating to the administration of public education in the United
States today stem from this dichotomy. In American private Christian
schools any subject can be discussed, whereas in the public schools a discussion of the teachings of Jesus Christ would be off limits, for example. It is plausible that public provision of health care could conceivably lead to similar limitations on the amount and type of medicine that could be provided, sometimes for similar reasons. For example, the use of holistic or herbal medicine might be restricted in a government facility in the same way that a discussion of a worldview that is not universally accepted might be prohibited in a public school. Once the payment for a service is separated from its provision, as would be the case if health care were funded by taxes, there is the risk that providers will ration its supply according to *their* needs and constraints rather than according to the user's.

> Once the payment for a service is separated from its provision, as would be the case if health care were funded by taxes, there is the risk that providers will ration its supply according to *their* needs and constraints rather than according to the user's.

Smith and Mill lead us to ask whether the state function of insuring health care can be similarly distinguished from the function of state provision. In the case of education, what caused the distinction to be blurred, and what rationales were put forward for public provision of a private good?

The U.S. Experience

The arguments for American government schooling reduced to a few, well-known contentions. Foremost was the argument of positive externalities. These were often called "neighborhood effects." Horace Mann is generally regarded as the most influential proponent of the public schools movement in the United States. According to E. G. West,

Much of Mann's reasoning, and that of the other protagonists, could be taken as constituting an early formulation of what has today become known as the "neighborhood effects" argument.[6]

[5] Lott, 1990.
[6] West, 1967, p. 109.

West goes on to say that those making the neighborhood effects argument "do not seem to have appreciated that the onus was upon them to give evidence and measurement demonstrating how deficient was the existing supply of education."[7] Often the external benefits cited were the necessity of education to the prosperity and existence of representative government and the benefits that one receives from living in a society of educated citizens. The Carnegie Commission on Higher Education wrote:

The elimination of religious, ethnic, and sex discrimination is closer to reality today in the college-student community than in society at large. Perhaps this simple example best illustrates the difficulty of defining (much less measuring) social benefits.[8]

The Carnegie Commission struggled with the difficulty that correlation does not prove causality and that those making the externalities argument did not have measures of their size but nevertheless believed that they must be large. Among those on the other side are economists like Adam Smith and Milton Friedman,[9] who acknowledge spillover effects but conclude that externalities are delimited and that private demand for education would result in the provision of large amounts of it. Charles A. M. De Bartolome (1985) in "The Public Provision of Private Goods" expresses a similar view of education.

At low levels of education there are public goods aspects, viz. that it is socially advantageous for everybody to be able to read instruction, stop-signs, etc. However, it seems likely that public goods aspects reach saturation at education levels below privately demanded levels. Education is probably an investment good with consumption aspects.[10]

> A stable society is required for protection of property, accumulation of wealth, uninterrupted commerce, economic prosperity, and happiness. Anything that promotes those objectives has great value.

One benefit of an educated public that seems surprisingly little mentioned might be its diminished willingness to follow demagogues or participate in mob actions of social unrest. Stated the other way, an ignorant population is probably more susceptible to harmful mass movements, insurrection, and manipulation. A stable society is required for protection of

---

[7] Ibid.
[8] Carnegie Commission, 1973, p. 80.
[9] Friedman, 1998.
[10] Ibid., p. 14.

property, accumulation of wealth, uninterrupted commerce, economic prosperity, and happiness. Anything that promotes those objectives has great value. The measurement problem remains, however, as well as the tricky question of proving that this requires governmentalization of the education process.

The other argument for public support of education had to do with the needy poor and thinly populated areas. Samuel S. Randall in his *History of The Common School System of the State of New York* explains that the argument was made in New York in the early 1800s that people "living far from each other, makes it difficult so to establish schools as to render them convenient or accessible to all. Every family therefore, must either educate its own children, or the children must forgo the advantages of education."[11] New York's experience is not unique and provides an object lesson. What began as a matter of some individuals' needing state aid ended with the view that there should be a state-supplied system for all areas.

The purpose of the original legislation in 1812 was to initiate an organization of common schools at state expense to "bring instruction within the reach and means of the humblest citizen."[12] Once a supplemental structure was enacted, the predictable progression began. It should be noted that at this time schooling was already almost totally universal, without having been made compulsory.[13] Under the plan, education was subsidized but was not free except to the very poor. Initially rate bills (charges to parents in proportion to the amount of education their children received) and town taxes provided the bulk of education support. As the number of state school districts expanded, many existing private schools became state schools to qualify for public money. In addition, pressure to increase the state's payments began, followed by pressure to make schooling completely free. The main opposition to rate bills arose not from the parents who paid them, but from the teachers and government officials who, once again, used the poor to argue that rate bills had a discouraging effect on poor families. Although state funding initially was made available in a way that included religious societies that supported or would establish charity schools, those speaking for the interests of the public schools such as the Free School Society objected to the competition. Under pressure, the state committee assigned to

[11] Randall, 1871, p. 18, cited in West, 1967, p. 103.
[12] Ibid., p. 105.
[13] Ibid.

investigate decided that entrusting state funds "to religious or ecclesiastical bodies was a violation of an elementary principle in the politics of State and country."[14] In response to the increase in public funding, the voluntary contributions of the inhabitants "declined with almost uniform regularity."[15] Thus, a system that began with universal private education was transformed by steps into an alternative that lobbied for full government support and viewed private competitors as rivals.

The consequence of public supply, according to West, included interest-group lobbying and monopoly-like behavior by providers of public education, less responsiveness to the "customers" of education, and distortion of voting decisions.

> The voting issue, of course, as it presented itself to each individual voter, appeared mainly as a demand choice. People would have been irrational indeed if, believing that they could really obtain something free merely by voting for it, they did not in fact do so.[16]

West's conclusion mirrors a nearly identical sentiment expressed by Bastiat more than a century earlier:

> In the first place, we note that always or nearly always public service eliminates, in law or in fact, private services of the same nature.... The reason is that the public will not buy what the state offers it for nothing.[17]

The original reasons given for public support of education – that poor students plus certain rural areas needed assistance, and that there were externality benefits – are arguments for subsidies of various kinds, not public provision. Because education went to minors, and externality subsidies would have to be supplied to parents, a voucher would have been the preferred format. Regarding needy parents, if low income is an issue that causes parents not to be able to pay for their children's education through grade 12, and one wishes to provide a remedy that retains appropriate incentives, then an Earned Income Tax Credit is the superior tool – certainly better targeted and cheaper than an entire public school system. Finally, if lack of a financial market for education loans is the impediment to parents' being able to pay for their children's education through grade 12 over time, then establishment of such a market is the implied tool.

---

[14] West, 1967, p. 106.
[15] Ibid.
[16] Ibid., p. 113.
[17] Bastiat, 1996, p. 17.34.

5.2. The American Ethical Base

Every man must decide whether he will walk in the creative light of altruism or the darkness of destructive selfishness. This is the judgment. Life's persistent and most urgent question is, What are you doing for others? (Martin Luther King, Jr.)[18]

We suggested in the chapter opening that many Americans would acknowledge their personal responsibility to engage in charity with regard to the charitable needs that they know exist. This is true independently of government activity. We are realists, however. Those who study American giving patterns note that "for many people, the desire to donate other people's money displaces the act of giving one's own."[19] Undoubtedly, learning to be personally generous is something with which we all struggle; those of us who have learned it better, such as Martin Luther King, must lead the way to draw in others.

The issue of government charity – whether it take the form of public provision of private goods, expropriation of property, or "taxes not needed for government expenses or to tax one man to enrich another" – raises different questions. Few have the time or the inclination to examine whether government charity is questionable because of the incentives it creates and because of its potential to undermine the effectiveness of government programs and functions. American thinking, however, has not been silent on this subject. This chapter began with statements by Presidents Cleveland and Kennedy and presidential candidate Bryan that suggest that the modern reliance on government as the giver of charity has not always been thought just or advisable.

We argue in what follows that government *does* have a part in facilitating almsgiving and charity based on efficiency considerations, but that its role is narrow, defined by information deficiencies and selective technical circumstances. By implication, this has relevance for programs that do not sit on their own base (see Section 3.3, "Principle 3: Every Pot Sits on Its Own Base"). For example, those who pay for Medicare are not eligible for Medicare themselves if they are under the age of 65 (unless they qualify as disabled or suffering from end-stage renal disease). If Medicare is intended to be charity rather than health insurance, then we must ask whether the Medicare program is the best way to deliver charity. Recall that the social goal is the best delivery method for medical care and for charity – separate objectives – at the appropriate level.

---

[18] Quoted in Brooks, 2006, p. 55.
[19] See Brooks, 2006, pp. 54–57 and surrounding discussion.

Incentives and Justice

Prior to the twentieth century, many prominent Americans rejected the role of government as a redistributor of wealth or of government in loco parentis for reasons of incentives and justice.

Benjamin Franklin is remembered best for his role in founding the American republic, but he was also a world-class scientist and observer of the economic scene, as well as an extremely successful entrepreneur. Regarding a public tax for the maintenance of the poor he said:

I am for doing good to the poor, but I differ in opinion about the means. I think the best way of doing good to the poor, is, not making them easy in poverty, but leading or driving them *out* of it. In my youth, I traveled much, and I observed in different countries, that the more public provisions were made for the poor, the less they provided for themselves, and of course became poorer. And, on the contrary, the less was done for them, the more they did for themselves, and became richer.... The day you passed that act, you took away from before their eyes the greatest of all inducements to industry, frugality, and sobriety, by giving them a dependence on somewhat else than a careful accumulation during youth and health, for support in age or sickness.

In short, you offered a premium for the encouragement of idleness, and you should not now wonder that it has had its effect in the increase of poverty. Repeal that law, and you will soon see a change in their manners.... Their circumstances will mend, and more will be done for their happiness by inuring them to provide for themselves, than could be done by dividing all your estates among them.[20]

Franklin favored assisting the poor. The basis for his views opposing a public tax for the poor was its false incentives. Making social policy with respect to the poor and poverty "leading or driving them *out* of it" (emphasis in original) is consistent with the intervention principle of Chapter 3: if you want more of something you subsidize it, and if less, you tax it.

William Jennings Bryan, populist candidate for president and political figure quoted at the beginning of this chapter, was well known to espouse the interests of the workingman and the disadvantaged of his day. Bryan also did not believe that government should use tax powers except to raise money needed for legitimate government expenses. Less well known is that Congressman Davy Crockett, famous frontiersman from Tennessee and patriot defender of the Alamo, was a consistent opponent of the provision of pensions by the government to the widows of veterans of the War of 1812 and the Revolutionary War. Among the reasons put forward by him and those he allied himself with was the fact that some of

---

[20] Benjamin Franklin, 1766.

the petitioners had simply fallen on hard times and now petitioned the government to bail them out. Crockett did not feel that it was proper for the government to single them out for relief. It is notable that in the case of government support for the family of General Brown, Crockett offered "to subscribe his quota, in his private character, to make up the sum promised" but felt he must oppose the principle of the bill.[21] We infer that he was in favor of helping the poor "in his private character" but opposed the use of public means. Davy Crockett's opinions about government charity are reported in *The Life of Colonel David Crockett* by Edward Ellis (1884), which, even if not reporting Crockett's verbatim words, gives representative evidence on Americans' thinking in the second half of the nineteenth century. (Crockett died at the Alamo in 1836.) At issue was Congress's vote to give money to the widow of a War of 1812 veteran. Crockett said:

> Mr. Speaker... we must not permit our respect for the dead or our sympathy for a part of the living to lead us into an act of injustice to the balance of the living. I will not go into an argument to prove that Congress has no power to appropriate this money as an act of charity. Every member upon this floor knows it.... I am the poorest man on this floor. I cannot vote for this bill, but I will give one week's pay to the object, and if every member of Congress will do the same, it will amount to more than the bill asks.[22]

America is a large country. There is no such thing as a universally held position on something as emotionally laden as charity enforced by government. It is significant then that the views of Grover Cleveland were often repeated and unequivocal: "It is the responsibility of the citizens to support their government. It is not the responsibility of the government to support its citizens." Cleveland, like Bryan, believed that "when more of the people's sustenance is exacted through the form of taxation than is necessary to meet the just obligations of government and expenses of its economical administration, such exaction becomes ruthless extortion and a violation of the fundamental principles of free government." Cleveland was concerned with economic incentives and dependence:

> "It is the responsibility of the citizens to support their government. It is not the responsibility of the government to support its citizens" (Grover Cleveland).

---

[21] *Debates in Congress*, p. 2086.
[22] Ibid., pp. 138–139.

When we proclaim that the necessity for revenue to support the Government furnishes the only justification for taxing the people, we announce a truth so plain that its denial would seem to indicate the extent to which judgment may be influenced by familiarity with perversions of the taxing power. And when we seek to reinstate the self-confidence and business enterprise of our citizens by discrediting an abject dependence upon government favor, we strive to stimulate those elements of American character which support the hope of American achievement.

Cleveland's views on the Texas Seed Bill in 1887 are particularly relevant because they deal with a regional natural disaster. This bill voted $10,000 to buy seed grain for government distribution to farmers in Texas who had suffered from drought. Cleveland vetoed the bill, saying that he found "no warrant for such an appropriation in the Constitution; and I do not believe that the power and duty of the General Government ought to be extended to the relief of individual suffering which is in no manner properly related to the public service or benefit. . . . Though the people support the Government, the Government should not support the people." He affirmed that "the friendliness and charity of our countrymen can always be relied on to relieve their fellow citizens in misfortune."[23]

Once again, incentives and the real purpose and consequences of our actions are central to their accurate assessment. It is easy to lose sight of both. Medals in war, for example, are *not* given to recognize bravery and heroism – though recognition is their ostensible purpose. Their true purpose is to increase the efficiency and effectiveness of the nation's fighting forces. This implies that the right number should be given; too many become meaningless, and too few have little effect on behavior. Other examples are possible. Foreign aid, for example, is not international government charity – though that is its ostensible purpose. Foreign aid is justified by the benefits to the nation of maintaining allies, cementing international friendships, and establishing international goodwill, objectives that benefit all citizens in public good fashion.

Having more experience with personal charity and less experience with government charity, Americans of earlier eras had less need to warn that mixing charity with government created a sense of entitlement in the recipients. President Franklin Roosevelt, however, did have experience and warned about its incentives: "continued dependence on [government support] induces a spiritual and moral disintegration fundamentally destructive to the national fiber. To dole out relief in this way is to administer a narcotic, a subtle destroyer of the human spirit."[24] More

---

[23] Grover Cleveland, 1887, p. 1875.
[24] Franklin Roosevelt, quoted in Brooks, 2006, p. 85.

recently, President Clinton's successful welfare reform elicited very elo-
quent statements about the pitfalls of government charity. Such charity
also often interferes with the ability of programs to function effectively in
their primary mission. We will return to this issue in some detail when we
talk about insurance in the section "Community Rating, Charity Transfers,
and Pure Insurance" in Chapter 7.

Alexis de Tocqueville also believed that the effects of institutionalized
charity were harmful to the permanent underclass. *Pauperism* was the term
used in his day. Here is G. Himmelfarb's summary of de Tocqueville:

> Public relief as a legal right, he explained, is *more* demoralizing than *private charity*.
> It is demoralizing not only because the assurance of subsistence undermines the
> incentive to work, thus making paupers out of the poor, but also because it is a legal
> public testimony to the individual's dependency.... *Charity*, on the other hand,
> Tocqueville said, being *private*, involves *no* such acknowledgement of inferiority.
> Because it is personal and voluntary, it establishes a moral tie between the donor
> and the recipient, unlike public relief [emphasis in original]."[25]

Government charity encourages class warfare. De Tocqueville: "The law
strips the man of wealth of a part of his surplus without consulting him
and he sees the poor man only as a greedy stranger invited by the legis-
lator to share his wealth."[26] The recipient, on the other hand, "feels no
gratitude for a benefit which no one can refuse him and which could not
satisfy him in any case.... [Government charity] ranges each one under
a banner, tallies them, and, bringing them face to face, prepares them for
combat,"[27] not to mention the manipulation by demagogues who turn
the situation to their advantage by ever more generous polittroughing
promises.

More Difficulties

In the second half of the twentieth century, the view that government
charity (usually described as income redistribution), including public provision of private goods, is valid public activity has been so insistently taught
that it is difficult to believe any reevaluation of the topic is possible. As
an intellectual matter, however, re-evaluation of accepted beliefs is not
new. Thomas Paine felt that Americans were so accustomed to thinking

[25] Himmelfarb, 1996.
[26] de Tocqueville, 1997, p. 31.
[27] Ibid.

as British citizens that they could scarcely imagine independence. In the introduction to *Common Sense* he wrote,[28]

Perhaps the sentiments contained in the following pages, are not yet sufficiently fashionable to procure them general favor; a long habit of not thinking a thing wrong gives it a superficial appearance of being right, and raises at first a formidable outcry in defense of custom.

Paine nevertheless appealed to readers' reason. We likewise present reasons for difficulties with public provision of private goods before suggesting resolution in light of the efficiency approach of Chapters 3–4.

Rights, those that the government enforces as part of its justice mandate, can be classified as *freedom-preserving* or *resource-extracting*. *Freedom-preserving* rights protect the holder against improper actions by another (your neighbor does not have the right to swing his fist into your nose), while *resource-extracting* rights grant the holder power to demand resources from another agent (you must give me something). There is a difference between the two types of rights. This is de Tocqueville:

There is nothing which, generally speaking, elevates and sustains the human spirit more than the idea of rights. There is something great and virile in the idea of right which removes from any request its suppliant character, and places the one who claims it on the same level as the one who grants it. But the right of the poor to obtain society's help is unique in that instead of elevating the heart of the man who exercises it, it lowers him. . . . Ordinary rights are conferred on men by reason of some personal advantage by them over their fellow men. This other kind is accorded by reason of a recognized inferiority.[29]

The decision to provide a minimum standard of health care as a right requires action by others to provide such care. It engages three related issues: justification for forcing action by others to satisfy the moral right, rationing, and equity. While ethical questions are often discussed at the level of philosophy, application is almost entirely on a practical basis. Should a health care system provide equal heroic measures to a young and an old person with the same diagnosis? Should removal of tattoos be a covered procedure? Is it right for people who pay extra to get faster care? Many people consider abortion a sin equal to murder and a crime no less heinous than slavery was in antebellum America. Should abolitionists have been forced to return runaway slaves, and should pro-life advocates be forced to pay for abortions? Agreeing to make such decisions "public property" is to agree to subjugate one's own volition in matters where the details may be

---

[28] Paine, 1776.
[29] de Tocqueville, 1997.

better known to the individual and of great importance. It is well known that public attitudes are often unreliable because they are based on uninformed opinions. Even informed opinion is not perfect: "Historical choices, even historical choices made by most societies, may be wrong or misguided."[30] How public opinion is retrieved is frequently the determining factor. Did the question imply that the health care spoken of would be provided "free" by government, or did the question suggest that the person being surveyed would experience a tax increase? Consider the following account by a national newscaster:

I swear this is true. On an episode of *The Phil Donahue Show* some years ago, members of the studio audience were debating the merits of a certain federal program. One man stood up and interrupted angrily, "Why should taxpayers pay for this? Why doesn't the government pay for it?"[31]

In addition to relinquishing discretion over one's choices, public provision of private goods necessitates rationing and equity dilemmas. By definition, rationing health care implies denying beneficial care on grounds that the costs – opportunity or real – are too great. Equity is operationalized by identifying what should be equal. Should it be equality of opportunity or equality of outcome? It is a certainty that equality of outcome conflicts with the competing principle of merited reward. If the merit-worthy become rich, for example, should they be allowed to buy more? American thought historically justified moral rights – life, liberty, and the pursuit of happiness – because they are God given. But God does not give property (outcome) equally to all just as the ant and the grasshopper in Aesop's fable do not deserve the same reward.

Before suggesting a resolution in Chapter 6 to the questions raised in this chapter, we discuss another little-known problem inherent to relying on government as the agent of charity. We illustrate it with the following story from a black tie event that one of us (Grinols) attended in Champaign-Urbana, Illinois, a number of years ago. When the guest to my right learned that I was an economist, she settled on the "feminization of poverty" as her choice of dinner conversation. I listened to her account of national trends and the hardships experienced by women in the United States who suffered poverty and expressed sympathy, suggesting that she should make charitable donations to organizations that focused on combating feminine poverty and urge others to do the same. She responded that a bigger government effort was needed because not enough was being done without a

---

[30] Weale, 1998, p. 137.
[31] O'Reilly, 2002.

government effort. I then asked how much she gave in charitable gifts. Seven percent of her income was so used. This number favorably impressed me because the typical figure from U.S. tax forms was more in the 2–3 percent range. I, too, felt individual charitable giving was important, I said, indicating that my own giving was in line with treating the biblical tithe as a minimum.

I then made the point that for her to suggest that others should do more through a government program, however, when she was unwilling to do more had unforeseen implications. I knew from our conversation that she and her husband, both well-paid professionals, were a two-income house-hold without children in the home and suggested that they probably had a combined income significantly exceeding $200,000 annually, but that $200,000 would "do" for purposes of discussion, a number to which she assented. (Adjusting $200,000 for the price level would result in a much larger income figure for the present day.) Thus, by her own account, I said, she and her husband gave $14,000 to charitable causes, probably paid taxes in the neighborhood of $25,000–35,000 annually, and thereby demon-strated that they felt it was more important to keep $150,000 for themselves than for those in poverty to have even one more dollar of it. I think she was startled by this conclusion, but she reluctantly agreed after I explained that my deduction was nothing more than a revealed-preference obser-vation based on their actions. I then pointed out that her government charity proposal would include taking money from a young couple in their early twenties, just starting out in life, and earning less than $25,000. This would reduce them to live on considerably less than $25,000 annually when she, who had the concern for feminine poverty, was refusing to live on so little.

Undeterred, she replied that she had a sister who was not doing well finan-cially and that she helped her sister, action that no one else would know about. I doubted (but did not ask) that she gave $125,000 each year to her sister. Instead I said *the young couple also has a sister they help, about whom no one in government knows.* The conversation ceased at this point.

We are all human. I can understand why it is easy to believe (hope) that someone else should (can) give more, even if I myself choose not to. This conversation highlighted the following: Government charity requires taxes. The limit of progressive taxation is reached when it takes income from the highest earner, reducing his spendable income to the level of the next-highest earner, after which both give equally until their remaining income equals that of the third, after which all three give equally, and so on, down the income distribution until enough money has been raised. A program of

> A program of government charity *necessarily forces some who cannot afford it to live on less,* while others with more do not equally sacrifice to the same level. Only when taxes have reached the extreme limit of progressivity is this conclusion invalid.

government charity *necessarily forces some who cannot afford it to live on less,* while others with more do not equally sacrifice to the same level. Only if taxes have reached the extreme limit of progressivity is this conclusion invalid. Private charity does not suffer this criticism because it is voluntary.

Information, Social Insurance

Not all efficiency considerations work against government agency. Just as it is easy for members of the public to be naive about what the level of giving should be for others because they do not know others' circumstances, they may be underinformed about charitable needs. If households are fully informed about charitable needs, then they have the ability to allocate their income between their own needs and the needs of others. A fully informed public will select the right amount of charity because each agent will balance his or her own needs against the needs of others. If government (1) facilitates the flow of information about charitable needs and payment toward those needs in such cost-saving ways as check-off boxes on tax forms that many states and the federal government use, (2) prevents fraud, (3) certifies that dollars given in charity go to the uses intended, and so on, it serves an efficiency-increasing function. Action beyond this risks governmentalization, polittroughing, and forcing some to live on less than they can afford.

What remains to be said? Although our list of circumstantial requirements for efficiency does not include charity, we did touch on the related objective of provision for the incapable needy. For those unable to care for themselves in any circumstance, efficiency and incentives issues emphasized in this chapter are not considerations. This opens the way for true social insurance for which government may play a valid role. Social insurance creates no false incentives if the problem being relieved is not amenable to incentives. By social insurance we mean the collection of "premiums" from the public in amounts that equal expected benefits received by the payer on the occurrence of risky outcomes to which everyone is subject. If every family or household in society is equally at risk for being the beneficiary of aid, a social insurance program that does not encourage undesirable outcomes or more dependency only spreads risk across the entire population and sits on its own base.

Another example where considerations of economic efficiency support government agency might be immediate disaster relief that requires resources that are best socially insured. We mentioned ships and helicopters at the start of the chapter to provide immediate relief for calamities and catastrophes that private sector agencies would be unable to provide efficiently. Such standing resources are needed in any event for other national defense and coastal protection purposes, and their use is probably the least costly means at hand. This kind of relief is not permanent welfare, nor given in a manner to create local dependence.

5.3. Summary on Public Provision of Private Goods and Charity

Knowing what is proper for the state to do or not do regarding public provision of private goods and charity in order for the social system to achieve efficiency is infused with huge amounts of economics. It is not possible to do justice to all issues in a short chapter, and the example of public provision of education (primarily a private investment good with consumption elements) provides little guidance because the intellectual grounding was never done. Instead we have alerted the reader to principles that are relevant for the long-run success of providing every American access to health care. We list them in closing this chapter, continuing with their application to health care in Chapter 6.

- It is necessary to do what is sustainable and "best serves the welfare of the majority, not what rescues the few" (de Tocqueville).[32]
- Government charity creates false incentives through available tax structures, as well as being morally unjust.
- The appropriate amount of charity equals the sum of the voluntary individual gifts that a fully informed citizenry would give.
- Information is imperfect and charity needs are not always known to every individual. In the absence of other means, government can be appropriately tasked with aiding information flows. Government does not need to be the United Way of the economy but can encourage the function of the United Way.
- Government relief aid may be appropriate in narrow, technically defined circumstances.
- True, actuarially fair social insurance creates no false incentives if the problem being relieved is not amenable to incentives. Nevertheless, sustainability and efficiency continue to require that social insurance

---

[32] de Tocqueville, 1997, p. 36.

and government programs sit on their own base (be screened to avoid embedded efficiency-reducing charity elements). For example, if all citizens have equal prospects of receiving equal benefits from the social insurance program, actuarially fair premiums imply that they make equal payments into it.

- A social optimum does not require government redistribution, but the relevant theory presumes agent viability. Agent viability requires that each own sufficiently valuable tradable assets. Seeing to it that each agent is endowed with sufficient assets that he or she can make a living is a valid equipping role for government oversight attention if one includes as assets education and human capital.

This last item is taken up in Chapter 6 with respect to health care. As with education, government interest is that the equipping take place in the most efficient manner, not necessarily that it be done by government.

PART III

APPLICATION

SIX

Why Government in Health Care?

All around, there will be a big push for more government involvement in the health sector, which we believe is the source of many of the problems in the health sector today.

Grace-Marie Turner, President, Galen Institute, 2006

Summary: *This chapter concludes the necessary examination of the foundation for provision of health care. Conventional economics does not provide a rationale for public provision of private goods such as health care and education. Modern moral pluralism, likewise, fails to provide guidance about the ethical duty of government in such cases. An appeal to externalities and help for the poor do not themselves justify the public provision of either. If there is a rationale for government attention to the issue, it derives from an oversight function related to provision for equipping the capable needy with the means of independent survival in a hostile world and provision for the incapable needy through true social insurance.*

To think critically, we must think both abstractly and concretely. If we do, we are often led to conclusions and understandings that surprise and challenge our original point of view.

This chapter concludes our study of the rationale for government to have an interest in guaranteeing access to health insurance. As noted already, health care and health insurance are private goods, the benefits of which, as with an automobile, a home, or life insurance, accrue to the purchaser. Health services certainly have the property of being rival in consumption: when I occupy the operating table for my surgery, another cannot simultaneously occupy the same table.

As already noted, experience with the spread of infectious diseases suggests that preventive health care does include elements of "neighborhood benefits" or externalities. We point out, however, that the prescriptive economic response to such externalities is not nationalization of the entire sector, but the application of a subsidy to the purchase of preventive health care, or application of its incentive-symmetric equivalent tax.

If current events, interpreted through the eyes of the public, rather than economic understanding, are allowed by our political leaders to determine public choices, then unenlightened incrementalism will most likely dictate outcomes. For example, history teaches that price controls frequently lead to unhappiness. Historically, the public response to that unhappiness is to demand yet more control over prices. This is because even a deplorable system may take inordinate time before its deficiencies and internal contradictions grow to such proportions that the failings become evident to all, and opposing forces strengthen to the point where change occurs. Better to chart a course dictated by reason in harmony with principles that lead to success, and avoid the deficiencies and contradictions before they happen.

6.1. Efficient Collective Action: Reprise

Chapter 4 identified the sources of collective action as markets, voluntary private organizations (VPOs), and government. Government differs from markets and VPOs because it is not voluntary. Only in philosophical discourse would the fiction be employed that participation in government begins with a voluntary choice made from a hypothetical "state of nature." Consistently with Chapter 4, we start from the assumption that the goal of coordinated action is to achieve an optimal state of the economy for which it is impossible to improve the well-being of one household without harming another.

A major achievement of twentieth-century economics was proving under reasonable and general circumstances that optima existed for an economy, that a market equilibrium achieved such optima, and that *any* optimum could be achieved as a market equilibrium. Stated roundly, social optima and market equilibria are synonymous, and health care is but one of many services whose provision and distribution can be efficiently provided through payment for service, purchase, and sale. Government action – apart from assuring that there is a properly functioning health care market – can only be interpreted as interference that may make matters worse. The sociology of government and its adherents described in the Nobel laureate Friederick Hayek's *The Road to Serfdom*[1] is a practical (empirical) warning not to look uncritically to government to engineer social goals, just as we do not look uncritically to markets or VPOs. We therefore take a nuanced

---

[1] Hayek, 1995.

approach in this chapter to identify further the boundaries for market, government, and VPO function, recogniz- ing that government oversight to warrant an outcome does not imply that govern- ment itself supplants the function that ac- complishes the outcome of interest. Actions to guarantee universal health insurance, for example, might imply a supervisory role.

> Government oversight to warrant an outcome does not imply that government itself supplants the function that accomplishes the outcome of interest.

The technical approach to government – in some circles it would be called "scientific" – taken here rests on two foun- dations: The first is the mathematically identified ability of the private market to achieve a social optimum that places requirements on the social setting. The second is the inherent imperfection of government as a non-voluntary means of collective action. The latter is too complicated at present to have been reduced to demonstration by an elegant mathematical system as has the first. It has, however, been studied by those who have focused on the rel- evant incentives on the functionaries who constitute government."Power tends to corrupt, and absolute power corrupts absolutely. Great men are almost always bad men" (Lord Acton).[2]

Since the validity of the first and second fundamental theorems of wel- fare economics that state the equivalency of optima and market equilibria are not in dispute,[3] where does this leave us with respect to government? According to the Nobel laureate Milton Friedman, there remain a great number of necessary government roles.

A government which maintained law and order, defined property rights, served as a means whereby we could modify property rights and other rules of the economic game, adjudicated disputes about the interpretation of the rules, enforced con- tracts, promoted competition, provided a monetary framework, engaged in activi- ties to counter technical monopolies and to overcome neighborhood effects widely regarded as sufficiently important to justify government intervention, and which supplemented private charity and the private family in protecting the irresponsi- ble, whether madman or child – such a government would clearly have important functions to perform.[4]

Adam Smith himself distinguished between government as umpire (legitimate in our efficiency framework) and government as "coach" or

[2] Acton, 1887.
[3] Most good intermediate microeconomics textbooks with a section on welfare economics will have a thorough discussion on these efficiency theorems.
[4] Friedman, 1962.

"player" (unecessary, and even inimical to overall efficiency economy func-tion in our framework).[5] To Friedman's list we add in this chapter only two functions hinted at in Chapters 4 and 5: provision for the incapable needy and provision for equipping each economic agent for economic viability.

Provision for the Incapable Needy

Nowhere in the mathematical conception of a social optimum are the in-capable needy treated. We use the term "incapable" in a narrow technical sense to describe individuals who lack the innate capacity to provide for themselves in the world, even with proper training and preparation. They are always present in any sizable economy. Children, while they are still children and until they reach maturity, are temporarily "incapable" in this sense and therefore taken care of by their parents. If a child's parents are killed, and no close relatives exist to take him in, most economists would concur that the state has an obligation justified by social insurance argu-ments to provide for the child's education and rearing. In a similar vein, permanently mentally ill, retarded, or physically incapable individuals may be regarded as state responsibilities. The principle that seems to work in explaining state responsibility is

1. incapable: inability to be brought to the point of providing for oneself,
2. a risk-pooling-like feature: since an incapable individual might arise in any family, all of society rightly bears equal *ex ante* responsibility for the burden of his or her care (i.e., presuming that no household has a lower-cost way of dealing with the debility than does society at large – a Coasian notion – and that all households have paid equally into the fund from which support comes), and
3. deservingness: innocence in causing one's own neediness.

Most would agree that equal insurance levies (taxes representing social insurance premium payments) are a just way to provide for such incapable needy. Details remain; the degree of social insurance support, for example, might reflect degree of incapability. For most children, incapability is tem-porary; children are therefore equipped to prepare them for independence when they reach maturity.

---

[5] "What he suggested was that the State should both be strong, as a defence against sectional interests, but also not interfere too much. Ideally the State should be like a referee or umpire – able to punish or even expel, but not actually involved in the everyday contests and exchanges that led to wealth creation." Macfarlane, 2000, p. 43.

We have prominently quoted de Tocqueville in previous chapters. It is relevant, then, that he reaches a similar conclusion, based on what is effectively an efficiency argument:

I recognize that by regulating relief, charitable persons in association could infuse individual philanthropy with more activity and power. I recognize not only the utility but the necessity of public charity applied to inevitable evils such as the helplessness of infancy, the decrepitude of old age, sickness, insanity. I even admit its temporary usefulness in times of public calamities which God sometimes allows to slip from his hand, proclaiming his anger to the nations. State alms are then as spontaneous as unforeseen, as temporary as the evil itself.[6]

Provision for Equipping

Lao Tzu is credited with the maxim "Give a man a fish and you feed him for a day. Teach him how to fish and you feed him for a lifetime." The obvious societal deficiency in practice – and it is identified by Lao Tzu's maxim – is that children who are not equipped with the means to make a living, capable and incapable alike, can enter maturity unable to make their way independently. Oversight by government to ensure that equipping occurs – but not necessarily that government itself do the equipping (see Chapter 5) – is therefore a justifiable government function with respect to our framework.

We summarize the role of equipping through analogy to another ancient reference. The biblical book of Leviticus describes a distribution system whereby each family group was assigned land. Further, land could not be sold in perpetuity outside the family or clan. Every fifty years, land had to revert to the family or clan of original title. Land plus effort produced a reasonable living. Land plus no effort did not. An inalienable land endowment, therefore, meant that the endowed (equipped) individual would be poor only through lack of effort. Today, equipping individuals with human capital performs a similar function. Education plus effort equals a living, but education without effort does not. A society that equips all capable citizens with ability – teaches them how to fish – has moved in the direction of guaranteeing that no one is poor except by his or her own fault.

There is another important function of equipping that we now take up. Beyond the incapable needy, already considered, we must deal with the possibility that some capable individuals (i.e., those able to provide for themselves once equipped) are in the state of neediness through their own fault. Should the equipped capable needy be treated the same as the incapable

---

[6] de Tocqueville, 1997, p. 36.

needy? Can society distinguish? A screening device whose operation guaranteed that anyone who is needy is needy by his own fault would logically require that no "equipped-capable-needy" individuals are present whose neediness is due to another's "robbing (cheating)" him or her in some fashion, as well as that there are no "incapable needy" present.

Presuming that such a screen existed, it would serve the government function of isolating, identifying, and supporting the incapable needy. In fact, the requirements of the presumed screen can be satisfied and related to provision for equipping as follows: The idea of an optimal state of an economy presumes honesty of the agents described and absence of fraud; it is therefore necessary and uncontroversial for government to prevent dishonesty, including robbery and fraud, and make provisions ensuring that every agent can keep the wealth he or she creates. In a hypothetical world where people were born either endowed with the capability to make their own living or incapable, the operation of justice alone would be enough to satisfy the screening function: the incapable needy would be deserving of public aid; the capable needy would be needy through their own fault and would have the means to cease being needy by their own actions.

In the real world, because ability is created and transmitted to new citizens, ensuring justice alone is not a sufficient mechanism to distinguish incapable needy (deserving of state assistance) from the capable needy (perhaps deserving of private charity and compassion but undeserving of state assistance). A mechanism that adds equipping restores the screen.

Figure 6.1 shows how equipping limits government assistance only to the incapable needy. The following terminology is used in a carefully chosen technical sense:

- **Equipped-unequipped:** These are treatments, the endowing of an individual with the tools of economic independence.
- **Capable-incapable:** These refer to innate ability, the state of being able to be taken to the point of economic independence.
- **Unneedy-needy:** These are outcomes, the absence or presence of being economically independent.
- **Deserving-undeserving:** These are narrow assessments, relating only to the individual's worthiness to receive government aid transfers taxed from other individuals. The terminology is not pejorative and does not mean such individuals are unworthy objects of compassion and private charity.

The first three dichotomies produce eight possible categories of individuals. For example, "equipped-capable-unneedy" would be one group and "unequipped-capable-unneedy" another. Figure 6.1 summarizes what equipping, capability, and neediness imply about deservingness. If all are equipped, the unneedy, on the lower right of the diagram, constitute two groups (viz. "equipped-capable -unneedy" and "equipped-incapable-unneedy"). Since they are unneedy, they are undeserving of government aid. The two groups associated with "unequipped-needy" are nonexistent if government ensures that universal equipping of agents takes place (a condition that is satisfied if all are educated and have access to health care). Of the remaining groups, only the "equipped-incapable-needy" are deserving of government provision through social insurance, already covered.

The extension to health care is analogous: To the extent that a sick person may not be able to work or suffers work impairment, ensuring access to health care is justified as a valid object of government oversight in the same way that ensuring that everyone is equipped with an education as a precursor to making one's living is a proper object of government oversight. In the health context, "capability" means the ability of the person to be treated healthwise and taken to or maintained at the point of fitness for self-support.

> **In the health context, "capability" means the ability of the person to be treated healthwise and taken to or maintained at the point of fitness for self-support.**

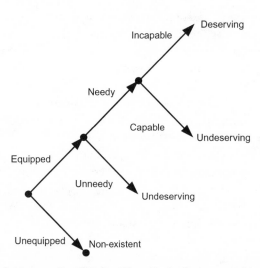

Figure 6.1. Equipping as a Social Policy Filter. Equipping agents with access to health care and education provides a screen so that only the incapable needy remain as deserving of government support through taxed transfers.

Because one's education and health are inputs for economic independence, there is a special equipping role for them by the government. Guaranteeing access to health care and education also serves the function of guaranteeing that the only individuals deserving of government aid are the incapable needy. The argument that government has an oversight interest, of course, does not imply that it should be the supplier. Rather, the most efficient supply method should be selected and should be based on the intervention principle and economic considerations.

Historical Setting of Government Involvement in Health Care Marketplace. The twentieth century witnessed in the United States a major expansion of government into areas that it previously had not entered. Social Security began in the 1930s; World War II led to the GI bill; the Hill-Burton Act passed in 1946 provided funds to build hospitals in parts of the country that had little acess to care in return for their providing a pre-determined amount of charity care; and Medicare and Medicaid were instituted with the Great Society programs of the 1960s, followed by expansions of Social Security in the 1970s. The expectations of the succeeding generation differed from those of earlier ones across a range of social issues including education and health.

Most histories of American health care point out that wage and price controls during World War II led to non-price competition, including bargaining over employer-sponsored health care benefits. These health benefits were given tax-preferred status by Congress in 1954, and the right to bargain for them was sanctioned by the Supreme Court. Predictably, workers did not want to give up what was considered a valuable fringe benefit. After the war, the practice expanded. At the time of writing, 59 percent of the population now receive their health insurance this way. The unintended consequence of employment-based, tax-advantaged health care was that healthy individuals outside an insurance group found it increasingly difficult to obtain reasonably priced coverage because they were pooled with individuals who were high risks. Being without a job, or changing jobs, meant going without health insurance. Especially for young citizens, such as those seeking their first job and those whose expected medical costs are likely to be much lower than those of older workers, this was an unjust and unfair situation.

Even as the nature of private insurance coverage was changing, publicly provided health insurance became the target of political attention. After repeated failures to produce a government-run plan, proponents passed legislation in 1964 creating a social insurance plan providing comprehensive coverage for the elderly and indigent. Since the creation of Medicare and Medicaid, the direction of legislation has been almost exclusively to increase the role of government in health care delivery and finance. Through time, laws were passed requiring public hospitals to provide services to all who showed up needing treatment, regardless of whether they had insurance or would pay. Inevitably, insurance determined whether a person would pay. There are many other unintended consequences. In San Diego County, for example, over 40 percent of babies born at Medi-Cal taxpayer expense in 2004 were to illegal aliens. Many plan their presence in the United States for this purpose.[7] A similar situation exists at many other hospitals across America.

Many Americans now believe that they should pay no out-of-pocket costs for any health care, whether the service is a routine check-up or a catastrophic emergency intervention. The State Children's Health Insurance Program (SCHIP) was created in 1997, providing coverage to low-income children through state administered programs. In 2005, the Medicare Modernization Act (MMA) expanded Medicare by creating an outpatient prescription drug benefit for the elderly known as Part D. The benefits provided under Part D represent the largest single expansion in government funding for health benefits since 1965. MMA was also responsible for providing a means of expanding the role of the individual in health care decision making. The legislation authorized the private sector offering of health savings accounts. Individuals who purchase a high-deductible insurance policy to cover catastrophic expenses may open one of these tax-free accounts to pay out-of-pocket expenses. The move away from third-party payment for first-dollar expenditures and the restoration of health insurance to its proper role have become the cornerstone of the consumer-directed health care (CDHC) movement.

6.2. Public Provision of Private Goods Cautions

We have explained that health care is primarily a private good, that provision for the incapable needy and provision for equipping are consistent with the technical or "scientific" efficiency framework of Chapters 4 and 5, and that there is justification for public interest and oversight in health care. Of what cautions should we be aware?

---

[7] Bennett, 2007.

Incrementalism, Unforeseen Consequences
Hayek and others warn of incrementalism – the creation of incentives that cause the system to drift toward an unacceptable end.

Elimination of Private Services
Once a service is publicly provided, it sets in motion a natural progression. Public provision creates incentives that tend to remove the service from competition and thus forgo the desirable consequences of competition. To an economist this is startlingly serious. In addition, governmentalization sets in motion the replacement of the corresponding private service. Citizens are taxed for the publicly provided private good. "The person who has already paid his share of the general assessment will certainly not pay again to have the same service performed for him by private industry."[8]

> Once a service is publicly provided, it sets in motion a natural progression. Public provision creates incentives that tend to remove the service from competition and thus forgo the desirable consequences of competition.

There is a second consequence of government provision. The public employees begin to view the private sector providers of the same service as the enemy that must be marginalized, crushed, and eliminated. This perspective, after all, is easy to justify: Advocates will claim that government employees are motivated by the good of the people; private providers, in contrast, seek nothing but profit; and private customers are the rich (and therefore should be viewed differently). In addition, the method to neutralize the private sector requires only that the bureaucrats work in their own interest: ask for more tax support to provide expanded services, ask for more money to attract and retain better employees (teachers, physicians, administrators, etc.), require that everyone participate in the government system (for the good of the system and therefore the good of the people, etc.), and so on.

Many of the invalid arguments for publicly providing health care could be applied to other private goods, and specious externality arguments are not hard to make for virtually any good that benefits its user. Claims that improved health for others must be a social responsibility because society benefits from a healthy population, healthy workers produce more, that doing so leads to lower prices, and so on, are dubious. Many of these

---

[8] Bastiat, 1996, p. 17.37.

arguments are naive and would apply without change to food, to clothing, to shelter, to newer General Motors assembly plants, to better shopping malls, and to any number of economic activities generally regarded as private. They confuse the benefits of living in a society – access to trade at favorable prices – to true externalities. The burden of proof rests with those asserting public goods or neighborhood effects to prove the amounts involved. My appreciation of the appearance of a new General Motors plant as I drive past on the freeway may, in fact, be a true externality but, sensibly considering the magnitudes involved, does not constitute a validation for establishing public tax programs to subsidize the construction of General Motors assembly plants.

Creation of Vested Interests

Publicly provided private goods confer acquired rights on certain groups. Reward is not acquired by market discipline, but by political activity. Bastiat asks, "See if the law benefits one citizen at the expense of another by doing what the citizen himself cannot do without committing a crime,"[9] a test that is satisfied by publicly provided private goods.

If such a law – which may be an isolated case – is not abolished immediately, it will spread, multiply, and develop into a system.

The person who profits from this law will complain bitterly, defending his acquired rights. He will claim that the state is obligated to protect and encourage his particular industry; that this procedure enriches the state because the protected industry is thus able to spend more and to pay higher wages to the poor workingmen.

Do not listen to this sophistry by vested interests.[10]

The threat works from both the demand and the supply side. The Medicare Catastrophic Coverage Act passed in 1988 is a case in point regarding the demand side. Public pressure from certain advocacy groups including the American Association of Retired Persons (AARP) led Congress to pass the measure. The unique feature of the plan was that the entire cost of the extra benefits was paid by the intended beneficiaries, the Medicare-eligible, unusually for a social welfare program. Instead of grateful acceptance, the elderly reacted with anger and indignation: it is true that they were in favor of the insurance, but they had not expected to be charged for it, apparently believing that younger workers should be taxed for their benefit. In addition, the program did not sit on its own base: it would be funded by an

---

[9] Bastiat, 1996, p. L.64–65.
[10] Ibid.

income tax to be paid by an estimated 40 percent of the elderly only. The measure was repealed one year later.[11]

Only the naive would believe that political parties are above using public measures to buy votes and campaign support. In June 2003, a stimulus package of $350 billion in tax cuts measured over ten years was passed by the U.S. Congress. The measure was reduced from the originally proposed $750 billion stimulus on grounds that the threat to the deficit and public debt was too great. A major component retroactively increased the dependent child tax credit from $600 per child to $1,000, meaning that taxpayers would be receiving rebates of $400 of taxes that they had already paid. One political party proposed to pass a second bill that would provide government checks of $400 to those who would not have received one under the original stimulus package because they had paid no income taxes or were receiving Earned Income Tax Credits already. In view of the party's earlier opposition to the original stimulus on grounds of adding to the national debt, their subsequent proposal can be viewed as an attempt to buy political support by handing out cash.

Productive Inefficiency

Economists are used to thinking in terms of production functions, forgetting that these are mental constructs that represent the outcome of an activity optimization process. A competitive firm has an incentive to minimize cost subject to its production function, as well as to ensure that the production function it uses is efficient. Government has no such discipline and therefore is subject to operating below its production possibilities frontier, sometimes referred to as x-inefficiency to distinguish it from other forms of productive inefficiency.[12]

> **Public Opinion Regarding Government Involvement.** Even though concepts like risk pooling with individuals of like risk (insurance is discussed in Chapter 7) or the negative consequence that employer-based insurance coverage is a contributing cause of uninsurance may not be

---

[11] Many already had comprehensive health insurance coverage and resented being made to pay for benefits they did not need to go to others. See Rice, Desmond, and Gabel, 1990, p. 76: "Many elderly resented the idea of paying additional taxes to finance the new coverage. This would have represented a hefty burden on some, and, unlike the rest of the Medicare program, the additional benefits mandated by the act would have been financed entirely by the elderly. Resentment appeared to be highest among people who already had comprehensive health insurance coverage from a previous employer."

[12] See Leibenstein, 1966.

universally understood, Americans do understand that there are problems with the present system and support some type of action to address them.[13] Their views on many issues, however, may surprise some. "Results suggest that in terms of priority for government action, health care is a second-tier issue. Today it ranks as the fourth most important issue for government to address, behind the war, the economy, and gasoline/oil prices/energy." Only 22 percent think the health system is in crisis, but most are critical of it and "want their government to do something about their rising health care costs and the problems of the uninsured." Americans are not as concerned about aggregate health care spending as they are about the amount that they pay out-of-pocket for their own health care (premiums, co-payments, and deductibles). Consider: the majority of Americans thought both that overall U.S. health care spending was too low (57 percent) and that the average American family had to spend too much (65 percent).[14]

Another relevant feature of public opinion is that "most Americans are satisfied with their own most recent medical care experiences."[15] Three-fourths received care in the past year and over 80 percent of them said that the medical services and physician care they received were good or excellent. This pattern has persisted across many different surveys and over time.[16]

With respect to actions, the majority opinion does not lean to government provision of health care. Only 39 percent of Americans prefer to replace the current system based on private health insurance with a government-run system.[17] Slightly more Americans (48 percent) think a plan similar to Massachusetts's recent reform would be a good idea for the country as a whole. Only 53 percent would be willing to pay higher taxes so that everyone could have health insurance.[18] The narrow majority support for higher taxes to pay for universal insurance coverage must be considered in light of the fact that 31 percent of Americans filing income tax returns pay no income taxes; 53 percent is only 22 percentage points above this number. In summary, Americans are happy with the care they personally get, say they are concerned about health care costs,

---

[13] Blendon et al., 2006.
[14] Ibid.
[15] Ibid.
[16] Ibid.
[17] Gallup poll, 2006.
[18] NBC News/Wall Street Journal, Poll, 2007.

and want everyone to have broader access to care. Seventy percent think
that government spends too little on health care, but at the same time,
most are not interested in spending more personally or being taxed more.

Destruction of Private Responsibility

One of the most damaging consequences of public provision of private
goods is perhaps the hardest to measure and prove: the destruction of
private responsibility and the social changes
this engenders, and its replacement with
an exaggerated sense of government of its
own importance. Individuals in the United
States who would not think of denying their
obligation to pay for other services that they
have contracted for abdicate their responsibility by refusing to pay for health care
services. They receive services from heart
specialists and refuse to pay their bill.[19] The
emergency rooms of America are filled with
clients who expect treatment without the
need to pay for it. There are both an abdica-
tion of responsibility and a loss of freedom
to the patient.

> One of the most damaging consequences of public provision of private goods is perhaps the hardest to measure and prove: the destruction of private responsibility and the social changes this engenders, and its replacement with an exaggerated sense of government of its own importance.

But, for man, responsibility is everything! It is
his motive force, his teacher, his rewarder and
punisher. Without responsibility man no longer
has free will, he is no longer perfectible, he is
no longer a moral being, he learns nothing, he
is nothing. He falls into inertia and no longer counts except as a unit of the herd.[20]

Paradoxically, if government provision should lead to adverse consequences, the correct diagnosis of the problem is confounded by public
attitudes.

The loss of responsibility has perverted public opinion. The people, accustomed
to calling upon the state for everything, accuse the government, not of doing too
much, but of not doing enough. They overthrow it and replace it by another, to

[19] Many physicians have passed to the authors their stories of intentional non-payers. The
services provided in this case, based on information provided to the authors, were highly
specialized and specific to the patient. They report to us that the refusal to pay is not
uncommon.
[20] Bastiat, 1996, par. 17.46.

which they do not say: *Do less,* but *Do more;* and thus the abyss that yawns before us becomes ever deeper.[21]

Thus, the public begins to believe that it is the government's responsibility not only to be just but to be philanthropic, a view that is easily tainted by self-interest and political manipulation, both by demanders and suppliers.

6.3. Is Health Care Different?

An economy must answer the triad of questions: what, how, and for whom? Few would assert that the answers should be "as much as needed, freely and efficiently, for everyone equally." But that is how health care is frequently seen. For example, Weale writes,

This basic principle can be simply stated. It is that comprehensive, high-quality medical care should be available to all citizens on a test of professionally judged medical need and without financial barriers to access.[22]

He continues his essay on this basis. Before considering Weale's ultimate point, however, it might be useful to substitute for other selected private goods and services. Would we say, for example, that

comprehensive, high-quality vehicles should be available to all citizens on a test of professionally judged transportation need and without financial barriers to access, or comprehensive, high-quality shelter should be available to all citizens on a test of professionally judged housing need and without financial barriers to access?

Weale says that the fundamental ethical problem of health care is the problem that only two of three objectives (comprehensive to all, freely available, and of high quality) can be simultaneously satisfied. His dilemma is not knowing which objective to drop. If treatment is denied because of cost, it is not comprehensive. If private insurance means that those in poverty or with pre-existing conditions do not buy insurance, then citizens are not equal and availability is lost. If too few diagnostic tests are run, or there is too much waiting, not enough screening, or unwillingness to use expensive therapies, then high quality is lost. He concludes, "There is tension among the three elements of the basic principle of modern health care, but it is not possible to resolve it by simply dropping one of the elements."[23] An economist would respond that refusing to choose is not an option. One,

[21] Ibid., par. 17.47.
[22] Weale, 1998.
[23] Weale, 1998, p. 149.

two, or all of the triad *must* be compromised or dropped, with or without a predetermined plan.

According to David Cavers, "For most people who work in the UK private sector, the American system is as remote from their ambition as it could be."[24] While Canadians and the British appear to describe their system one way, consider this story, told to one of us in May 2003, by Stephen Warhover, the president of Gorton Seafood Company, a Boston firm employing approximately 1,000 employees and owning a sister company under another name in Canada. Gorton manufactures and distributes seafood to grocery chains and stores nationwide. In discussing health care and my thoughts about ways that America might retain some of the better features of our present system, he expressed relief and strongly encouraged me. He explained that his Canadian employees "all wanted to get onto the American system," though they resided in Canada. When asked for something specific to explain why, he told of two Gorton employees – one in Montreal, the other in Boston – who were diagnosed with identical lower back problems at the same time. The recommended solution in both cases was surgery. The American was seen in two weeks, had outpatient microscopic surgery, and recovered in one week. The Canadian waited nine months. The employee asked for microscopic surgery but was told that it was not an option. The doctor said that the equipment was not available in Canada because the government did not consider it necessary. Older, conventional surgery involving a larger incision and an in-hospital operation was performed instead. After a hospitalization of six days, the recovery took six weeks, during which the employee was out of work. Warhover wondered whether the decision not to use microsurgery was truly cost-effective.

A report for the Brookings Institute states:

British doctors do not go looking for trouble: if the patient does not report symptoms, doctors are unlikely to order tests on their own.[25] British cardiologists are less likely than Americans to prescribe angiography on the basis of tests, and more likely to do so in response to persistence of symptoms after maximum medical therapy. "You can't be diagnosed as having hypertension if nobody takes your blood pressure," Lyn Payer summarizes. "But," she adds, "even when blood pressure is taken, the British have a higher threshold for disease."[26]

Economists recognize the impossibility of providing free, unlimited, and comprehensive high-quality health care. They emphasize the rationality and

---

[24] Cavers, 2000, p. 151.
[25] White, 1995. Reported in Weale, 1998, pp. 147–148.
[26] Ibid., p. 148.

suitability of some form of cost-benefit mechanism or rationing. However, efficiency and optimality do not enter into these discussions when conducted by ethicists or medical clinicians. This is true despite the fact that health care is a private service much like others treated by private markets. The view seems to prevail in many situations that the pressing problems of health care would be solved, if only the high-income members of society would stop their opposition and, presumably, pay for the care that the social planners want so much to offer. One study states, "We conclude that when the will exists, states can substantially expand coverage. However, as one moves up the income scale, political support and resources are harder to come by."[27] Another: "Only a radical change in the way the U.S. finances health care – specifically, a single-payer system – will permit the achievement of universal coverage while keeping costs reasonably under control."[28] Readers are referred to the tax numbers of Chapter 1 to decide for themselves.

> The unintended consequence of employment-based, tax-advantaged health care was that healthy individuals outside an insurance group found it increasingly difficult to obtain reasonably priced coverage because they were pooled with individuals who were high risks. Being without a job, or changing jobs, meant going without health insurance.

6.4. Conclusion

Formal twentieth-century economic theory is not fully enough developed to be able to offer a guide to the evaluation of public provision of private goods, per se, such as health care or health insurance. Working within the framework of utilitarian social optima, however, charts a course that allows the relevant issues to be identified. It is consistent for government to oversee the equipping function (provide agents with the opportunity through education and health care coverage to become self-supporting) and to provide social insurance for incapable needy (defined as we have in this chapter). Allowing for the raising of children to maturity, for example, suggests an equipping and health care role for public oversight to the extent that it

---

[27] Gold et al., 2001, p. 581.
[28] DeGrazia, 1996, p. 145.

ensures that each agent is endowed with adequate knowledge and health to attain the ability to make a living when combined with the agent's own effort. At the same time, public provision of private goods is fraught with incentives that lead to unintended consequences. It is appropriate that government policymakers see that action occurs, not necessarily that government takes action itself. In particular, the mechanism adopted to oversee equipping and health care must respect the structures that support social optima and avoid structures that destroy freedom and initiative and create harmful incentives for government and private sector abuse.

SEVEN

Insurance

Employer financing of medical care has caused the term "insurance" to acquire
a rather different meaning in medicine ... it has become common to rely on
insurance to pay for regular medical examinations and often for prescriptions.

Milton Friedman, Nobel Economist, "How to Cure Health Care," 2001

Summary: *Things are not always what they seem: Insurance is not pre-paid
care. It is not charity transfers. "Cherry picking" or "cream skimming" is an
indication of a healthy insurance market, while "utilization gatekeeping" –
denial of claims for covered services rendered – indicates a sick insurance market.
Moral hazard and adverse selection are concerns for underwriters, who should
not be expected to act against their own interests for the success of public policy with respect to health insurance. On the other hand, legally enforced ethical insurance requires guaranteed renewability of health insurance at standard
rates.*

*Separating pre-paid care, charity transfers, and utilization gatekeeping from
the pure function of risk sharing and pooling, allowing freedom to underwrite,
and addressing selected intertemporal issues combine to place health insurance
on a solid footing. Health insurance in America cannot be said to have failed,
when it has not been tried for years.*

7.1. What's Wrong with This Tale?

The insurance agent related the following story. A client arrived at his office
to buy health insurance. In the interview process the client was asked about
pre-existing conditions. Yes, the client's wife was eight months pregnant.
Yes, he wanted insurance to cover the expenses he expected to have in the
next month. And, yes, he was definitely not happy when the agent explained
that, of course, this pre-existing condition could not be covered. "Well,
something is *really* wrong with this country if you can't even buy insurance
when you need it."

Background

This story would be humorous if it were not true. It highlights two preva-
lent contradictory understandings about health insurance that continue to
appear in the debate about how health care spending should be financed. The
agent represented the indemnity insurance view whereby clients pay actuarially fair premiums for the insurance benefits they receive, and the client
the "subsidy" view. Indemnity insurance is risk-rated insurance (sometimes
called "experience-rated" insurance) in which premiums are determined
according to the expected spending the client can anticipate receiving on
his behalf. The purpose is to mitigate risk. Social insurance, as described
in Chapter 5 in Section 5.2 in the discussion "Information, Social Insurance," and in Chapter 6, Section 6.1 in the discussion "Provision for the
Incapable Needy," is indemnity insurance administered through government auspices, often forcing participation through taxes and covering the
entire population. The "subsidy" view of insurance, in contrast, sees insurance as involving risk-related charity where payments are event-dependent
and charity elements are combined with true insurance. Instead of those
who are expected to receive lower insurance payouts paying lower premiums, premiums are set according to other measures – usually ability to pay.
"Winners" – as the subject of our story wanted to be – are those who get
more on an *ex ante* expected basis than they pay for in premiums; "losers"
are those who get less on an *ex ante* expected basis than they pay for in premiums. Private insurance programs typically follow indemnity insurance
principles. Government-run programs often incorporate subsidies, for reasons discussed in Chapter 3 in Section 3.3, "Principle 3: Every Pot Sits on its
Own Base," thereby failing to sit on their own base. In this chapter we dispel
various misconceptions about insurance before explaining how insurance
is incorporated into a national health care framework in a way that meets
the economic principles discussed in Chapter 3.

Today, U.S. health care financing combines subsidy elements with
indemnity (experience-rated) insurance. Individuals are typically pooled
with others to share the risk of extraordinarily high spending. Private insurance (covering about 68 percent of the population)[1] is partially risk rated
with premiums based on the expected spending of the average member of
the pool. Medicare and Medicaid (covering 20 percent of the population)
are social insurance programs funded primarily from payroll and income
taxes. Health status is unrelated to the amount a person pays.

---

[1] A total of 67.9 percent were covered by any private plan in 2006. See U.S. Census Bureau,
    2007, p. 20.

This chapter examines the structure of health insurance, its consequences, and the implications for reform. We discuss the nature of insurance –
what it is and why people buy it – then look at features of insurance markets,
including moral hazard, adverse selection, and community rating, and their
consequences. After a discussion of the best design for an insurance plan,
we summarize reform options.

7.2. Essential Insurance

Chapter 6 (see the box "Historical Setting of Government Involvement in
Health Care Marketplace") described the beginnings of employer-based
health insurance and the unintended consequence that healthy individuals
outside an insurance group found it harder to obtain reasonably priced
coverage. Because of the historical paths chosen and where they have led,
health care reform inevitably requires a discussion of the merits of private
indemnity insurance versus government-run insurance.

> **The Benjamin Franklin Model.**[2] Among Benjamin Franklin's accom-
> plishments are the creation in 1736 of the Union Fire Company in
> Philadelphia and the creation in 1752 of America's first fire insurance
> company. A metal medallion marked insured homes to direct respon-
> ders in event of fire.
>
> Imagine 1,000 homes, each with equal 0.1 percent chance of suffering
> $100,000 fire damage in a given year. Rather than one homeowner suf-
> fering enormous loss in the event of a fire, and the rest none, the home-
> owners band together. Each pays $100 for fire insurance (the actuarially
> fair amount) to cover damages in event of fire. All homes have an equal
> chance of collecting an equal payout. Working from a measure of utility
> (well-being) that declines with probability of fire and at an increasing rate
> with size of loss, the homeowners would have 10 units of utility without
> insurance. With insurance, utility rises to 14. In fact, premiums could be
> $230 per year – leaving the insurance company plenty for its operating
> costs – and utility would still be higher than 10 in this example. Risk is
> costly and people will pay to reduce risk.

Individuals enter into insurance contracts to share risk with one another.
The traditional insurance contract is purchased for a premium based on the

---

[2] Franklin Institute, 2007.

expected payout if a specific event takes place. The most straightforward application of the traditional insurance contract is term life insurance. The purchaser pays a specified premium for a life insurance policy that pays a predetermined amount to named beneficiaries in the event that the insured person dies. A second application is property-casualty insurance, where the payout is based on the cost of restoring the value of a damaged asset to its undamaged state.

Health insurance shares many characteristics of traditional indemnity insurance with a few notable differences. Indemnity health insurance policies pay a predetermined amount for a list of covered conditions. If the insured broke a leg, the policy paid a pre-set amount, fulfilling the insurance function of transferring purchasing power from the healthy state to the sick state of nature. We use the term "state of nature" in this context to represent the outcome of a random event that determines which situation an individual is in. Two problems arise with the indemnity insurance arrangement. The first is difficulty verifying the validity and/or seriousness of the health event that initiates the claim. The second is the wide variation in the cost to treat similar medical conditions and the high risk that this leaves with the insured individual. Thus, the indemnity health insurance policy was replaced by the service benefit policy, one that covered billed expenses for a given episode of illness. This form of insurance and its cost-sharing features, including deductibles, co-insurance, and stop-loss (out-of-pocket limit) provisions, grew in popularity until the early 1980s. As a college student, one of the authors bought such a major medical policy for himself on the private market before 1980 but, checking recently, found that the company no longer sells such insurance.

> Moral hazard – the need for increased payout for insured events caused by the presence of the insurance – arises when there is opportunity for the payout recipient to gain from the contract by altering behavior in some fashion.

"Moral Hazard"

One of the most common information problems that influence insurance markets is "moral hazard." Moral hazard – the need for increased payout for insured events caused by the presence of the insurance – arises when there is opportunity for the payout recipient to gain from the contract by altering behavior in some fashion. It can also arise from events set in motion by the presence of insurance that relate to prices of insurance-covered purchases.

Moral hazard can result from intentional improper acts but also can be the natural (and moral) response of economic agents to insurance-created incentives. Moral hazard is the result of post-contractual self-interested behavior. Several implications of moral hazard are of interest. Not only are the insured more likely to seek medical services, they use more services, including services that cost more to provide than the value they receive from them.[3]

> **Moral Hazard.** Return to Ben Franklin's Philadelphia. If a policyholder intentionally burns down his insured home, that is criminal fraud and violates the contract. But what if the insured simply fails to be as careful as before to prevent fire once the home is insured? If the probability of a fire rises because the homeowner is insured, this is a form of moral hazard. (This is equivalent to the increased probability that a person with health insurance will seek medical care.)
>
> It may be that the contract allows the homeowner to rebuild after a fire. If the contract does not specify otherwise, the homeowner has an incentive to build a larger home or use more expensive materials than he would if rebuilding without insurance. This is also a form of moral hazard. In the case of medical care, a patient who asks for a private hospital room instead of sharing one, or who gets an additional procedure, or selects a more costly intervention, because the expense is covered by insurance also exhibits moral hazard.
>
> Assume that indemnity insurance transfers \$750 of purchasing power to the patient in the sick state of nature. Figure 7.1 shows the value that the patient receives from treatment (and hence demand for service) with the \$750 insurance payment in hand. When the patient pays the true cost of service rendered, p^0, the level of treatment chosen is q^0. Since $p^0 q^0 = \$750$ in this example, indemnity insurance has performed its function. Now presume that coverage is provided in the form of service benefit insurance. When the co-insurance rate is 20 percent, the patient pays price p^1 and selects quantity q^1. The insurance company now pays \$750 plus an additional amount equal to the shaded area. The patient demands additional care, even though its cost exceeds the value to the patient, because the third-party payer

---

[3] See Pauly, 1970, pp. 414–416, for a discussion of risk-increasing, quantity-increasing, and price-increasing moral hazard.

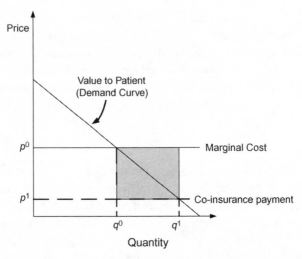

Figure 7.1. Service Benefit Insurance and Moral-Hazard-Induced Use of Medical Care

(insurance company) is footing part of the bill. The shaded area above the value-to-patient line is the excess cost (waste) over value received.

In general, if *ex ante* payout is $\pi p q$ where π is the probability that a covered event occurs, p is the price of the covered purchase, and q its quantity, moral hazard occurs if one or more of π, p, or q rises because insurance is present. We can therefore distinguish the different avenues through which moral hazard occurs.

It is important to design insurance plans to deal with moral hazard.[4] Ideally, insurance would pay only for care that would be selected had the individual chosen to self-insure. For example, consider the situation where two health states are possible, sick and healthy. Suppose the probability of becoming sick is 10 percent and that it requires medical spending of $20,000 to return to full health. The risk-averse individual prefers to pay the fair premium of $2,000 rather than self-insure.[5] If medical spending is actually

[4] "As has been noted in several places, an optimal solution in this kind of 'moral hazard' situation is for the insured to retain some part of his losses." Pauly, 1974, p. 45. The welfare losses of moral hazard can be mitigated if some risky medical events are not fully insured. Pauly, 1968; 1974, p. 45; 1986 discusses alteratives that include the use of deductibles, co-insurance, quasi-indemnities. See "Deductibles, Co-insurance, and Other Explicit Financial Benefit Limits" in Pauly, 1986, pp. 641–642.

[5] This is a standard implication of risk aversion and expected utility maximization. See, for example, Von Neumann and Morgenstern, 1944.

$30,000 when the person has insurance, the additional $10,000 spending is due to moral hazard.

There are several distinct aspects to understanding the incentives that cause quantity (as opposed to price or probability) moral hazard. Reducing the price seen by the insured for medical care, even if the probability of the insured event and the quality (and hence price) of any covered good or service are unchanged, has both an income effect and a substitution effect. The income effect transfers income from the healthy state to the sick state and allows the insured individual to purchase medical care that would be unaffordable without the income transfer. Moral hazard results from the substitution effect, the additional spending undertaken by the insured beyond the amount that would have been contracted for with the income transfers present but the non-contract price imposed.

To manage moral hazard, insurers use deductibles and co-insurance. The presence of a deductible imposes costs on the insured if a health event arises. There is therefore an incentive to prevent insured events. If an insured event occurs, however, the co-insurance amount encourages patients to make choices about care that balance the value of the additional care with its out-of-pocket cost. Patients with chronic conditions especially have the knowledge and ability, if the incentive is present, to find ways to reduce the costs of their long-term interventions and care. If a catastrophic event occurs, however, incentives have very little impact on the choice of treatment, and costs beyond the out-of-pocket limit are paid in full. Catastrophic coverage – effectively income transfers to the sick state of nature – leads to little or no moral hazard if purchased goods and services are priced at their marginal cost of provision. See Chapter 10 for a discussion of what is needed to cause this to happen. If providers have market power, however, the presence of insurance can cause them to raise prices in response.

Well-designed insurance, therefore, recognizes that in situations where the patient has no choice or control over the care received – for example, the onset of appendicitis requires an appendectomy for which there is no choice, and no one would choose to have two appendectomies merely because the cost of the operation to the insured is zero – co-insurance rates can be zero. In situations where the insured has a choice about the quantity, quality, or likelihood of care – this might include chronic situations, situations of routine care, and/or an identifiable selection of covered services – deductibles and co-insurance rates should be set to induce appropriate use of care by reflecting the true cost of care to the insured balanced by the need to transfer purchasing power to the insured in the sick state (balance the benefits of greater risk sharing with the costs of moral hazard).[6] "With a properly designed insurance plan, people will self-insure for expenses for which individual choice is appropriate and desirable."[7] Of course, in the present environment, this may require various legislative innovations (health savings accounts, though imperfect, are a current example) to correct tax and incentive distortions.

For those with insurance coverage, first-dollar coverage reduces the direct costs of risky behavior and choice of treatment. Excess coverage changes the risk-taking behavior of all parties involved in a transaction. Patients with comprehensive insurance will seek more care than those who are uninsured and providers will recommend higher levels of care to those with more generous coverage. The reader should revisit Figure 7.1 and the lunch plan example in the discussion before Section 3.4 to consider the effects on lunch spending when the "lunch insurance" program is established. More spending will take place, and, in fact, all will spend more for lunch than they have demonstrated (shown by their previous actions) it is actually worth to them. All is due to the moral hazard created by the incentives of the program.

Higher deductibles and co-insurance rates result in greater user responsiveness to limit overspending in medical care. Short of a pure indemnity plan with fixed dollar payouts, no service benefit insurance is perfect in eliminating moral hazard, but recognizing moral hazard and the incentives that the insurance product creates, coupled with learning through time by the issuer, will allow much better outcomes than observed at present in many insurance products.

Adverse Selection

The other information problem relevant to insurance, adverse selection, refers to the inability of the insurer to distinguish prospective risks accurately and charge each insured party a premium appropriate to his or her risk. As is the case with moral hazard, asymmetric information between the insurer and the insured allows the insured to act in ways that the insurer would prefer to avoid.

> **Adverse Selection.** Assume that one-third of Philadelphia's homes are made of straw, one-third of sticks, and one-third of bricks. Brick houses have 0.1 percent chance of burning each year, while houses of sticks and straw have 0.25 and 0.5 percent chance, respectively. Presume further that

---

[6] Cutler and Zeckhauser, 2000.
[7] Goodman, 2006.

homeowners know the construction material of their own homes, but insurance companies cannot observe this (we abstract from reality for pedagogical reasons. Asymmetric information is more understandable in the medical insurance context where the individual knows his or her own health status better than insurers do.) If we retain the $100,000 of damage assumption for each house should a fire arise, the actuarially fair premium for brick houses is $100 per year, for stick houses $250, and for straw houses $500. It can be shown that $333.33 \times 0.001 + 333.33 \times 0.0025 + 333.33 \times 0.005$ implies 2.833 houses will burn each year, causing $283,333 dollars in damage. The insurance company would therefore have to charge each homeowner a yearly premium of $283.33. This premium is actuarially unfair for the owners of brick homes, whose utility drops from 10 without insurance to 8.48 with insurance, causing them to drop coverage and self-insure.

Meanwhile, the policy offered for $283.33 per year experiences adverse selection, attracting only the higher-risk homes. Instead of being able to offer the policy for the intended price (based on incorrect information), the insurer must charge more. Now $333.33 \times 0.0025 + 333.33 \times 0.005$ implies 2.5 insured homes will burn each year, requiring premiums to be raised to $250,000/666.66 = $375 per home. Stick and straw homeowners still find it worth their while to carry insurance at this price.

If it could identify them *ex ante*, the insurance company could make money by separating out the low-risk brick homes and offering members of this homogeneous group separate policies for actuarially fair rates. "Cherry picking" or "cream skimming" (the profitable separation of the insured into homogeneous groups by insurers) improves efficiency and is welfare-enhancing because it eliminates the pool of uninsured, raises brick homeowners' welfare, and does not alter the ability of the stick and straw homeowners to buy insurance exactly as before. Were the stick and straw homes likewise separated, efficiency would rise further. In a perfect world, each type of home would insure with others of its kind for actuarially fair premiums all around.

If this story referred directly to health insurance, the low-risk (brick) homes would be the young and healthy, who would be uninsured because of actuarially unfair premiums but through "cherry picking" and the elimination of adverse selection and asymmetric information issues would be able to obtain low-cost, fair insurance.

Insurance-financed medical care fundamentally changes the market. Insurance premiums are determined by the need for payouts, and this spending is determined by the composition of the insurance pool. Efficient insurance *wants* to sort individuals into similar risk categories and charge premiums based on risk. Those who know they will need more frequent and bigger payouts are disproportionately attracted to more generous insurance plans. As long as the insured can be sorted into homogeneous groups, the incentives are aligned to offer both high-risk and low-risk groups what they want at actuarially fair premiums. Empirical evidence suggests that individuals are sensitive to price differences and will switch plans for small premium savings.[8] These studies also show that price sensitivity makes comprehensive plans vulnerable to a so-called death spiral resulting from adverse selection. Some change in the market starts the process, such as increasing the comprehensiveness or generosity of a plan. Healthy enrollees are forced to drop out of the comprehensive plan because of actuarially unfair higher premiums. Premiums in those plans rise to cover higher expected costs of the less healthy. More drop out and premiums rise further. Ultimately, the comprehensive plan may be cancelled if only people with known extensive needs remain for whom paying the premium is as burdensome as going without insurance or who simply do not have the ability to pay. Often such individuals are "uninsurable" – a technical term and situation that we will take up next.

From a social perspective, the problem with a death spiral is *not* that premiums rise or that people with known extensive needs have to pay actuarially fair premiums, but two other consequences that are important to understand properly. The first is that insurable individuals are prevented from insuring. The second is that the insurance issuers are, in effect, reneging on their contract to insure against the risky outcome that an insured individual enters the state of permanently needing higher payouts. The latter has to do with the intertemporal nature of insurance and the fact that health insurance covers two kinds of events: the first is the event that occurs in the covered year and needs treatment in that year, but the second is the event that the individual will need payouts that extend beyond the coverage year. The appropriate response is described in more detail in the discussion of

> From a social perspective, the problem is that insurable individuals are prevented from insuring by the failure to separate potential insureds into homogeneous risk classes.

[8] Buchmueller, 1998; Cutler and Reber, 1998.

reclassification risk ("Time and the Uninsurable: A Curious Connection" in Section 7.2). Before turning to it, however, we discuss several other important features of insurance.

Community Rating, Charity Transfers, and Pure Insurance

Heterogeneous risk pools usually result from the inability of insurers to distinguish one group from the other. Sometimes they are formed intentionally as the result of tax distortions. Either way, actuarially unfair premiums are the consequence for some members of the group. Meaningful use of the terms "high-risk" and "low-risk" implies the ability of *some* agent to distinguish between members of the two groups *ex ante*. If no one can distinguish *ex ante*, then the terms are meaningless: when individuals are indistinguishable from one another in terms of the probability of experiencing an insured event, they are, by definition, a homogeneously pooled group.

The special tax preference granted employment-based health insurance, well-meaning as it is, nevertheless creates perverse incentives for heterogeneous insurance groups. Such pools are "community rated" or "group rated" because, even though it is possible to distinguish *ex ante* between low-risk and high-risk members, the pool sets premiums according to the average expected payouts for the group. As the example of straw, stick, and brick homes shows, community rating can lead people to face higher prices for their insurance than is actuarilly fair, resulting in their going without insurance because they cannot affort it and/or it is not worth the price they are asked to pay.

> **Community Rating.** Intentionally grouping high-risk, high-cost individuals with low-risk, low-cost individuals leads to actuarially unfair premiums for the latter. These individuals often have no choice but to forgo insurance coverage when they could afford to buy insurance that reflected their needs. In many places, for example, young people in their early twenties can buy adequate insurance for $50–$65 per month ($600–$800 per year). Being forced into insurance pools with older individuals and paying for coverage they do not need or want such as three physicals per year or hip replacements for degenerative conditions (almost exclusively used by those beyond their late fifties) cause their insurance premiums to rise to the level of $4,500 or more per year. Basic coverage at each age should reflect desired usage by that age group as well as be distinguished from "extras" that can be offered as add-ons to those who want them, retaining homogeneous pooling and equal expected benefit payouts to

policyholders. Placing individually purchased insurance on an equal tax basis with employer-sponsored insurance would make it even more affordable to those just starting out in life.

Profit incentives for insurers encourage them to establish homogeneous risk pools, a good insurance principle. Furthermore, the satisfaction of the insured rises with the establishment of homogeneous risk pools. What does this imply for high-risk, high-cost individuals and those with conditions that guarantee high medical expenditures? The answer is found by recognizing that satisfying two separate objectives with two separate tools is better than trying to satisfy both with one.

Community rating (heterogeneous grouping) creates a de facto condition of forced charity tied to the insurance function that damages the effectiveness of both. In our example, straw house owners received benefits valued at $500 per year and would have willingly paid actuarially fair premiums of $500. Charging them $283.33 implied that they were given a mixed product that consisted of "pure" insurance (premiums that paid for expected benefits received) plus charity of $216.67. This money resulted from overpayments by stick and brick homeowners, some of whom consequently became uninsured.

Each type of homeowner is better off compared to the non-insured state through purchase of actuarially fair insurance offered through homogeneous risk pools. A program of voluntary charity that allows stick and brick homeowners to give money to straw homeowners to help them pay their premiums can be implemented in a fashion similar to existing programs that help the needy pay utility bills in many cities. When paying a utility bill, the homeowner can check off a box that directs the utility company to add an extra payment that is directed to this program. Actuarially fair, pure insurance coupled with separate charity transfers, can achieve a social state where no one is made worse off and some or all are better off. Separating insurance from charity allows homeowners to assess rationally how much charity they are able to provide, another advantage of keeping insurance on a "pure" basis.

Table 7.1 shows that the best social outcome is achieved by actuarially fair insurance offered to homogeneous pools of individuals with similar risk. No insurance is the worst social state among the comparisons of Table 7.1.[9]

[9] Appendix B shows that badly designed insurance programs, for example, those with inappropriately generous benefits, inappropriate group rating, costly insurance overhead, and/or suppliers taking advantage of insured patients by increasing their charges, can be worse for everyone in society than no insurance coverage at all.

Table 7.1. *Superiority of Fair Insurance + Separate Charity over Combining Charity with Insurance*

Insured type	Actuarially fair insurance	Actuarially fair insurance + charity	Low-risk homes uninsured	No insurance
Brick	14.0	12.5	10.0	10.0
Sticks	9.5	5.7	5.7	−0.5
Straw	1.9	5.7	5.7	−18.0
ALL HOMES TOTALS	8,468	7,970	7,138	−2,834

Note: Figures shown are annual expected utility for the homeowners described in "The Benjamin Franklin Model," earlier in this chapter.

When insurance is mixed with charity, the efficiency of insurance is affected and low-risk homeowners go without. A better outcome can be created by separating the charity and insurance functions. In the case displayed in the third column, brick homeowners buy actuarially fair insurance at price $100, and give separate charity transfers of $50. Stick homeowners likewise buy actuarially fair insurance and make charity transfers. The third column is superior to the fourth, where combining charity and insurance creates a pool of uninsured. As discussed in Chapter 5, another advantage of engaging in charity in a separated and transparent way is that individuals are empowered to evaluate the needs of other households relative to their household's needs and determine what they should give and can afford. Every household does the same for itself, building up to the total that reflects all such information and does not interfere with insurance market functioning.

Pre-Paid Care Is Not Insurance

John Doe is a healthy, active 22-year-old. Guidelines say that he should have a routine physical exam every three years. He is unmarried and does not need in vitro fertilization, breast implants, elective cosmetic surgery, or a host of other specialized services that apply to those who are older, married, or of a different sex. He does, however, need medical insurance to cover catastrophes such as car accidents. A physical exam costs $180. If three per year are required to be part of his medical insurance, the premium he would pay would rise by its cost plus the administrative overhead in collecting his money and returning it to him for exams. Assuming 20 percent overhead, $[(3 \times \$180)/12] \times 1.20 = \$54$ per month. This is not his insurance premium; this is the *increase* in his premium from just one added feature to his policy – three covered physicals a year. Were he forced to pay for other coverages – some of which he may well want or need at a later stage in his life but does not want or need now – through being pooled with those older or of a different sex, it could add hundreds, even thousands, of dollars a year to the costs he would pay for the basic coverage that he wants at his current age.

The prevention benefits of routine physical exams are the increased likelihood of identifying diseases and medical problems early. These benefits accrue to the individual. Individuals therefore have an incentive to get those procedures that provide them with sufficient benefits to warrant the extra cost. Pre-paid care is not insurance because it covers care that is predictable, certain, and not subject to medical randomness. In most cases, it also carries a relatively small price tag. If John wants an extra physical, it is much cheaper for him to pay for it directly. The exception would be pre-paid care that is premium reducing. It makes sense for premium-reducing pre-paid care to be included in an insurance policy. For pre-paid care that is not premium reducing, pre-paid care should be a voluntary option to purchasers of insurance, but not a mandate.

The argument is sometimes raised that individuals will forgo the preventive care that is in their own interest to get. The argument requires for its validity that individuals will fail to do what is in their own interest. If so, this is a matter for education (why would informed, rational individuals not get care that provides benefits exceeding its cost?) or, possibly, an adequacy of income issue. The response to these problems can be separated from health insurance. The need for education or aid to those with low income is not a reason for destroying the effectiveness of health insurance to offer products that meet customers' actual needs.[10]

> The need for education or aid to those with low income is not a reason for destroying the effectiveness of health insurance to offer products that meet customers' actual needs.

---

[10] In the presence of medical care substitutes and complementarities, improperly insuring some types of medical care but not others could distort demand and create an efficiency rationale for coverage to relatively certain types of expenditures with highly elastic demand. The base insurance product should be chosen to take account of sales and administration costs ("loading") as well as moral hazard, and this may require a balancing of forces, the discussion of which is the subject of much attention in the health care insurance literature. In insurance matters we recommend the work of Mark Pauly, 1968, 1970, 1974, 1986, 1991, 2002, 2004.

Time and the Uninsurable: A Curious Connection

We have saved what is often considered the greatest challenge for last: the uninsurable. A *high-risk (high-cost)* individual is one whose expected future payouts are high relative to those of others. An *uninsurable* individual is one whose future payouts are certain, or virtually certain. A *high-needs* individual is one whose expected future out-of-pocket payouts are high relative to his or her ability to pay. Often, all three descriptions apply to a single individual.

Uninsurability and time are intimately tied in a way that can best be explained by considering a hypothetical person's experience from birth onward. From the birth vantage point, all of us start life alike, with sex an obvious difference. The few who could be meaningfully distinguished and identified before the moment of birth for significantly higher than average lifetime health spending prospects are rare enough that they can be ignored for purposes of the discussion here. Thus, all of us start life in a common risk pool identified by our age (here, zero year), sex, and geographic location of residence. All three determine expected payouts but are not the result of risky, harmful medical events that have already occurred.

The medical risks we face from birth onward relate to health incidents that might need to be treated in the coming insurance period (typically a year) but do not change our risk prospects thereafter, and they relate to the different risk that in the coming insurance period we might permanently enter a higher medical risk state that reclassifies us into a group that requires a lifetime of future higher medical costs. This "reclassification risk" is different from the risk of experiencing a medical event that requires care in the coming insurance period but leaves us thereafter with the same future health prospects as others for the succeeding period. At any moment in time, an individual therefore needs *two* insurance policies, one against each type of risk. Public discussion of health insurance frequently fails to explain this important distinction. How would the two kinds of health insurance work?

To see, consider a large group of male babies born at the same place on the same day. They each pay the same for a reclassification-risk insurance policy (call this policy *A*) and a standard health insurance policy (policy *B*). Policy *A* promises to pay the increase in policy *B* premiums at policy *B*'s renewal time, should the holder become reclassified during the coming year. A year passes. Some babies are treated for health events on their *B* policies and others not. In addition, some babies experience medical events that reclassify them as "group 2" boys for the second year, meaning that their expenditures for the second year are expected to be two times the average for boys of their age. The reclassified boys should expect to pay more for their *B* health insurance in the second year, but, from their *A* policies they will receive payouts that exactly offset the higher *B* policy premiums. The net effect is that all boys, regardless of experience in the first year, pay the same total in premiums for their *A* and *B* policies that cover the second year. In fact, carrying policies *A* and *B* from birth onward *through all subsequent years of life* would imply paying the same net premiums annually as anyone else of the same age, sex, and location of residence. Guaranteed renewability of insurance at standard rates leads to the same outcome. We therefore need to consider the effects of guaranteed renewability, and why it should be a required feature of health insurance.

Presuming you have health insurance coverage of both types from birth onward, you would be covered against short-term medical risks, *and* against a change in your risk classification. Were you to have to pay a higher net total for your policies *A* and *B* in the following year, it would imply that your insurance company had reneged on its commitment. However, an insurance company cannot legally refuse to honor its obligations with respect to a covered condition once the condition has occurred. Thus, if insurance companies honor their contract, an insured population would consist of individuals who progress through life paying the same health insurance premiums as anyone else of their age, sex, and geographic location of residence. (To this list, we might add certain relevant lifestyle choices such as smoking that add to risk if they are administratively feasible and verifable.) Mandating guaranteed renewability as an insurance feature is equivalent to mandating that insurance companies honor their reclassification risk policy contracts. It implies that no one would find himself or herself paying more for insurance coverage by reason of reclassification because "reclassification" is a covered medical event.[11] Uninsurable and high-needs individuals disappear as a concern because, while there may be high-risk, high-cost individuals, they will be paying the same premiums for insurance as everyone else their age, sex, and geographic location of residence.

> No one would find himself or herself without insurance coverage by reason of reclassification because "reclassification" is a covered medical event.

[11] "If a plan guarantees to everybody a premium that corresponds to total experience but not to experience as it might be segregated by small subgroups, everybody is, in effect, insured against a change in his basic state of health which would lead to a reclassification." Arrow, 1963, p. 964.

It is important to distinguish the effects of experience rating in the presence of reclassification risk insurance where risk pools are distinguished by age, sex, and location of residence from the operation of community rating, where different age groups and sexes may be lumped together. Community rating charges all members of the community, even those in different age and sex pools, the same premiums regardless of risk. The result is that some individuals receive benefits that they did not pay for on an actuarial basis and others make payments for which they receive no benefits.

Experience-rated insurance plus reclassification risk insurance, on the other hand, starts from a situation of homogeneous risk pools of indistinguishable individuals. All individuals are charged identical premiums because they have actuarially equal expectation of future benefit payouts. With the passage of time, some individuals are reclassified, but they begin receiving income transfers equal to their higher actuarially expected benefit payouts, appropriately leaving them to pay the same (out-of-pocket) premiums in future years as others of their age, sex, and location of residence. Individuals receiving payouts on their reclassification risk policies are not receiving charity because they have paid for their benefits on an actuarially fair basis by past premiums. In a normal life cycle, we expect actuarially fair insurance costs to vary through life. Guaranteed renewability as described earlier honors this variation and leads to actuarially fair premiums. Community rating, on the other hand, ignores this variation and leads to deviation from actuarially fair insurance premiums.

When private insurance was a prominent part of the American health insurance market, 80 percent of private policies included a guaranteed renewability feature that required insurers to renew policies at standard premiums regardless of future medical status.[12] Reclassification risk is now a looming problem in American health care. The solution is to require guaranteed renewability at standard premiums, just as we legally require insurance companies to pay on claims for covered conditions once they occur. After the health insurance market is rationalized by this change, everyone will have the ability to buy insurance rated for his or her age, sex, and location of residence. Risk adjustment by itself is no longer a problem if everyone has insurance coverage from birth that includes reclassification risk coverage. In fact, efficiency *requires* that premiums reflect the demographics (age, sex, and location) of the individuals who are a part of the

---

[12] "Federal law now requires states to ensure guaranteed renewability for individual (but not group) insurance policies. But even before the spread of such state laws, industry observers estimated that about 80 percent of policies voluntarily (on the parts of both buyers and sellers) contained such provisions (Pauly, Percy, and Herring, 1999)." Pauly, 2004, p. 8.

risk pool. It will still be the case that *high-needs* individuals may be present, but dealing with high-needs individuals is a separate problem that can be handled separately from the problem of *uninsurable* individuals. We discuss in Chapter 8 how to resolve the problems of high-needs individuals without impairing the effectiveness of the insurance market. They include (1) the problem of individuals whose premium payments exceed their ability to pay, (2) the problem of transitioning from our current system to one with efficient insurance, and (3) the problem of how people can move back and forth among plans.

7.3. Summary and Evaluative Discussion

Americans rely on a health insurance system that would never have been deliberately created. Health insurance began as a means of providing a predictable revenue stream for hospitals. Employers used it to attract and retain workers during times of labor shortage. Ultimately, an employer-based system became the dominant way most Americans received coverage because of political decisions to grant special tax subsidies, amounting to over $200 billion in 2004, or approximately $1,400 for every member of the work-force.[13]

Conventional coverage, the kind that most insured Americans have, does not make much economic sense at all. The income tax subsidy encourages the system to provide more insurance than rational risk aversion would prescribe. Coupled with the employer contribution (on average, about 75 percent of the premium), the arrangement creates the illusion that insurance is less expensive than it actually is. Most workers would be better off if their pay were not reduced because of their employer's contributions and they were free to choose coverage in a competitive insurance market on an equal tax basis, accessing market experts that would be better informed than many of their employers now are. By collecting premiums for the expense of routine medical bills, conventional insurance forces excess spending. Many find insurance unaffordable and its purchase a poor use of money.

The employer-based insurance system has other unintended consequences. There is evidence that it reduces labor mobility[14] and crowds out other pooling arrangements that do not qualify for the employer-based subsidy. Interestingly, the arrangement does provide a partial way of dealing with reclassification risk. Premiums in employer-based systems tend to rise with the age of the insured, but not in proportion to the rise in

---

[13] Sheils and Haught, 2004.
[14] Gruber, 2000; Adams, 2004.

expected spending. Some firms, for example, charge premiums according to income groupings, and higher-earning workers tend to be older. Premiums imperfectly mimic, therefore, a market with guaranteed renewability. Moral hazard and adverse selection are considerations in the design of a health care system, but government-run systems are equally susceptible to moral hazard and, for that matter, adverse selection.

The value of health insurance derives from managing the unpredictability of high medical spending. Risk-averse individuals find it in their interest to pool risk with others who have characteristics similar to their own. Insurance companies likewise have an incentive to offer insurance that pools homogeneous individuals. Both incentives are aligned to efficient insurance function. The value of risk pooling is positively related to the degree of risk aversion in the population and the variability in the cost of treating a given medical condition.

The term "insurance" has acquired a different meaning in the medical sector. Instead of covering low-probability, high-cost events, "insurance" now includes payment for routine care. Forcing pre-payment of a certain high-probability, low-cost event in order to buy insurance coverage of low-probability, high-cost events is expensive. We generally do not buy insurance that pays for routine maintenance on our automobiles, so why would we want to be forced to do so for routine medical costs? Equity considerations aside, premium payments would reflect the demographic risk and health status of the insured. The standard for this model is the diagnosis-based risk adjustment adopted by Medicare+Choice[15] and the Swiss approach to risk adjustment.[16] Were those who suffer from re-classification risk insured for such risk prior to re-classification, the costs of their current state would be covered by past premiums. In that case, every individual would progress through life paying premiums determined by his or her age, sex, and geographic location.

Health spending increases with age, implying that older individuals get greater benefits from medical spending and should be expected to pay more for their medical care. Using 2002 Medical Expenditure Panel Survey (MEPS) data, per capita health spending for the over-65 age group was $7,400, almost five times the per capita spending for the under-45 age group. The typical Medicare enrollee can expect to spend 18 years in the system, obligating taxpayers to fund $142,500 of medical care spending. With the rapid aging of the U.S. population it is no wonder that the

[15] Ellis et al., 1996; Fowles, et al., 1996.
[16] Beck et al., 2003.

unfunded obligation of the government's health insurance program is over \$32,300 billion. (See Section 3.4, "Principle 4: No Polittroughing.") According to U.S. General Accountability Office numbers, \$32,300 billion represents a per-full-time-worker obligation of \$255,842. Using all civilian employment, the obligation is hardly much better – \$221,162, or almost \$7 for each billion.

In addition to providing protection against the financial risk of a catastrophic health event, insurance should contain *ex post* incentives to consume efficiently. Policies can be designed to reduce moral hazard by offering higher deductibles and co-insurance payments for medical care with greater demand response (higher price elasticities). We need not worry about moral hazard in those cases where the demand for care is relatively inelastic: that is, beyond the ability of incentives to affect the insured's choices.

For contract design to be effective, insurance must be transparent. Americans know more about the price of gasoline than they do about the price they pay for health insurance or covered procedures. Yet, which ultimately matters more? Most recipients of employer-based insurance have a single choice of carrier, and that choice is made for them by their employer.

The employer contribution to premiums is effectively hidden from the worker and removed from any meaningful responsiveness to worker preferences. Placing individually purchased health insurance on an equal tax basis with employer-based insurance and providing the opportunity for employees to decline employer-based insurance and apply the employer's contribution to an individually purchased policy would allow freedom of choice to workers and ultimately result in better risk pooling and actuarially fair insurance. Institutional arrangements such as insurance exchanges would improve welfare. An insurance exchange is a multi-employer arrangement where individuals and small groups can get the benefits of risk spreading along with choice of insurance plan. See Chapter 9.

Against the current imperfect system of health care insurance are the ideals described in this chapter:

- Efficient insurance, coupled with an independent mechanism for charity and income transfers, is superior to the present arrangements that mix two unrelated functions to the detriment of both. Many of the perceived "problems" of health care are not health care problems, but problems of too little income that can better be addressed through dedicated separate income programs. See Chapter 8.
- Efficient insurance pools individuals of like risk, charging actuarially fair premiums (plus an administrative margin that is restrained by competition among insurers).

- Individuals have an incentive to resist the inclusion in their pools of those with higher expected payouts than theirs. Young individuals have an incentive to leave insurance pools where the product mix includes benefits that are not worth the cost to them, and firms have an incentive to offer lower-cost insurance that is tailored closely to their needs based on age, sex, and location to low-risk, low-cost individuals who want to leave a pool where premiums are above their actuarially fair rates (cherry picking/cream skimming).

- An effective insurance system recognizes the efficiency-supporting role of natural incentives and does not require working against them for its success. In particular, the social system chosen should not force community rating and should not resist freedom of underwriting.

- Moral hazard is a concern in service benefit plans that is primarily addressed by constructing plans that meet consumer needs through appropriate choice of covered services, deductibles, co-insurance rates, and out-of-pocket limits.

- Reclassification risk is a special kind of insurable health risk. Individuals who are insured against reclassification risk do not become uninsurable, because they receive what are essentially payouts from their reclassification risk policy upon a reclassification "event." Just as insurers are prevented by law from refusing payment once a covered condition has arisen (fraudulent breach of contract), so insurers should be prevented by law from refusing to offer insurance at standard rates to anyone because of a change in his or her health status (fraudulent breach of contract regarding reclassification risk).

- The concepts, or categories, of
  1. high-risk individuals (versus low-risk individuals),
  2. high-needs individuals, and
  3. uninsurable individuals

  are distinct notions. Homogeneous risk pooling is accomplished by rating on age, sex, geographic location of residence, and possibly lifestyle choices. High-needs individuals are treated by dedicated programs addressing the issue of too little income, and uninsurability is removed from concern by insurance against reclassification risk.

- Moving from current conditions to an efficient health insurance regime requires addressing transition issues. See Section 8.4, "Transition Issues," in Chapter 8.

EIGHT

The Targeted Intervention Plan

The best ideas are common property.
Seneca, *Epistles* (5 B.C.–65 A.D)

Society is always taken by surprise at any new example of common sense.
Ralph Waldo Emerson (1803–1882)

Summary: Working from the list of attributes that Americans want and applying efficiency principles generates a virtually unique health care framework that resembles a free market except for those few particulars that need to deviate to accomplish the objective that everyone has health insurance. We call it the Targeted Intervention Plan.

Earlier chapters followed a demanding solutions-based, patient-focused agenda. A solutions-based, patient-focused agenda is justified, however, because we are dealing with health and welfare. To review:

1. Good health insurance needs to satisfy the four Ps: patient-centered, personal, portable, and permanent.
2. The arrangements we choose must provide access for anyone for insurable services on the same terms as everyone else. Those who may be receiving program help should not be identified or disadvantaged by this fact.
3. Available choices must respect incentives for high-quality provision of care. Market forces, including in the insurance market, are the guardians of patient interests, needs, and freedom.
4. Health care arrangements must be sound, providing assured cost containment features for government and program flexibility. The program should benefit from the economic insights and efficiency principles of Chapter 3.
5. Above all, health care arrangements must be sustainable – capable of thriving in perpetuity. Thus they must avoid inducements to

polittroughing, governmentalizing, and Ponzi schemes. (See Chapter 3, Section 3.4, 3.5, 3.6, respectively, for technical meanings of these terms as used here.)

8.1. The Plan

Often the greatest error lies in the perception of difficulty, not in the project itself. Solutions to health care issues are attainable in a relatively straightforward manner once an efficiency framework is adopted. No more community and legislative input is needed than is required by other proposed alternatives that are only partial solutions or short-term corrections.

> Often the greatest error lies in the perception of difficulty, not in the project itself.

When the appropriate provisions are in place, the largest of the issues will be resolved by the direct actions taken. Others will self-correct, and yet others that depend on the first two will disappear altogether.

Step 1: Identify the Precise Objective and the Least-Cost Tool to Achieve It

We start with the objective that all households purchase health insurance and the best way to accomplish it. If that objective is dropped, meaning we decide to accept that millions of Americans are uninsured, then parts of the resulting framework described here will change. We address that in Section 8.5, "Mandates versus Incentives versus Leaving Some Uninsured." Whichever way we decide, however, it is helpful to know in advance what efficiency principles identify as the *best* way to reach the state of full insurance coverage, before we decide whether the cost is too high in terms of some other objective. We will see that efficiency leaves intact everyone's freedom of choice and alters the relative prices of those choices only for those for whom we want to make the purchase option relatively more attractive.

There are multiple ways to create an incentive to purchase health insurance that will accomplish the objective, but they are not equal in their effects.

The intervention principle directs us that to encourage more of an activity at least cost – in this case, the voluntary private decision by those currently without insurance to purchase it – we should subsidize the desired activity, but only for those individuals who would not purchase insurance without the intervention.[1] Finally, the intervention should be just great enough to induce insurance purchase at the desired level and no greater. The incentive symmetry principle gives us significant flexibility about the form in which the incentive is implemented.

How does this description of efficient intervention compare to existing proposals? Four approaches have been prominently suggested to induce insurance purchase.

1. The first is a refundable tax credit – meaning that everyone, whether he or she owes taxes or not, will receive money from the government that can be used for the purchase of insurance. This suggestion has the positive feature that it gives personal health insurance purchases the same tax-preferred status as insurance obtained through place of employment. It has three disadvantages, however.

   (a) The first disadvantage is that it fails the intervention principle because it subsidizes everyone rather than just those who would not buy insurance without help. This means a wastefully over-large program is needed to support the payments. As discussed in "Deadweight Loss of Taxation" in Chapter 4, Section 4.3, every additional tax dollar imposes more than a dollar in cost to the private sector. Fifty-one cents on the dollar (to use the mid-range estimate of the numbers reported there) is a sizable added burden. The larger the subsidy program and the more money run through government hands, the larger is the unnecessary cost to the private sector in deadweight loss.

   (b) The second disadvantage was first noted in Section 3.2, "Principle 2: Incentive Symmetry." It is that once everyone is subsidized, it is no longer possible to observe who would have bought insurance without the program. As shown later, it is not necessary to blur these two groups.

   (c) The third disadvantage is that a refundable tax credit creates an entitlement and the appearance that it is government's duty to buy health insurance. Public provision of private goods such as health care encourages polittroughing. Once politicians realize the personal benefits of promising their constituents increasing subsidies at other constituents' expense, we edge down the proverbial slippery slope to pollitroughing and political abuse.

---

[1] See Chapter 3 and Grinols, 2006.

2. The second prominent approach uses the points of contact between the individual and the government to create incentives for the insuranceless individual to buy it. For example, in the Massachusetts plan (see Section 9.2, "Massachusetts: Leveling the Playing Field"), individuals lose their personal tax exemption (worth approximately $219) if they do not have health insurance. In subsequent years, the cost of the penalty rises to approximately half the cost of the lowest-priced plan. In this approach, the selection of penalties and their size can be adjusted.[2] Penalties can also be applied when the individual tries to get a driver's license or obtain other state privileges. This approach has the advantage that it targets just the uninsured and leaves them distinguishable as a self-identified group. It also retains the purchase of insurance as an individual obligation. It fails to match the efficiency description, however, because it does not create an incentive that is equivalent to a subsidy of health insurance purchase. By incentive symmetry, an efficient subsidy to health insurance purchase is equivalent to a tax on *all* non-insurance purchases paid by those who have not bought health insurance. The Massachusetts approach comes closer, but, because it is not based on all purchases, it is not as strong an incentive, is not a daily reminder, and does not apply to the same base. It also requires that individuals engage in the targeted points of contact for it to be effective, whereas virtually everyone buys non-health-insurance goods and services.

3. President Bush proposed a $15,000 family tax deduction for taxpayers who have insurance. Those who do not purchase insurance do not receive the deduction. This approach has the advantage that it is narrowly directed – it imposes penalties on only those who do not buy

[2] The "New Year, New Penalties" page (accessed at http://www.mahealthconnector. org/portal/site/connector/template.MAXIMIZE/menuitem. 3ef8 fb03b7fa 1ae4a7 ca7738e 6468a0c/?javax.portlet.tpst=2fdfb140904d489c8781176033468a0c_ws_MX&javax.portlet .prp_2fdfb140904d489c8781176033468a0c_viewID=content&javax.portlet.prp_2fdfb1409 04d489c8781176033468a0c_docName=Changes%20for%202008&javax.portlet.prp_2fdfb1 40904d489c8781176033468a0c_folderPath=/FindInsurance/Individual/&javax.portlet .begCacheTok=com.vignette.cachetoken& javax.portlet.endCacheTok=com.vignette.cache token) reads, "Penalties are higher in 2008. As drafted by the Massachusetts Department of Revenue, they equal half of the cost of the lowest cost Health Connector plan available in your income range. The penalties will add up for each month that you don't have a health plan in 2008."

For example, someone who earns more than $30,636 (or 300% of the federal poverty level) could face penalties of $76 for each month that they remain uninsured. That's $912 per year. Lower-income people will face lower fines, and some won't be penalized at all. Visit the Department of Revenue's website to learn more."

insurance – and it has the advantage that it provides less of an attraction to polittroughing because it does not suggest that health insurance should be government provided. It, too, fails the intervention principle, however, because it does not provide as strong an incentive as efficiency requires. Many of the individuals who do not buy health insurance need more than a once-yearly reminder, and many do not file tax forms now.[3]

4. The fourth approach is that implied by the intervention principle. The form and appearance that efficient intervention takes can vary on the basis of incentive symmetry. Recall that incentive symmetries are already used in other contexts such as bail bonding (see Section 3.2). According to incentive symmetry, subsidizing a desired activity is equivalent to avoiding a tax of the same size on alternative activities (see Appendix C). In the case of purchasing health insurance, alternative activities are the purchase of non-health-insurance goods and services. The incentive to purchase insurance therefore can be presented in different ways, depending on whether we want the incentive to appear as a subsidy (carrot) to those who buy insurance or as a penalty (stick) to those who do not. The alternatives are economically equivalent, though psychologically they may differ in public perception. Thus, whichever is more effective can be selected. In our description we will assume 10 percent is the incentive differential, but the precise rate is an implementation choice that should be set just high enough to accomplish the objective.

Subsidy Version. In this version, prices for non-health-insurance goods and services are computed and paid by buyers at the point of purchase exactly as they are today. The only difference is that those who present evidence of current health insurance pay a gross price that is 10 percent lower than the standard price. In other words, the "subsidy" to insurance purchase is delivered to households in the form of a 10 percent rebate on their purchases. The evidence of insurance coverage can be provided at point of purchase, perhaps by scanning a credit card or card similar to ones used for grocery store promotional programs. In addition, individuals who forget their card could be allowed to file for rebates of the relevant amount annually, perhaps when filing income taxes, by proving that insurance was held at time of purchase. Other implementation options are possible.

---

[3] An estimated 7.4 million individual taxpayers that should have filed did not voluntarily file a tax return in tax year 2003 (U.S. Treasury Inspector General for Tax Administration, 2005).

Tax Version. In the tax version, prices are computed exactly as they are today, but those who do not present proof of current insurance coverage pay an additional ad valorem compliance levy (tax surcharge).

It is important to emphasize that in the tax version, the compliance levy is an exaction that no one needs to pay; its purpose is not to collect revenue. Anyone can avoid the levy by purchasing health insurance. Because the Targeted Intervention Plan provides for income aid to those individuals who need it to buy insurance, the intervention can be set as needed to accomplish its objective: be an efficient incentive and constant reminder for every individual, family, and household to buy health insurance. Proceeds from the levy, if there are any, can contribute to support of the health care program.

> The intervention can be set as needed to accomplish its objective: be a constant reminder and incentive for every individual, family, and household to buy health insurance.

Equivalence of the Two Versions. How are the two versions economically equivalent? The answer is that in the subsidy version, an 11.11 percent (i.e., 0.1/0.9, for example purposes – the actual rate is an implementation choice) value added tax (VAT) is inaugurated at the outset of the program. The VAT is therefore embedded in the prices seen by retailers; hence retailers apply sales taxes at the register as they do now, not changing their behavior in any way. However, only the consumer without health insurance actually pays the VAT: the consumer with insurance is rebated the exact VAT amount. For example, let C be the base cost of an item. In the tax version, the insured customer pays $C(1 + s)$ where s is the sales tax rate. In the subsidy version, $(1/0.9)C(1 + s) = P$ is the gross price with sales tax s included. Rebating 10 percent of P for customers with health insurance implies that they pay $0.9P = C(1 + s)$, exactly the same as under the tax version.

Though they appear different, both versions have the same outcome. In each, there is an efficient price incentive to buy insurance. In each, if everyone buys health insurance, net taxes collected are zero. In each, the incentives have no net effect on those who buy insurance. In each, the obligation to buy insurance remains the individual's. And in each, the program collects no money if the rate has been set high enough to induce everyone to buy insurance. Should a few remain uninsured, then both programs collect a small amount of cash. Importantly, both do not create any dedicated program to subsidize with tax dollars the health insurance purchases of 300 million Americans because of the few who do not buy insurance.

Applying the intervention and incentive symmetry principles produces a framework that rewards those with insurance at the point of their purchases. We personally prefer carrots (the subsidy version) to sticks (the tax version) because they provide a positive reason for individuals with insurance to reap rewards for their good behavior. Proof of insurance is no more difficult to carry than cash, check, or credit/debit card, and private purchases now cannot be conducted without providing proof of ability to pay in the form of presenting cash, a check, or a credit/debit card. Because a card when swiped at point of purchase would be connected to a central database that verifies current insurance, a counterfeit card alone is not sufficient for fraud. A card must belong to the person whose picture, signature, or other identifier is on it, and it must link to data showing current insurance. Having another individual purchase for you may work for a short period, but having someone purchase for you every day, indefinitely, is another matter. Balancing the risks that the principles help avoid against the differential costs of other approaches leads us to prefer the subsidy version that the intervention principle of Section 3.1 of Chapter 3 implies.

Step 2: Provide Aid Because Some Need It

Most poor are only temporarily poor.[4] Whether the condition is permanent or temporary, however, those who cannot afford health insurance will need assistance to purchase it. Program aid to those who cannot afford health insurance is provided in the Targeted Intervention Plan. As was the case with the inducement to purchase insurance, the form that the aid takes is guided by efficiency considerations and by the way the aid affects incentives.

The degree of aid and the rules for who qualifies for it are program implementation choices. As a nation we spend 14.5 percent of our income on personal health care expenditures and 11.7 percent of disposable personal money income on food.[5] Health care is arguably as important as food. It seems reasonable, therefore, that once a household has spent a predetermined percentage of its income on health insurance and still falls short, the difference could be made up by program aid.[6] In any event, this detail is a program implementation choice that can be adjusted as desired.

---

[4] A number of studies have documented the turnover rates within income groups: Hungerford, 1993, Duncan and Morgan, 1984; U.S. Treasury Department, 1992; Gottschalk, 1997; Cox and Alm, 1995; U.S. Census Bureau, 1989, 1990, 1991; Council of Economic Advisers, 2003; Ladd and Bowman, 1998.

[5] USDA, Economic Research Service, 2007, Table 8.

[6] Switzerland provides assistance to households that spend over 8–10 percent of income on health insurance.

Equity Considerations. Americans have shown in various ways over the years that they are uncomfortable allowing those without health insurance coverage to go without medical care. Using incentives to induce everyone to buy health insurance, rather than mandating that they do, changes the relative attractiveness of buying health insurance, but without enough income some people still will not be able to purchase coverage.

This is an equity issue that the Targeted Intervention Plan addresses by ensuring that everyone has enough income to afford basic insurance coverage. The capable needy receive income subsidies in a manner that maintains their incentives to work. Maintaining work incentives is not as critical for the incapable needy, who receive direct income aid that enables them to purchase insurance. In both cases, the plan provides the needed assistance in the form of income in the economically most efficient manner available.

A second way that the plan promotes equity and fairness is in the pricing of services. Under the current system, those who least can afford medical care are often charged the highest prices. The fully insured have large insurance carriers negotiating discounted price schedules with suppliers, while self-payers and the uninsured have no one looking out for their interests and are billed higher prices. The Targeted Intervention Plan requires that providers treat everyone alike by charging everyone the same price.

While the determinants of the plan focus on efficiency and spend more verbal resources describing it, equity is not ignored. One is tantamount to the other in the development of the plan, where inducement to insurance purchase and disbursement of income aid are addressed in the most efficient manner available. Those with adequate insurance now are left largely untouched by the proposed changes, except to the extent that market rationalizations improve market function for them, and those without adequate insurance benefit from improved market function plus the acquisition of insurance. While no reform or change can be strictly fully welfare-improving to everyone, the changes here come close.

What efficiency rules apply? In the discussion "Provision for the Incapable Needy" in Section 6.1 of Chapter 6 we distinguished between the *incapable needy* and the *capable needy* when we discussed collective action and efficiency. Once an individual is certifiably in the class of the incapable needy, providing for that individual's health insurance purchase through the program is consistent with the efficiency approach of Chapter 4 (see

"First and Second Fundamental Theorems of Welfare Economics (FTWE)" in Section 4.2, and Section 4.4, "Implication for Efficient Intervention in Health") and cannot alter their work/self-help decisions. To the extent that it provides medical care for those who are incapable of providing for themselves, even after being equipped with an education and the normal social tools of modern life, Medicaid is a model. As noted in Chapter 6, individual giving and charitable foundations are also critical to deliver health care support to the incapable needy. This can be channeled through the government budget or given directly.

For the capable needy, the social objective is to induce full work effort and provide income aid only if the result of their full efforts is insufficient for their needs. The efficient tool is *not* any of the seemingly obvious prescriptions such as the minimum wage, subsidized child day care, Medicaid to the working poor, subsidized housing, food stamps, aid to the purchase of heating fuel, or aid attached to any number of other goods. The *efficient* tool is a subsidy to work effort by the low-income capable. Again, an appropriate tool already exists. For the capable needy, the Earned Income Tax Credit (EITC) is close to ideal. Modifying this to ensure that the capable needy have enough total income to purchase health insurance in light of their other needs is the economically efficient tool. For example, the existing EITC could be augmented by an amount that was calculated to allow the recipient to buy, combined with his or her own income and existing EITC money, the basic insurance policies that applied to the individual and list of family or household members dependent on the individual. For both incentive and efficiency reasons, however, it is important that no money be explicitly earmarked or stated to the recipient to be for health insurance. The incentive to purchase health insurance and the calculation that the individual has enough total income are sufficient to induce purchase and retain the individual's discretion and responsibility to buy the targeted private good, in this case, health insurance.

Step 3: Manage the Government Budget Responsibly and Sustainably

The objective that everyone buys health insurance implies a subsidy (applied in the Targeted Intervention Plan in an incentive-equivalent form) and aid to the capable and incapable needy provided in an incentive-compatible form through modification of the Earned Income Tax Credit. This, in turn, requires a program budget. As is the case in the Massachusetts plan (discussed in Section 9.2 of Chapter 9), the Targeted Intervention Plan accesses cost-shifting dollars already present in the health care system (see Glossary and Definitions) to help cover government expenditures. If everyone purchases health insurance, there is no longer need for those cost-shifting dollars.

Money that was previously devoted to cost shifting is accessed through a revenue tax on health care providers and health care insurance policies. The tax is set at a level that balances the budget. The likely rate, 3–5 percent of revenues, is similar in size to the share of revenues that not-for-profit hospitals must now devote to charity to

> The Targeted Intervention Plan accesses cost-shifting dollars already present in the health care system.

retain their charitable status. Details, such as how credit will be given toward the revenue tax obligation for charitable care, are program implementation choices. An example that shows how big the tax would be for a particular program choice is given in Appendix D.

There is a reason for using a revenue tax. Goal 5, Sustainability (see Section 2.5 of Chapter 2), is that the government budget be indefinitely sustainable and that the program allow *ex ante* selection of the amount of government expenditure to be devoted to the plan. The provider tax is necessary for this level of cost control. Consider: the amount that the plan puts into the health care sector – call this amount A (i.e., through augmentation of the Earned Income Tax Credit program) – is adjusted by the amount that the plan removes from the health care sector through the revenue tax – call this B. Both A and B are program choices, thus the net injection, $A - B$, is a program choice. If tax B is unavailable, then $A - B$ is not under program control. Tax revenues B could be modified relatively easily, perhaps even on a quarterly basis, to meet budget objectives.

Provider revenue taxes also supply an indirect method to access rents in the health care sector because the amount the government selects for net payment can be set equal to the true cost of care (including relevant margins) used by the supported population.[7] If injections by government into the health care sector cover the true cost of care received by the population receiving aid, the remainder of the revenues in health care comes entirely from the private dollars and personal choices of consumers. As in other sectors, competition will cause these amounts to reflect cost of service as well.

---

[7] Economic "rent" is payment received by a factor that exceeds the amount needed to keep the factor in its current employment. If I earn $110,000 in my current employment and $100,000 is the most I could earn in the next-best equally pleasant job, then $10,000 of what I earn is economic rent.

A revenue tax spreads the public costs of the program uniformly to everyone who uses health care or buys health insurance – all of us – because we all will have insurance under the plan. This is a desirable feature relative to the current system, which forces the privately insured to pay for cost shifting. The precise details and extent of the provider tax base are a program implementation choice but logically should include any provider whose revenues derive partly or wholly from program-injected dollars.

Step 4: Insurance Is the Right Kind

Insurance companies and individuals in the marketplace can be relied on to work out the kind of insurance they want. The original Blue Cross plans based on the original Baylor University Hospital plan were private initiatives in response to a need. The objective to create a twenty-first-century incentive to purchase insurance, however, makes it necessary to identify when an individual has satisfied the purchase requirement. What kind of basic insurance is enough? While this is a program implementation choice, it is one that must be made carefully. For example, one might want to include in the basic plan all benefits that are premium-reducing (selected preventive care is premium-reducing because it lowers the probability of future insurable events). One might also want to include benefits currently recommended by the U.S. Preventive Services Task Force, but one might want to undo many existing state mandates that add expensive, unneeded, unwanted coverage that serve only to bloat the cost of policies that otherwise would be affordable.

We state here a few observations related to insurance market rationalization: underwriting freedom, guaranteed renewability, a commonsense base plan, an employee protection feature, tax neutrality toward employer-based or individually purchased insurance, and portability/transferability. The conception of the base insurance plan follows the "responsible national health insurance" plan described by Pauly, Damon, Feldstein, and Hoff (Pauly, et al., 1991, p.14). There is no adverse selection in the market for the base plan, though, as they point out, adverse selection might persist in markets for supplemental coverage. "Since this is optional coverage, however," they note, "it is not a matter of social concern."

- The principles of Section 3.3, the introductory summary of Chapter 7, and Section 7.3 explain that a national framework for health insurance cannot depend for its success on insurance companies and other firms acting against their own interests. Underwriting freedom, entry, and exit are critical to market contestability and competition to deal effectively with moral hazard, to lower costs, and to lower administrative overhead. Groups having efficiency-producing ideas or technology must remain free to benefit from their improvements. Research shows, for example, that in some circumstances self-insurance for a group benefits from within-group commitment to reduce moral hazard.[8] Such efficiency gains are welcomed and in no way prevented.

- Health is an individual matter and so is health insurance. In an ideal framework, dad, mom, sister, and brother each has his or her own individual base policy that begins at birth, continues throughout life, and is rated on age, sex, geographic location of residence, and possibly a few observable health-related lifestyle choices.[9] The coverage of the base plan is an implementation choice, but we would reasonably expect that base coverage might vary by age and sex. A policy is portable for the individual and does not terminate on the basis of employment.[10] Of course, supplemental insurance can be bought at any time, but this is not a social concern.

Not all incentives of an unregulated market are desirable, however. For example, an insurance company has an incentive to deny a claim for a covered condition once the condition arises but is not allowed to act on that incentive by law. Likewise, a dishonest merchant might have an incentive to provide faulty merchandise, so such behavior must be prohibited. The discussion "Time and the Uninsurable: A Curious Connection" in Section 7.2 of Chapter 7 explained that a comparable situation in the health care sector occurs when a healthy person experiences the onset of a costly permanent medical condition. Reclassification risk is a medically insured risk. Thus, legal mandates are needed that guarantee renewability of coverage at standard rates – meaning that regardless of change in medical status in a given year, the holder pays the same premium based on age, sex, and location

---

[8] Philipson and Zanjani, 1997.
[9] To say that rating is based on a list of descriptors means that anyone to whom the description applies can buy coverage at the premium rates that apply to the described pool. If I am a 42-year-old male living in New York, then I can buy insurance from any company offering insurance (and they must issue it to me) at the same rates that they offer insurance to any other 42-year-old male in New York.
[10] The question-and-answer section later in the chapter discusses several portability options for individuals who want to change insurance companies. Precisely how portability is guaranteed is an implementation choice.

as everyone else. According to Pauly,[11] and as already noted, *guaranteed re-newability* is a feature that historically 80 percent of privately available commercial insurance contracts carried without government mandates. In the Targeted Intervention Plan guaranteed renewability is a matter of adequate insurance and ethical underwriting.

- Health insurance typically consists of a deductible, co-insurance rate, out-of-pocket limit, and list of covered items or benefits. We hold it to be self-evident that any benefit that reduces premiums should be included. Many types of preventive care, as noted, lead to lower long-term medical expenditures. The size of the deductible, co-insurance rates, and out-of-pocket limits are program implementation choices that can be guided by what constitutes a *commonsense base plan* for each age and sex, features that lead to responsible use of insurance, and social norms.[12]

  At the same time, there are benefits that are not universally needed that lead to higher premiums. These should be available to those who want to supplement their insurance coverage at a price but should not be a required part of the base plan. For example, it makes little sense to force 85-year-old widows or single men to pay for in vitro fertilization benefits they do not want. Those who want such benefits can add them to their base plan if they wish.

- As noted, the Targeted Intervention Plan provides help to purchase health insurance for those who need it (see step 2). There is no intrinsic need for direct charity transfers to be embedded in the health insurance products that individuals buy. If employers want to contribute to health insurance purchase and employees want to accept it, they are free to do so. However, if individuals wish to take the employer contribution and use it instead to purchase individual insurance, they may still take advantage of the same tax treatment that the dollars received when offered through the firm. There are various ways to accomplish tax equivalency (a program implementation choice). One method, for example, would be to eliminate the tax preferences applied to employer-provided health insurance. Another would be to exempt

[11] Pauly et al., 1991; Pauly and Hoff, 2002, Pauly, 2004.
[12] See Chapter 10. Pauly et al., 1991, describe the features of a "responsible national health insurance plan." Since adverse selection is not a consideration for the basic insurance treated here, moral hazard and avoiding excessive overhead ("loading") costs are the primary concerns. Good insurance references include Manning and Marquis, 1996; Ma and McGuire, 1997; Cutler and Zeckhauser, 2000; Pauly, 2000; and Zweifel and Manning, 2000.

a specified amount of income from all federal, state, local, and payroll taxes if the individual purchases insurance.[13]

This employee protection feature has a number of beneficial implications. It implies that insurance arrangements for everyone are fully voluntary and guaranteed to be no worse than what is available in the market. Further, there is reason neither to encourage nor discourage insurance offered through place of employment. *Insurance source tax neutrality* accomplishes that objective, either by ending the tax exemption of employer-based insurance or by extending equivalent exemption to private purchase.

- We want a *freedom of choice protection* feature so that insurance claims may not be denied by the insurance provider. That is, in a free market, prices tell the consumer what he or she must pay to purchase a given product. If individuals choose to buy, they are free to do so if they are willing to pay the price. The same freedom of choice applies to health insurance. If insured individuals wish to purchase a covered service and are willing to pay the required co-pay or co-insurance rate, then they may decide in consultation with their physician to purchase the service. This feature is especially important when second opinions are sought on major health interventions such as surgery. It follows that the base insurance plan should exclude nonessential or "frivolous" services and not include deductibles and co-insurance prices that are too low. That is, moral hazard always must be kept foremost in mind when designing the insurance product. Once a benefit is part of an insurance package, however, and the price to the insured is set, individuals have the same market freedoms as they do in other markets.[14]
- Insurance portability and transferability require that individuals can move freely among insurance companies whether they are sick or healthy. Under these conditions a risk adjustment mechanism must exist. Otherwise insurance companies have an incentive to expend valuable resources in an attempt to select risks (normal "cherry picking" or "cream skimming") that will work against the provisions for insuring against reclassification risk (see the discussion "Time and the Uninsurable: A Curious Connection" in Section 7.2) and the portability objective.

---

[13] This feature is similar to the proposal presented in the president's 2007 State of the Union address.

[14] Should individuals want to select a plan with a utilization gatekeeping feature, they should be allowed to do so, however, with this feature prominently notified in advance to the buyer, who presumably would pay a lower charge for the plan, ceteris paribus.

One solution regarding portability is to require that insurance companies accept everyone, charging rates based only on age, sex, location, and lifestyle choices as described. In other words, the unlucky company presented with the high-risk individual wanting to buy a policy would simply have to accept him or her, even if this worked against company interests. It is not inconceivable that a company presented with enough such bad risks would be forced to close or close with the objective to restart later under a new name with a fresh pool of insured. Thus, we prefer another approach, shown in Table 8.1 and explained in the following.

A better solution would be to make the increased perpetual liability of a high-risk insured person the responsibility of the original company. Here is how this could work through a form of reinsurance. In Switzerland sickness funds that have a favorable mix of relatively healthy individuals must pay into a risk equalization fund. Those that have a disproportionate number of high-risk individuals receive a subsidy from it. For example, assume that John Doe insures with Old Reliable Insurance Company and pays a premium of $120 (which includes Old Reliable administrative costs of $20). Expected spending for his risk class is equal to $100. Suppose John contracts a condition that raises expected spending to $150. He has experienced a reclassification event that puts him in a higher risk pool. He now wants to shift to Western Vista Insurance Company, which is in another part of the country. Old Reliable is liable for some payment, in this case, $60 (= $50 + $10 for the administrative overhead), to Western Vista Insurance Company. Suppose the normal premium that applies to healthy individuals of his risk class in the new region is also $120. Since rates $100 and $120 are public knowledge, ensuring the transfer of $60 to Western Vista is the responsibility of the companies. Various institutional details would deal with the setting and transfer of $60. For example, Old Reliable might be required to pay $60 into a national pool (much like the Swiss risk equalization fund). Western Vista would ask for $60 from the pool when it takes the transfer. These types of features can be worked out in different ways.

Table 8.1. *Insurance Transferability*

	Premium
John Doe without medical condition	$120
John Doe with medical condition	$180
Old Reliable Insurance Company low-risk premium	$120
Western Vista Insurance Company high-risk premium	$180
Implied transfer from Old Reliable to Western Vista upon John's purchase of a Western Vista policy	$60

Steps 1–4 are summarized in Table 8.2. Reading down the left column displays the logical progression that determines the pieces of the Targeted Intervention Plan. In the bottom of Table 8.2 is a row devoted to step 5 of the plan, which is just as important as the steps that precede it.

Step 5: Create a True Market in Health Care

Anyone who is familiar with health care and who knows what a market is knows that the health care system in place in America today is not a market. Even the first requirement of a market – that a common price be publicly known for a given service – fails. We have reserved for the chapter on prices (Chapter 10) an example from our personal experience of how health care is deficient on this account (the interested reader can refer to Section 10.2).

Many of the deviations from market are caused by government policies. These and more can be corrected by adjustments that rationalize health care provision. Rationalization of the market and proper structuring of insurance imply savings such that the cost to the system of extending coverage to all is low or even negative. There are many improvements that could be cited. In Chapter 1 we explained that utilization savings on the order of 2 percent of GDP exceed the estimated costs, which are on the order of 1/2 to 1 percent of GDP, of extending insurance coverage to everyone (in a proper fashion that prevents crowding out of existing coverage and its absorption into the public program). Any reform that increases market contestability (see Section 9.2, "Markets") and competition is desirable. These range from reforming graduate medical education in the United States, to allowing greater competition across state lines for insurance companies, to modernizing Stark II limitations (restricting referrals by physicians to entities in which they have a monetary interest), to modernizing Medicare and Medicaid, to allowing the establishment of clinics and hospitals on the basis of business profitability.[15] Minimally, the most far-reaching rationalizing changes in terms of their implications include:

1. price transparency (prices must be publicly known and easily accessible),
2. most favored customer pricing (a term derived from international trade policy implying that the price a customer pays is the price charged by the provider for the service to the most favored customer),

---

[15] In the past, Medicare has imposed a moratorium (the 18-month moratorium ended in June 2005) on opening physician-owned niche hospitals. The need for the moratorium ultimately had to do with inappropriate pricing and reimbursement structures across services within Medicare.

Table 8.2. *Summary: Targeted Intervention Plan Components and Rationales*

Step	Need	Response	Rationale
1	Everyone should purchase health insurance.	Subsidize health insurance purchase: Reward those who buy insurance.	A subsidy to purchase insurance is equivalent to a tax on all other goods if insurance is not purchased. Creating the incentive through a price differential retains individual responsibility to buy insurance and discourages polittroughing. If all have health insurance (the goal), no one pays any levy.
2	Some cannot afford health insurance.	Provide income assistance efficiently to those who cannot afford insurance.	The aid plan is a program design choice that respects incentives.
3	The program budget must be covered, cost shifting dollars in the current health care system must be accessed, and the program must not create uncontrolled liability for expenditure.	Levy a revenue tax on health care providers and health insurance. Accomplish all three objectives.	The provider revenue tax spreads program costs evenly to everyone, not just to the privately insured. Program budget expends A in aid and collects B in provider taxes. Since both are under program control; $A - B$ is under program control.
4	Good coverage is patient-centered, personal, portable, and permanent.	Make insurance policies individual and insure against medical and reclassification risks.	Policy coverage is a program choice. Guaranteed renewability (see insurance features discussion, "Step 4: Insurance is the Right Kind," earlier in the section) deals with reclassification risk. Affordability is provided by underwriting freedom and competition.

Step	Need	Response	Rationale
5	The health care sector does not exhibit necessary features of a market or competition. Market rationalization is needed.	Rationalize the health care market and health care insurance underwriting. Rationalization includes: 1. price transparency 2. most favored customer pricing 3. guaranteed renewability 4. equal tax treatment across all pools 5. health care insurances connector (see "Health Care Connector" in Section 9.2 of Chapter 9)	The government's job is to institute conditions of competition. Inadequacies of the current non-market are addressed by creating the right environment.

3. guaranteed renewability (already discussed: the provision that insurance is renewable at the same rate available to others of the same age, sex, and geographic location),
4. equal tax treatment across insurance pools and methods of accessing health insurance,
5. freedom to underwrite, and, as a market-creating aid,
6. an insurance "connector" patterned along the lines of Massachusetts's recent example, which will help join those seeking insurance to those providing it. See Section 9.2 of Chapter 9 for a discussion of the Massachusetts Plan.

We have frequently stated that no plan that requires economic agents to act in ways that are against their own interests (except dishonest behavior) can succeed. Apart from meeting the minimum coverage requirements and limiting risk rating to age, sex, and location cohorts companies are free to offer additional benefits in supplementary policies. Additional coverage can be offered on market terms. As discussed in "Step 4: Insurance Is the Right Kind," earlier in this section, insurance consists of a list of covered events, a deductible, a co-insurance rate, and an out-of-pocket limit. Increases in system-wide costs of covering the uninsured and reductions that result from market rationalization provide the opportunity to cover everyone, and at the same time decrease spending from current levels.

8.2. Enabling Compassion

The individual's choice, in spite of the "Samaritan's Dilemma,"[16] to provide charity or to withhold it is addressed positively in the direction of encouraging charity by providing a mechanism for concerned individuals to supplement in a charitable way the public budget. (The budget supports incentive-compatible income transfers that make it possible as a matter of policy for everyone to buy health insurance that includes the responsible and necessary coverage for his or her age and sex.) This is appropriate because the efficiency approach suggests that charity is a function of individuals and VPOs that government serves in an efficiency-determined facilitating role. The right amount of charity is the amount that individuals fully informed of their own circumstances and the circumstances of others would choose to give.

As described in this chapter, the logical consequence of choosing the most efficient means to induce everyone to buy health insurance leads us to an incentive subsidy/levy (there are cosmetically different forms that it can take) and a provider revenue tax. The Targeted Intervention Plan therefore treats the revenues (if any) collected from the compliance levy, the revenues collected from the revenue tax on health care providers, and charitable donations of VPOs and individuals as dedicated funds for use in the incentive-compatible income transfers to the needy to allow them to have sufficient income to buy health insurance.

There is an enlarged role for VPOs to play. In the past, charity for health care consisted of the creation of hospitals and free clinics. While these will still be available objects of charity, the more modern role will be for charitable foundations, individuals, and VPOs to add their money to the flow of program income transfers. That is, individuals and groups who want more to be done for the health care and health insurance needs of the needy will

---

[16] The Samaritan's dilemma is the phenomenon that the act of giving charity may cause the recipient to expect and become dependent on more of it. Buchanan, 1977.

have the opportunity to augment the public flow of funds with their own funds. We have suggested that this could be done using tax form check-off boxes but feel that creative ways for individuals and VPOs in partnership to enlarge the income program support offered to the capable and incapable needy have only begun to be worked out. The point that we would like to make is this: The Targeted Intervention Plan offers a natural point of entry that is consistent with all of the efficiency considerations that led us to separate problems of too little income from problems of failure to buy health insurance. Everyone who feels that too little is being done for the health care needs of the poor has access to an efficient way to donate their funds to fulfill those needs.

8.3. Financing the Targeted Intervention Plan

Working through plan financial implications is not as difficult as might be imagined. In fact, Baylor University M.B.A students, using U.S. Medical Expenditure Panel Survey Data and a little guidance, were able to "price out" a system for themselves just prior to our beginning work on this book. Details can be found in Appendix D.

Before considering broad-brush financial implications, however, we emphasize that while estimates are useful (reported here in terms of per-centages of GDP), the arrangements described are a framework within which the sizes of various components are choices of the implementer. The feasibility and success of the chosen specifics depend not on the estimates but on the fact that the framework

1. does not require injections of external funds (top-off costs need be the only budget obligation),
2. sits on its own base (i.e., apart from income transfers related to top-off costs and the risk-reducing effects of insurance, all pay for their own health care over their lifetime),
3. allows the deliberative choice of program budgetary expenditures, and
4. has four control points (levers) for administrative fine-tuning.

This means that the program can be adjusted according to circumstances and the "numbers" are less critical than the capacity to make mid-course corrections in light of judgments from experience and monitoring of new post-implementation information. Under program control are:

1. its choices about what the base insurance policies will be for each age-sex group,

2. the selection of the program's budgetary spending limits and rules for dispensing income support,
3. the choice about the size of the revenue tax rate, and
4. the choice about the size of the incentive price differential (incentive levy).

Table 8.3 lists the sources and uses of funds. The framework is simple. The program determines its rules for dispensing income support, A, and its desired level of net expenditures into the health care sector, B. Observations of A and choice of B determine the amount to be collected by the revenue tax, t, according to $tR = A - B$, where R is provider revenues and t is the revenue tax rate. Appendix D (see discussion in "Funds Used to Insure the Uninsured") explains that t is likely to be a number on the order of 3–4 percent. However, the size of t will vary, depending on the selections of A and B, which are implementation choices. The lower bound for choice of B is the true cost of the additional program-induced medical care that results from expanded insurance coverage (this is the top-off cost discussed in Chapter 1). To the extent that the VAT/compliance levy collects revenue, it will marginally reduce it. The income received by individuals through the incentive-compatible earned income tax credit–type mechanism equals A plus C, where C is foundation support for individuals' health care and private charity channeled through the government program.

What are the aggregate welfare implications? Again, feasibility is not dependent on knowing these numbers in advance, and it is not our purpose to estimate numbers – that is the job of the Congressional Budget Office and the Council of Economic Advisers when the program that is passed by Congress has been defined in detail. It is nevertheless sensible to want to know what may be expected about the order of magnitude of costs and benefits. Table 8.4 lists the main components of welfare consequence.

Of the numbers in Table 8.4, only the efficiency gains have not previously been explained. Markets exist to facilitate trade and the re-distribution of

Table 8.3. *Sources and Uses of Funds*

Sources	Uses
Revenue tax	Income support
Foundation and private charity	Program administration costs
VAT/compliance levy (if any, *de minimis* revenues)	

Table 8.4. *The Welfare "Budget"*

Costs, benefits	($\approx$ % of GDP)
Top-off costs[a]	−0.58 to −1.16
Moral hazard gains[a]	+2
Efficiency gains[b]	+1.4
Total	+2.2 to +2.8

[a] See discussion of top-off costs and moral hazard gains in Chapter 1.

[b] Distributive efficiency gains; see text in this section.

goods to those who value them more highly. Voluntary exchange is always welfare-creating because one party or the other can refuse to trade if it does not think it is improved by the trade. Unifying a market by causing a single competitve price to prevail over a larger group of participants increases the welfare of the group's members because there are more options available for trade. Moving in the reverse direction – fragmenting a market into smaller separated groups – lowers welfare. We have argued that rationalizing health care markets encourages greater competition and common prices. To gauge how much could be gained this way, Table 8.4 reports numbers based on eBay. By linking buyers and sellers in a market that sets a common price, eBay improves efficiency. Some of the value created accrues to eBay as operating profit, and the rest goes to the buyers and sellers who use eBay. The operating profit of eBay as a percentage of sales is a lower bound estimate for the efficiency gains. Applying the eBay lower bound to personal health care expenditures gives the number in the table.[17] Working from this back-of-the-envelope first approximation, were the recommendations in this book enacted together, the net impact would be to expand health insurance coverage and improve health care satisfaction at a net gain of 2.2–2.8 percent of GDP.

8.4. Transition Issues

Implementing the proposed framework affects in no way – other than by overall market improvements in the health care sector – the majority of Americans who already have acceptable health insurance; its changes impact only the currently uninsured by creating an efficienct price incentive

---

[17] Merchandise sales on eBay in 2006 were $52.47 billion. Operating profit in the same year was $5.06 billion. See Internet Retailer, 2007, and Ebay Inc Annual Income Statement, 2007. $0.145 \times (5.06/52.47) = 0.014$.

for them to buy insurance that they have adequate income to purchase through a separate income mechanism. The selective impact of the program is a positive feature, as well as being necessary for efficient intervention. Those who have adequate coverage and who are happy with their current arrangements can be left alone. At the same time, transition flexibility is available. For example, Medicare and Medicaid recipients can continue to be covered by Medicare and Medicaid, though in the long run, these programs can be replaced by the proposed framework if desired. Costs for the program are spread uniformly, instead of borne by the privately insured. Providers and consumers are free to offer and seek care as they wish. Health care market features are enhanced and, through them, costs contained. Government will be able to plan for its health-related program expenditures with perfect foresight and assurance. Importantly, the framework provides enough points of control and flexibility that adjustments can be made as needed and as experience with the new system grows.

> Implementing the proposed framework in no way affects the majority of Americans who already have acceptable health insurance; its changes impact only the currently uninsured.

A question that would have to be addressed before implementation is how to insure those who have preexisting conditions that make them uninsurable with private companies. It might be necessary for government to establish regional high-risk pools, at least initially while the new system is phased in, to deal with individuals who cannot acquire private coverage for this reason. The pool is likely to serve relatively few individuals but will guarantee that no one slips through gaps during the transition.[18] In this way, everyone is guaranteed continuous coverage at the lowest cost he or she can achieve by healthy behavior. Thereafter, insurance renewal is guaranteed at premiums based only on age, sex, geographical location (and possibly verifiable health-relevant lifestyle choices such as smoking), but not on medical conditions that arise after the start of the program. Insurance plan choices could be made to include level premium plans for terms of 5 years, 10 years, or more.

---

[18] Kaiser Foundation, 2004, reported that 182,381 individuals participated in high-risk pools across the entire United States. Even multiplying participation by 10 produces a number that is less than 1 percent of the population.

Because the plan makes minimal demands on most agents and is transition-friendly, a few remarks about its philosophy and impact on the stakeholders are in order.

- An incentive is created for individuals to purchase health insurance. Purchase is a personal obligation. The incentive for those who do not buy insurance and intentionally free ride on others is the failure to receive a lower price on all their other purchases. For most of us, who already have adequate insurance, nothing changes. The fraction of the population that needs income assistance gets it. Everyone in the same age-sex-location pool pays the same price for the same health care services.

- Insurance companies must underwrite insurance policies that meet or exceed prescribed coverage standards for the policy-relevant basic plan. They cannot adjust premiums in response to medical experience, hence the need for guaranteed renewability and a basic benefit package.

- Health care providers are subject to a revenue tax. Because everyone has insurance, there is little need for charity care provided by health care suppliers. Providers can set their prices and pass on costs according to the market. The net impact on providers is zero. Presuming competition, prices will reflect marginal cost plus the revenue tax.

- The revenue tax gives government perfect, in-advance control over its net injections into the health care sector. It also provides a fiscal tool to address sector rents, should this be a concern.

- A list of desirable features includes the implication that everyone with insurance enters the health care sector equally. Providers set fees as they see fit. Issues of market power – as in patented pharmaceuticals facing customers who have low co-pays – can be addressed. See Chapter 11 for a specific proposal.

Four control points guarantee that the program is sustainable, flexible, and controllable. Different efficient implementation options exist that are consistent with the framework and objectives. Some options may be more acceptable politically.

1. The insurance contract terms for basic coverage is a program choice. We have explained that basic insurance, the focus of policy, should be bought and sold on an actuarially fair basis. Basic coverage should vary by the age and sex of the policyholder group, include only necessary coverage for true insurance (protection against medical events with catastrophic financial implications), and remain affordable by not

including "budget-busting" lists of benefits and services that are unneeded and unwanted, even though at other ages such coverage might be appropriate.

2. The rules for dispensing income support and qualifying for program aid are a program implementation choice.

3. The provider revenue tax rate is a flexible choice.

4. The incentive price differential/compliance subsidy/levy rate is a program implementation choice. Its level needs to be high enough to induce insurance purchase in the targeted population. For those who already have insurance, the non-targeted population, it has no financial implications. It is important to note that the higher the rate chosen, the greater the compliance it induces and, ultimately, the less revenue it raises. A rate high enough to induce full compliance collects zero revenue and raises consumer prices for no one.

The Targeted Intervention Plan leaves in place virtually all of the well-known advantages of the market and does so in a sustainable way. It satisfies the *no-Ponzi-scheme principle* (see Section 3.6 of Chapter 3) and the *every-pot-stands-on-its-own-base principle* (see Section 3.3 of Chapter 3), provides for underwriting with *homogeneous risk pooling*, and requires *transparent* prices. It leaves the current employment-based system intact for those who desire that approach (including the practice of self-insurance by large employers.)[19] The plan also allows for further development of consumer-based options to control moral hazard. Those alternatives are left to the market. Apart from insurance events and charity transfers, sustainability requires that every person pays his or her own health costs over his or her lifetime, as the plan provides.

8.5. Mandates versus Incentives versus Leaving Some Uninsured

The health care debate over the uninsured has raised terms like *mandates, incentives, individual responsibility, fiscal responsibility*, as well as concern about whether any should be allowed to remain uninsured. There is a false impression of conflict among the various goals that these terms imply. In fact, there is no conflict. Because an efficient intervention can be selected that is "self-eliminating" when it achieves its targeted objective, leaving

---

[19] The success of self-insurance depends – as it should – on its efficiency-generating ability and whether participants are better off than they would be with market-provided insurance.

none uninsured implies no tax penalty for anyone, no mandates, and the retention of individual responsibility and fiscal responsibility.

The word "mandate" implies the presence of an authoritative order or command enforced by law from a superior (the government) to a lesser (the individual). An "incentive" is not a mandate, but an inducement or reward for taking a certain action. The inducement can take the form of a positive financial reward or the avoidance of a negative one. Using tax consequences to create an incentive does not convert the incentive into a mandate because the individual can choose not to comply and no police will appear to enforce the unchosen action, though it does arguably lean the incentive in the direction of a mandate because it is *government* enacted.

Price incentives leave the individual free to choose. An ideal price incentive would induce the desired behavior, with no financial consequences if the desired behavior is chosen. The subsidy version the Targeted Intervention Plan (see discussion "*Subsidy Version*" in Step 1 of Section 8.1) has this property: it creates a price incentive to buy health insurance that alters no price to complying consumers and costs them no additional charge. That is, those who buy insurance without government help are unaffected in any way and those who need an incentive are left with no penalty once they have complied. Those who buy insurance have done so as an individual responsibility, they have sufficient income to afford it, and they receive the benefits of their insurance. The government program budget is under its prior control, is sustainable, and has sufficient points of flexibility. In particular, it does not create an entitlement or unfunded mandates for the private sector.

We see little to object to in such an arrangement and much that is appealing. First, what has changed relative to laissez faire? Only one thing: in the subsidy arrangement, there will be a VAT in place that returns the funds it collects to the consumer at the point of purchase. It therefore can be set high enough to incentivize insurance purchase as a rewarded action. There are considerations for the implementation of a VAT, as for any tax, but the experience with VATs is favorable relative to that with other taxes.[20]

---

[20] Many nations have had a VAT for many years. The VAT avoids tax cascading, is superior in exempting business-to-business purchases, is self-enforcing because sellers want to receive credit for embedded tax on their inputs, collects tax at many points along the production stream (tax avoidance is more difficult), functions well in collecting rates of tax as high as 15–20 percent, can be rebated to foreign visitors and on exports, creates a paper trail, and suffers less resistance than sales tax of the same magnitude. There is a large literature on the effectiveness of the VAT relative to other taxes. See, for example, President's Advisory Panel on Federal Tax Reform, 2005; Agha and Haughton, 1996; and others.

Second, the intervention is intentionally small – in fact, it has no tax or price consequences to anyone if executed properly – and it satisfies the dictates of an efficient price incentive for individuals to buy health insurance. This means that other interventions to accomplish the same objective impose greater costs on the citizenry. This leaves only one efficiency comparison: the intervention has induced individuals to buy insurance who, by their choice not to buy in the laissez-faire state, demonstrated that the insurance was not worth their expenditure. This, of course, is the source of the efficiency cost that we want to minimize by the choice of intervention. *Some cost* must be imposed, however, if everyone is to be induced to buy insurance. As long as the cost is as low as possible, the policy has been a success. If the objective is dropped that there be universal health insurance, then the corresponding intervention can be dropped, income aid eliminated, and the plan budget set to zero. The remaining Targeted Intervention Plan features will lead to a rationalized health care market and health insurance market. With prices for insurance set on an actuarially fair basis, with benefits varying only according to need by age and sex of the insured group, competition in health care and its insurance will lead to greater voluntary purchase of insurance and better ability of the health care sector to supply value to the American public. There will remain a non-zero pool of uninsured, but it will be smaller.

Before concluding this chapter, we take time to anticipate and answer potential objections. We also provide a parable that compares the plan to providing access to a sector of the economy with least impingement on market functioning possible.

8.6. Answers to Questions

Won't some people fall through the cracks?
Everyone is encouraged and able to buy insurance under the plan. Those who cannot afford a base policy will receive government help so that everyone has enough income to buy insurance. No one is left out.

Will indigent people get enough help?
Everyone will be able to afford insurance satisfying a minimal set of coverage requirements. Again, no one is left out.

Won't rich people buy better care?
Coverage beyond the basic policy is not a necessity. Those who do not want to pay more for features that are not required should not be required to

buy more than they want. Those who want extra features should be free to supplement their coverage and buy what they want.

Won't some people free ride on the contributions of others?
Everyone is encouraged and able to buy health insurance. A compliance subsidy/levy can be selected that induces everyone to buy insurance but results in no price or cost consequences for those who carry the basic health insurance or better.

Isn't showing proof of insurance to earn the price reward burdensome?
Showing proof of insurance is no more burdensome than making a purchase now. People carry cash, checks, or credit/debit cards to "prove" their ability to make a purchase. Proof of insurance coverage, perhaps the credit/debit card itself, can be presented the same way that credit cards are swiped to establish credit at time of purchase. Counterfeiting a card will not work because the data bank that the cards connect to must also show current insurance status for the indentified individual. An individual who did not want to carry the card or forgot the card could also file for a rebate based on receipts. This could be done at time of paying annual federal and state taxes as is done now for state sales taxes in some cases. If desired, rebates could be arranged for on a shorter-term basis.

What about illegal aliens? Won't they end up getting free care at taxpayer expense?
All residents must purchase health insurance or be subject to the price differential on their purchases. This applies to illegal aliens.

Won't visitors to the United States end up paying a tax they shouldn't have to pay?
Tourist visitors to the United States can be rebated the levy in the same way that vacationers to Europe apply to have their value-added taxes rebated when they leave.

Wouldn't a refundable tax credit for health care insurance be more direct? Why not use that?
A refundable tax credit subsidizes the purchase of insurance of the entire American population in order to cause a relatively tiny number of Americans to buy insurance. The larger a government program requiring taxes is, the larger is the deadweight loss from the taxation added to the costs of the program. Mid-range estimates place this extra cost at 51 percent of the taxes raised – a sizable consideration. In contrast, the intervention

principle says that the efficient way to induce those to buy insurance who do not do so now is to subsidize the insurance purchases of only those who do not now buy health insurance, a much more targeted response. This is accomplished by imposing a value-added tax that is rebated to buyers who show proof of current insurance. Comparing the two approaches, we note the following additional consideration: a refundable tax credit creates the appearance that it is government's obligation to provide health care and is subject to polittroughing; the compliance subsidy/levy with income aid through the Earned Income Tax Credit does not.

Should workers have to buy insurance? Shouldn't their firms buy it for them?

Empirical evidence suggests that workers pay for their own insurance already. Under current arrangements, those who really pay the premium are not obvious. Regardless of who pays, however, workers may want and firms may offer employer-based insurance as before under the proposed arrangements. In fact, if premiums are lower because firms offer coverage, the savings accrue to the workers and firms who create the savings. This is the market at work, creating incentives for firms and workers to find better ways to offer insurance.

Will the system stifle the practice of medicine?

Medical providers are free to practice medicine as they wish. Buyers are free to select whatever services they want.

Won't the revenue tax be a burden on providers?

As the number of people without insurance falls, the provision of charity care will also diminish because there is less need for it. The revenue tax can be set as needed and should never exceed the current outlay for charity care.

Will the required insurance be good enough?

The level of required basic coverage for each age and sex cohort is a legislative decision in the same way that the level of mandatory automobile liability insurance is in most states. Individuals who desire more coverage beyond the basic level are free to purchase supplementary policies with their own money.

Won't demogogues subvert the system for selfish reasons?

Transfers and subsidies are the necessary element of any system that provides free services to indigents. Some politicians will inevitably try to subvert such a system by promising free benefits to their constituents. This always-present problem is not unique to health care. Requiring the transfers to be visible and transparent, offering them through the Earned Income Tax Credit rather than tying them to the health care product, provides some degree of protection against abuse.

8.7. How the System Works: A Parable

Although no analogy is perfect, consider an amusement park or state fair and its enclosed grounds as representative of economic life. Different attractions are available, including entertainment offerings, food courts, recreation activities, and a fenced-in rides section. At the park, entertainments are accessed with tickets purchased at the entrance to the entertainment section; more expensive shows require more tickets and less expensive venues fewer. Most people navigate their way to the entertainment section and buy what they want for themselves and their children without help, but some do not. Generally no single attraction such as the food court or rides would be considered essential, but for purposes of discussion let us assume that it is important for everyone and his or her children to have access to the entertainment, and when selecting it, everyone will be treated equally. That is, the amount and quality of the entertainment selected will not vary regardless of whether members of the audience purchased tickets with their own money or are receiving assistance.

Beyond the concern that everyone access a reasonable and appropriate range of shows, the show concessionaires and the public are happy with the offerings their amusement park provides and the way the park works. That is, they want to continue to make their own choices and decide their actions in the park as before. Moreover, as they, their neighbors, and their children grow up and grow old, they want their access to entertainments to be a continuous feature of the park. Being conscientious and dependable, they are willing to pay for their own shows as well as participate in providing for others, but they do not want their compassion to be abused, and they do not agree to establish an unlimited obligation to pay for an entitlement to shows without accountability.

Thus everyone buys a minimal number of tickets, but those who cannot afford them will buy their tickets after receiving income support according to their work circumstances. This ensures that everyone can attend shows while preventing abuse by those trying to slip in without paying at all. Concessionaires remain free to set ticket prices for their shows and compete as they always have. A market continues to exist. Competition keeps prices low relative to the true costs of provision. As they were before, consumers are free if they wish to buy entertainment beyond the universal minimum. The money gathered at the show window equals what the consumers have spent on tickets from their own pocket and includes the amount provided to them in income subsidies.

Those who pay the full cost for their shows are indistinguishable from others who receive help in their purchase. This satisfies a horizontal equity condition that those receiving equal treatment pay equally and are treated equally at point of treatment. The use of tickets performs this function because concessionaires will not know which buyers were subsidized. As long as everyone uses tickets to buy access to entertainment, the provider makes no distinctions among audience members.

There is another requirement. Government wants the net amount of money injected into the entertainment sector to be able to be set in advance. To meet this requirement, at the end of the day concessionaires turn in the tickets they have earned and the money collected at the ticket window is divided among them according to proportion of the total tickets turned in. This feature is equivalent to the functioning of the revenue tax. The net amount injected into the entertainment sector is under the perfect control of the park.

The amusement park has met its objectives fully. Everyone has access to entertainment. Everyone remains free to purchase as much or as little as wished in other parts of the park. Entertainment concessionaires set prices as they want, consumers buy what they want, subsidized purchasers are indistinguishable from other purchasers, and no one can view a show without paying. Everyone must buy tickets, and net subsidies are determined at the end of the day. The net subsidy can be set to reflect the actual costs of subsidized entertainment.

Everyone has access to entertainment, no one free rides, and the sector as a whole gains by the requirement that everyone has tickets.

Back to Health Care

It is a short step to translate from the amusement park parable to health care. Health care access is gained through health insurance. The entertainment sector represents health insurance services and the minimum purchase consists of buying a policy that covers a specified list of conditions and procedures. The basic ingredients of health insurance are a deductible, a co-insurance payment schedule, an out-of-pocket limit, and a list of covered events, conditions, and services. The required limits can be made to vary by cohort group and individual income levels to minimize moral hazard or for any other consideration.

Everyone purchases health insurance coverage that meets or exceeds the required standard. Anyone who wishes to is free to purchase more extensive coverage than the minimum policy.

In the amusement park, tickets were used as currency and the entertainment window transferred money to the concessionaires for their tickets at a rate that reflected the income subsidies to some customers. In the real world, tickets are unnecessary. To access cost-shifting dollars, government taxes the revenues of firms engaged in the sale of health insurance and health goods and services, setting the tax rate so that government subsidies minus the taxes collected equal the desired net injection into the health care sector. Physicians, hospitals, pharmaceutical manufacturers, and other health care providers are all free to set prices, practice fee for service, and compete as they wish. Because control over the net payment made to the health care sector is the objective, health care is the only sector subject to the revenue tax.

> To access cost-shifting dollars, government taxes the revenues of firms engaged in the sale of health insurance and health goods and services.

8.8. Conclusions

While most people said it could not be done, within a few years of the Wright brothers' and Glenn Curtiss's first powered flights everyone was getting into the air and wondering why it was ever thought impossible. The same can be said of animal cloning now that we are in the post–Dolly the sheep era.[21] Cynicism about creating a health care framework that Americans can embrace is equally understandable but unfounded. We restate the chapter summary: working from the list of attributes that Americans want and applying efficiency principles generate a virtually unique health care framework that resembles a free market except for those few particulars that need to deviate to accomplish the objective that everyone has health insurance.

We have addressed two distinct problems for selected individuals – failure to purchase health insurance and too little income – and solved them efficiently using the intervention and incentive symmetry principles. No Ponzi scheme features, unsustainable elements, or inducements to governmentalization or polittroughing were introduced. A third need – the

---

[21] Dolly (5 July 1996–14 February 2003), a Scottish sheep, was the first mammal to be cloned successfully from an adult cell. Her birth was announced 22 February 1997.

need to rationalize the health care market and health insurance market-place – was also addressed by introducing key features into the Targeted Intervention Plan. The plan is composed of already-tested components that are manageable in number. They are combined here for the first time in a form dictated by economic efficiency and the objectives of Chapter 2:

- Subsidy/tax-equivalent incentive to purchase insurance that affects only those who do not buy insurance as the intervention principle directs (i.e., there is no subsidy to the entire population's purchase of health insurance),
- Earned Income Tax Credit modification to account for insurance purchases of the capable needy/direct aid to the incapable needy,
- Provider revenue tax to fund the program aid. This also establishes budget control for government and accesses cost-shifting dollars in the current health care system.
- Market rationalization and consumer protection features to re-establish a market in the health care sector.

The inducement to purchase health insurance and the provider revenue tax represent the contact points between government and the private sector. Health care providers receive program dollars from patients who receive income subsidies from the government, so it is appropriate for providers to pay a revenue tax that on a system-wide basis is equivalent to the amount of free care currently provided. Apart from these contact points, consumers have complete freedom to seek the health care that they want; providers have complete freedom to find innovations that improve the care they provide and/or reduce its cost; and the government has complete control over its health-related expenditures. Safeguards are built into the separation of purchase incentives and provision of income assistance. Competitive concerns remain, as do concerns over improving efficiency and quality, but these concerns are concerns of any health system. The Targeted Intervention Plan has flexibility so that changes to improve the system can be made. Incentives are aligned for all stakeholders, and incentives for making further beneficial changes remain.

For the interested reader, Appendix D addresses the issue of plan feasibility by briefly describing the product of research presented in Washington, D.C., in 2006 to an audience of representives of Washington think tanks, the Council of Economic Advisers, and senatorial staff (the venue was arranged by Texas senator Kay Bailey Hutchison's office). Response could be described as cautiously positive, as might be expected for an expert audience that knows a great deal about the issue and has heard a great deal.

One comment that stands out was that unlike many other "plans" that the commenter had heard, this one addressed how it could be paid for and justified the way its components interacted. The Targeted Intervention Plan is the framework that results from satisfying the list of objectives described in Chapter 2 by applying the principles of Chapter 3. We are satisfied that it is economically and financially feasible and has enough programmatic points of flexibility to succeed in its objectives.[22]

---

[22] Programmatic points of flexibility include (1) the choice of insurance product for each age-sex cohort, (2) the size of the provider and health insurer revenue tax, (3) the size of the incentive levy, (4) the qualifying rules for income aid, and (5) the extent of aid.

PART IV

PROTECTIVE MEASURES

NINE

Forestalling Free Riders

I shall be telling this with a sigh
Somewhere ages and ages hence:
Two roads diverged in a wood, and I,
I took the one less traveled by,
And that has made all the difference.
Robert Frost, "The Road
Not Taken," 1920

Summary: *Those who go without health insurance burden more than just themselves. Persuading individuals to purchase insurance removes this burden on others. Massachusetts and Switzerland demonstrate that universal access to high-quality medical care is possible without turning to single-payer or a purely public sector approach.*

9.1. Background

The patchwork quilt of plans and programs that is the current U.S. health care system, where access is secured primarily through employer-sponsored insurance supplemented by myriad government programs targeting vulnerable population groups (primarily indigent and elderly), has produced unique problems of affordability and choice. With family premiums at or above $10,000 per year, many Americans go without insurance, instead burdening taxpayers and those with private coverage to fund their care via cost shifting. Many uninsured are doubtless unable to absorb the cost of a standard health insurance policy in their monthly budget. But many, upward of 30 percent of the total number of uninsured at any given time, have annual household incomes that exceed $50,000 (approximately 300 percent of the federal poverty level for a family of four). For individuals who can afford coverage, unwillingness to accept personal responsibility to purchase insurance must explain going without coverage. The "free rider" option is possible because no one is refused necessary care.

The challenge for U.S. health care reform is to improve access to care significantly without jeopardizing quality and patient choice. Advancing these goals requires clear understanding of what government involvement cannot accomplish. Where the private sector can succeed, government should accept a subordinate role and allow the market to function.

This has not been the political direction taken. Historically states have taken a regulatory approach to health care. State actions include liberalizing Medicaid eligibility requirements to expand access to low-income residents and other vulnerable population groups, mandating that insurance cover specific medical benefits, and establishing guidelines governing how insurers price their products, evaluate their risks, and administer their plans. Too often this approach has left little room for market incentives. Created inefficiencies are the result.

This chapter examines two related, but different approaches to health care delivery. We discuss first the recently enacted Massachusetts Health Plan. While the plan is not yet fully implemented, we can speculate on its likely impact. We are more definitive in discussing the Swiss plan, given that it has been operational for over a decade. We offer important lessons for U.S. policymakers from both. Similar in size, demographics, and the socioeconomic status of their respective inhabitants, Massachusetts and Switzerland have each taken an innovative approach to health care – each in its own way, the road less traveled.

9.2. Massachusetts: Leveling the Playing Field

The Massachusetts legislature, overwhelmingly Democrat, joined forces with its Republican governor to enact a comprehensive plan to increase insurance coverage and improve the quality of care, while creating a sustainable cost structure that rationalizes the financing of medical care. The plan represents a major expansion in coverage relying on individual responsibility and social solidarity. Legislation passed in April 2006 and fully operational by July 2007 provided a mechanism to achieve universal insurance coverage for all residents of the state.

Characteristics

The key components of the Massachusetts Plan include (1) creating strong incentives for individuals to purchase health insurance, (2) requiring that employers (with more than ten employees) make provision for insurance coverage for their workers, (3) merging the individual and small-group markets to create a state-level health insurance clearinghouse, and

(4) relaxing several regulatory features applying to the state's health insurance industry.

Elevating Individual Responsibility

The most notable component of the Massachusetts Plan places responsibility on the individual to purchase health insurance or face economic penalties. Establishing an expectation that all individuals purchase insurance is a legitimate response to free riders in health care and over $40 billion nationwide in uncompensated care required to cover their health care needs.

During the first year of the plan individuals who remain uninsured lose their state income tax deduction valued at approximately $180. Beyond the first year, however, the incentives increase to one-half of the annual premium on a standard insurance policy, approximately $2,000 for an individual and $5,500 for an entire family at the time of writing. Individuals can avoid these costs by purchasing any health plan approved by the state insurance commissioner. Approved plans include catastrophic insurance sold in conjunction with a health savings account (HSA) and managed care plans. For the program to work effectively, low-income residents must have the ability to pay for coverage and insurance markets must be deregulated for flexibility and lower costs. The Massachusetts Plan has chosen to tie the transfer of income to the purchase of insurance – a linkage that we have explained in Chapter 8 can be better accomplished with separate instruments – and will provide full subsidies to those households with incomes less than 100 percent of the federal poverty level (FPL). Those with incomes up to 300 percent of the FPL will be subsidized on a sliding scale. Households with incomes greater than 300 percent of the FPL (approximately $58,500 for a couple with two children) receive no subsidy.

Proponents argue that individual responsibility backed by a subsidy tied to health insurance purchase is the least obtrusive way to reach the goal of universal insurance coverage. They are nearly correct: An incentive to purchase insurance coupled with a work effort subsidy are superior tools for the capable needy according to the intervention principle. For the incapable needy, where work effort is not the same concern, the Massachusetts approach is equivalent in its efficiency properties. Nevertheless, the Massachusetts approach is an improvement. Rather than subsidizing providers for the uncompensated care they offer, Massachusetts uses those resources to subsidize individuals to purchase their own insurance coverage. With a law requiring community rating already in place, the reliance on individual responsibility will serve to strengthen the state risk pool by requiring the young and healthy to participate. Critics counter that the free rider problem is overstated; that the plan imposes a legal mandate that takes us a step closer to a government-run health care system (Tanner, 2006); and that our main concern should be cost and quality, not access. We would argue that the difference between a *mandate* – enforceable by the legal system – and an *incentive*, such as a subsidy to purchase insurance, is obvious and significant. If a subsidy to buy insurance (a favorable price differential) is socially acceptable to critics (i.e., not considered to be an individual "mandate"), then the same policy in its tax equivalent form should logically be acceptable for the same reasons by incentive symmetry.

Employer Mandate

The new law also places a "fair share" contribution requirement on employers who do not provide health insurance for their workers. Firms with more than ten employees that do not offer health insurance must pay up to $295 annually per worker into the state's uncompensated care pool (UCP). The "play-or-pay" feature is intended to replicate the premium tax that employers who arrange insurance for their workers pay into the UCP already. Additionally, these same employers are subject to a "free rider surcharge" if their employees use free care. The surcharge is imposed when a single employee receives free care more than three times in a year, or when as a group a firm's employees receive free care more than five times. The surcharge can be up to 100 percent of any spending that exceeds $50,000. Employers may avoid the surcharge by setting up a Section 125 plan, often referred to as a "cafeteria plan," so employees can pay their premium share with after-tax earnings.

In view of the fact that most or all of employer-paid health insurance is really paid by the worker in the form of reduced take-home wages, and recognizing that employer costs for health care are essentially equivalent in their effect to payroll taxes (also paid largely by the worker), the attempt to place greater reliance on the employer as the point for health insurance purchase – a private good – creates inefficiencies and paves the way for problems that will probably have to be addressed in the future.

Health Care Connector

The more innovative part of Massachusetts's legislation is the creation of the Massachusetts Health Care Connector. The Connector is a central clearinghouse – a single market for individual and small-group insurance. Here private insurers will compete for customers, offering a choice of plan designs. California Choice and Benu serving Oregon, Washington, Virginia, Maryland, and the District of Columbia have insurance exchanges, multi-employer arrangements, that are already in existence. By allowing small groups the benefits of risk spreading, an exchange decreases a plan's vulnerability to risk segmentation, adverse selection, and high administrative costs. Individuals benefit from improved portability and more flexible payment rules (ability to receive contributions from multiple employers).

The restructured health insurance market in Massachusetts has been described as similar to the CarMax auto market, where many different types of automobiles are available from one giant dealership (Haislmaier, 2006). A more accurate analogy, however, is the Federal Employee Health Benefit Program, a working example of Enthoven's model of managed competition (Enthoven, 2003).

Health insurance markets require a large concentration of potential consumers to facilitate exchange effectively. By merging the individual and small-group markets, the Connector provides a mechanism that lowers transaction costs by establishing uniform rules of engagement and managing the administrative function relating to marketing, enrollment, and payment. This allows insurance providers to focus their competitive efforts on improving the quality and efficiency of health care delivery. Risk pooling through the Connector is expected to provide more affordable choices to individuals, lowering their premiums by an expected 28 percent. Unfortunately, community/group rating will still dominate insurance. Because health insurers will not be able to adjust premiums on the basis of age, sex, or other risk factors, actual competition will be limited.

Regulatory Reforms

Massachusetts has one of the most heavily regulated health insurance markets in the United States. It is widely acknowledged that this regulation, however well meaning the motivations behind it, drives up costs and inhibits the insurance markets from doing their job as well as they could. The new law provides some relief to the regulatory burden by relaxing several of the more onerous provisions. Firms with fewer than fifty employees may utilize the services of the Connector to arrange their insurance coverage, and those employers making a premium contribution may do so through the Connector. In addition, households may receive premium contributions from more than one employer. Managed care plans may offer high-deductible plans that are HSA qualified, and young adults (between the ages of 19 and 26) may purchase policies that cover fewer of the state's 40 mandated benefits.

Selective contracting is allowed for plans sold through the Connector, enabling insurance providers to avoid the any-willing-provider provisions required of insurance sold in the state. The law also establishes a two-year moratorium on the creation of any new mandates while the legislature reviews all the state's existing mandates.

Issues and Further Considerations

Believing that better insurance coverage improves access to health care that should, in turn, improve health, the Massachusetts plan seeks to cover an additional 550,000 residents, half of whom earn more than 300 percent of FPL. The cost of providing uncompensated care to Massachusetts uninsured was $1.3 billion in 2005, or $2,364 per uninsured individual. On average, each of the 4.82 million privately insured residents was required to pay an extra $270 (taxes plus cost shifting) to cover the state's uninsured. The Massachusetts plan makes much better use of this money.

Unless more legal flexibility for insurance underwriters to establish better risk pools and fewer insurance mandates are made part of the Massachusetts health insurance scheme, it is likely that health insurance in the state will remain overly costly and an impediment to the outcomes that the state seeks. Nevertheless, in a culture that has drifted, probably unintentionally, to the present situation, where individual responsibility is downplayed and discouraged when it comes to the purchase of health care, Massachusetts legislators have crafted a plan that reverses this expectation. Everyone is now expected to have insurance coverage: If you do not, you purchase it. If you are below 300 percent of FPL, your purchase will be subsidized. If you continue to go without insurance, your free riding will trigger payments into the system that go toward the $2,364 (current average) of unpaid care that you receive from the people of Massachusetts. The intervention principle mentioned at length throughout this book implies an incentive that differs from the Massachusetts approach. The principle implies a reminder to buy insurance that is brought to mind *daily*, or at least as often as non-insurance purchases are made in the absence of health insurance coverage.

> The intervention principle mentioned at length throughout this book implies an incentive that differs from the Massachusetts approach. The principle implies a reminder to buy insurance that is brought to mind *daily*, or at least as often as non-insurance purchases are made in the absence of health insurance coverage.

Despite excitement among proponents of the new law, successful implementation presents formidable challenges for other reasons as well, among which enforcement stands out. The legislation establishes for the first time a requirement to purchase a specific product as a requisite for living in the state.

The legislation is similar in some ways to legislation in states that require drivers to carry automobile liability insurance. Two obvious differences are that driving on public roads is a privilege, not a right, and car insurance is enforced by the legal system rather than through subsidy incentives. Massachusetts's citizens verify health insurance coverage by reporting their health insurance status when they file their state income tax returns. This approach uses the contact point between the individual and the state to create the plan's incentives. Because filing taxes occurs once per year, this requirement is complicated by the temporary nature of being uninsured by many who find themselves without coverage. It also places the incentives out of mind for much of the year, except for the astute few.

The Massachusetts approach has another implication that is worth mentioning. At the national level, over 20 percent of the nation's uninsured are foreign-born non-citizens (9.5 million, U.S. Census Bureau, 2006). It is not known how many uninsured are illegal aliens, but their total is estimated at 11 million by some and as much as 30 million by others.[1] Presumably, each uninsured individual costs as much on average as other uninsured, which in Massachusetts is $2,364 per year. Massachusetts's legislation challenges such individuals' entitlement to free health care based solely on illegal residence in a state.

9.3. Switzerland: Individual Responsibility in a Federalist Framework

Switzerland is divided into 26 political entities – cantons and demi-cantons – sovereign, like the American states, in all matters not directly granted to the federal government by the constitution. The Swiss enjoy unusual decentralized decision-making authority. Voters are able to affect policy through a political process of continuous referenda, providing them with unparalleled influence. Policy change requires voter approval. Most of its 7.3 million citizens live in the Swiss Plateau, the narrow region between the two mountain ranges that dominate the landscape, the Jura in the north and the Alps in the south. From its inception in 1911, Swiss health insurance has avoided the link between health insurance coverage and employment and relied instead on personal responsibility.

The Swiss approach leads to a lot of medical care. Second only to the United States, health care spending was 11.5 percent of GDP and $3,781 per capita in 2003. The generous supply of medical resources provides unprecedented access to medical services. Whether measured in terms of physicians

---

[1] Passell, 2007, estimates 11 million.

per 1,000, acute care bed density, or access to medical technology, resource supply is among the highest in Europe.

Characteristics of the Swiss System

The Swiss, like the people in Massachusetts, base their health care on the individual's purchase of insurance. Switzerland has operated successfully on this basis for many years and is therefore a model from which we can learn.

Individual Mandates

Permanent residents of Switzerland are subject to an individual legal mandate to purchase compulsory health insurance. Refusal to do so results in forcible assignment to a health insurance plan. Compulsory insurance covers a generous package of medical benefits, including inpatient and outpatient hospital care, unlimited hospital stays, and complementary and alternative medicine. Despite the generosity of the basic package, between 25 and 40 percent of the Swiss purchase supplemental policies, paying risk-rated premiums. The most popular supplementary policies allow patient choice of physicians and private hospital rooms among other features. Plans cover medical services for those traveling abroad, dental services, and prescription drugs that are not covered under compulsory insurance. Compulsory insurance is provided by 93 sickness funds operating on a not-for-profit basis. Insurance funds have established a centralized risk-adjustment mechanism, called Foundation 18, subsidizing funds that suffer disproportionately from adverse selection. The subsidies are based on a fund's deviation from average cost across 30 age-sex categories.

The public-private mix with respect to Swiss health care expenditures is unique among European nations. The proportion of expenditures from private sources at 42.1 percent is the highest in Europe – two to three times that of other countries in the region. The breakdown in spending is similar to that experienced in the United States. The major differences occur in spending on physician services and nursing home care.

Physician fees are based on a uniform nationwide relative value scale (RVS). Negotiations between physician groups and health insurance associations within each canton determine the monetary conversion factor applied to the RVS. Physicians are paid on a fee-for-service basis and are not allowed to charge more than the negotiated fee. In over one-half of the cantons physicians have freedom of prescription. These dispensing physicians are able to supplement their incomes by approximately one-third. Cantons finance approximately 80 percent of all hospital investment and one-half of all hospital operating expenses directly through taxation. In terms of European standards, the Swiss hospital system has a well-developed hospital infrastructure.

Financing

Individuals pay community-rated premiums within a canton. Approximately one-third of all individuals receive means-tested subsidies when premiums exceed 8–10 percent of their total income.[2] In 2001, almost 20 percent of enrollee premiums were financed through these government subsidies.

Policies feature six different deductibles, ranging from 300 SwF ($240 U.S.) for the standard policy, or *franchise ordinare* (FO), to 1,500 SwF ($1,205 U.S.). Policies also include co-insurance provisions of 10 percent for spending over the deductible, with an annual cap on out-of-pocket spending of 700 SwF ($562 U.S.). As the deductible increases, consumers receive premium discounts off the standard FO policy. Premium discounts range from 8 percent for the 400 SwF ($322 U.S.) deductible up to 40 percent for the 1,500 SwF ($1,205 U.S.). The average annual premium for the standard FO policy in 2003 was $2,388. Children under age 18 and students under age 25 paid lower premiums. Premiums can vary as much as 50 percent among cantons. While the standard FO plan is the most popular, the majority of the population has chosen either the higher deductibles or one of the managed care plans offered.

Two types of managed care plans are available to Swiss consumers – a plan similar to the staff-model health maintenance organization and a plan based on a general practitioner network. The latter utilizes a gatekeeper model in a risk-sharing arrangement between physicians and insurers. Surpluses and deficits are shared equally with an annual cap on losses absorbed by physicians of 10,000 SwF ($8,040 U.S.).

The Role of Markets

In theory, three markets exist in Swiss health care. Physicians compete for patients, insurers compete for customers, and as a result of selective contracting, insurers compete for primary care physicians. While the competitive rhetoric in the Revised Health Insurance Law is notable, the reality of competition has fallen somewhat short of the promise. Swiss physicians have virtually no latitude in the fees they charge nor the services they provide. Competition among insurers is almost nonexistent. The generous

---

[2] All of the numbers reported in this section are from Herzlinger and Parsa-Parsi, 2004.

nature of the compulsory benefits package allows little competition based on benefits offered. As expected, the appeal of supplementary insurance has been shrinking because of the expansion of the basic benefits package.

Competition among insurers is based on premiums charged and not benefits offered. The only exception to this rule is the ability to offer managed care plans that restrict access to certain providers. Since all policies are individually purchased, enrollees are aware of the full cost of their insurance.

There is some empirical evidence that high deductible plans enroll a relatively larger number of healthy individuals, as would be expected in a flexible insurance market. In 1999, high-deductible plans transferred an average of $510 per enrollee to low-deductible plans, who in turn received an average of $174 per enrollee.

Something to Like

There is much to like in the Swiss health care experience because it allows for freedom of patient choice and appropriate insurance underwriting to a greater degree than other European countries. The Swiss system, like the others, however, is subject to political pressures that continue to push for superimposing non-market features. Risk rating is based on age, sex, and geographic location, though rising numbers of legislatively mandated requirements raise insurance costs for the general population. The revealed preference of only a portion of the Swiss for additional coverage – those who want particular coverage and benefit from it demonstrate their demand by paying for its provision – shows that insurance could be kept more affordable for those who do not.

9.4. Lessons from Massachusetts and Switzerland

Deriving lessons for health care delivery and finance from other places – no system is perfect – is always a risky proposition. There is a danger in thinking that all the elements of a system can be imported from a foreign counterpart. Regardless, there are lessons that can be learned.

1. If universal coverage is the goal, incentives (or, failing that, mandatory participation) are essential.
2. Universal access to high-quality medical care is possible without reliance on a single-payer system or a pure public sector approach.
3. If insurance coverage and personal responsibility are linked (insurance through place of employment weakens the link), price transparency provides the incentives for responsible consumers to emerge.

4. Price-conscious behavior is encouraged as long as consumer choice and individual responsibility remain prominent in the system. "Crowding out" – the replacement of consumers' market choices with the government program – is a concern.
5. Controls over benefits and premiums mitigate competitive incentives.
6. Enrollees in high-deductible plans use substantially fewer medical resources. In 1999, spending was 60 percent lower per capita in the 1,500 SwF deductible plan (including risk adjustment) than in the basic FO plan.
7. People who cannot afford to purchase health insurance on their own can still have access to essential services within a system that provides transfers. Tax-financed, means-tested transfers can be designed to be consistent with promoting the efficient delivery of health care services.

TEN

Preserving Prices

All that a man has will he give for his life.
Satan, quoted in Job 2:4

Competition and market forces have been absent from our health care system, and that has hurt working families tremendously. We are excited to take the lead in doing what we do best – driving costs out of the system – and passing those savings to our customers.

H. Lee Scott, Chief Executive Officer, Wal-Mart, 2006

Summary: *Two things are certain: People can be made to pay more for health care than it costs to provide, and prices can be restrained and made useful only by re-establishment of competitive forces, or their approximation, that rationalize the current (dysfunctional) health care market.*

10.1. Background

The patient entered the doctor's office with a fishbone dangerously caught in his throat. Desperate, he waited anxiously until the doctor skillfully removed it. "How much do I owe you, Doc?"

"About half as much as you were willing to pay when you came in." [1]

The story makes a good point: if health care were priced according to willingness to pay alone, doctors and hospitals could extract far more than the cost of providing services. The same can be said for many equally vital commodities. We do not price water at willingness to pay, for example, and neither should we do so for health care. Water can be purchased quite reasonably in grocery stores everywhere at prices roughly comparable to

---

[1] We thank our colleague Tom Kelly for providing this anecdote as we began to think about health care pricing.

its cost of provision because competition among suppliers acts as a self-correcting force.

Controlling prices may be the most important element requiring attention in the attempt to control inappropriate health care spending. According to standard neoclassical economics, pricing affects resource allocation and is the transmitter of economic efficiency. To perform their job, prices should reflect the value of the good or service and its cost of provision. The value individuals place on any item is determined by the price they are willing to pay. In functioning markets, however, consumers pay less than this amount, and the surplus they retain is a benefit of the efficiency created by the system. If willingness to pay for improvements in health (depending on wealth, life expectancy, and current health status) were the only determinant, the allocation of medical resources would be badly biased in favor of those who are wealthy, older, and in poor health.

Prices signal both demanders and suppliers. Numerous studies have used data from the RAND Health Insurance Experiment to examine this issue,[2] and the answer is always the same: when it matters, consumers of medical care do in fact consider price when making purchasing decisions. But with so many people receiving discounted or free care, third-party payers making payments to suppliers, and prices difficult to determine, can prices do their job? The issue examined in this chapter, therefore, is not whether prices matter, but whether prices have been allowed to work in medical markets and whether medical markets have been allowed to work on prices.

We do three things: First, we review how prices are currently established in the medical marketplace, using hospitals, physicians, and pharmaceuticals as our reference. Second, we summarize approaches to restrain medical prices at the industry level: competition, countervailing market power (negotiated pricing), and administered pricing. Third, we provide recommendations based on theory about how to "restrain" medical prices, in other words, cause them to reflect marginal cost of supply more closely.

10.2. Pricing

Chapter 4 explained that effective competition in markets is associated with four features: a standardized product (meaning that goods of different suppliers are close substitutes from the perspective of consumers), price-taking behavior by firms and households (buyers and sellers do not base their actions on how they might appreciably influence the price of the market),

---

[2] Newhouse et al., 1993.

contestable markets (there is free entry and exit of firms in response to profit incentives), and perfect information (consumers have access to information about the product, its price, quality, and availability, and firms are informed about potential profit opportunities).[3] In competitive markets, equilibrium price reflects the true marginal cost of provision. The most basic requirement of a market is the existence of a common price. Medical markets fail on even this first condition. They also fail on so many others that it is difficult to catalogue. Consider, however, the first requirement: prices must facilitate market function. One of the authors at the time of writing was advised to have an MRI (magnetic resonance image) made of his hip joint. The following account results:

> *Day 1.* To test how well prices performed in medical markets, I asked my doctor the price of the procedure he had just recommended. He said he had no idea. Perhaps his administrative officer could answer. After finishing my exam, I went to the main desk to ask. The administrative officer also had no clue what the price was but suggested that I should call the MRI radiology center that would perform the scan and ask them. I did so the next day by phone.

> *Day 2.* The radiology center did not know what the price was either. They suggested that I call the radiology center's billing office in another city, and I did so the same day. The radiology center's billing office did not know what my price would be but were able to tell me that their listed charge would be $1,548.00. I would have to call my Blue Cross/Blue Shield processing division to find the price that would actually be paid, and my share of it.

> *Day 3.* I called the billing office of Blue Cross/Blue Shield, which was able to verify that $1,548.00 was not the applicable price, but they could not tell me the rate that would apply. They would call me back within one to five days.

> *Day 5.* The insurance billing office reported that the price was $416.14. Without knowing the applicable co-insurance rate, however, they did not know what my price would be.

> *Several Weeks Later.* I ultimately received my Explanation of Benefits Form, which informed me that my payment was $41.61 because my applicable co-insurance rate at that time was 10 percent.

Medical markets do not conform to the characteristics of the competitive model. There is no uniform price, making price comparisons impossible, and charges paid do not gravitate naturally toward marginal cost. Market failure in medical markets, exemplified by the experience described, is the result of widespread availability of insurance coverage and how it has come

---

[3] See Grinols, 1994, pp. 265–268.

to be used. From the consumer's perspective, insurance is certainly important in reducing the financial consequences of an illness, providing access to medical services, and preventing uncontrolled health care spending. But the implication of insurance as currently practiced is the inability of prices to allocate resources efficiently.[4] Competition, the normal mechanism for controlling and eliminating economic rent (payments for resources that exceed opportunity cost), cannot function if even the most basic feature of a market – price information – is absent.

> Competition, the normal mechanism for controlling and eliminating economic rent, cannot function if even the most basic feature of a market – price information – is absent.

In discussions of health care, hospital services tend to dominate because of the relative importance of hospital spending – approximately one-third of total health care spending is hospital related in most developed nations. Combined with spending on physicians' services (20 percent of total spending) and pharmaceuticals (10 percent), these three components of spending are responsible for almost two-thirds of overall health care spending. Explaining pricing in these three sectors, therefore, goes a long way in furthering understanding of medical markets.

Hospital Services

The cost-based system of medical service pricing was a standard practice in hospital markets until the mid-1980s. Under cost-based pricing the amount paid to a provider is based not on billed charges, but on the cost of the service. The most common cost-based method starts with a per-diem cost calculation and bills each patient according to the length of the inpatient hospital stay. Added to the cost calculation is a factor based on the opportunity cost of capital. Thus, the method is often called "cost-plus."

At the time Blue Cross and Blue Shield became household names in health insurance in the 1950s, hospitals were paid on a per diem basis an amount determined by the average cost of a hospital day plus a small increment. Medicare and Medicaid adopted cost-plus pricing from their inception in 1965, solidifying this approach as the standard method of payment for hospital services for the next two decades. By 1983, however, the government abandoned cost-plus pricing in favor of a fixed payment per case determined by the principal diagnosis at the time of admission.

---

[4] Ellis and McGuire, 1990.

Procedures are bundled into approximately 600 diagnosis-related groups (DRGs) and given a relative weight that is intended to reflect resource use. The price of a DRG is the product of the relative weight and a "monetary conversion factor." The monetary conversion factor is set nationally, updated annually, and adjusted for geographic location and other factors that affect the cost of providing care. Private insurance went in an entirely different direction, negotiating prices based on discounts from billed charges. These two approaches exist simultaneously, each relying in part on the billed charges established by the individual hospital.

> By the early 1990s, while Medicare and Medicaid were both paying approximately 90 percent of hospital costs, private payers were being charged 130 percent of costs.

After an initial period of overly generous payments, hospitals saw their margins on Medicare services drop from an average of 13 percent in 1985 to −2.4 percent by 1991 as Medicare lowered payment rates.[5] To compensate for this shortfall, hospitals began increasing the payments demanded from privately insured patients faster than costs were rising, a practice commonly known as cost shifting.[6] By the early 1990s, while Medicare and Medicaid were both paying approximately 90 percent of hospital costs, private payers were being charged 130 percent of costs.

With the growth of managed care and the bargaining power it represented, hospital pricing moved from charged-based to negotiated rates determined by contract. The result was a shrinking percentage of patients paying billed charges and a growing gap between billed charges and the prices paid by most payers. The shrinking pool of self-paying patients is still an important revenue source, so hospitals continue to raise charged-based rates. The American Hospital Association (AHA) estimated that in 2004 gross patient revenues at U.S. community hospitals (based on billed charges) were *260 percent higher* than net patient revenues (based on actual receipts).[7] Hospitals keep track of the prices they charge for procedures through a file system referred to as the chargemaster. While the form and content of the chargemaster may vary from hospital to hospital, the goal of a successful pricing policy is to cover costs and generate a positive margin to guarantee flexibility for future operations. But when billed charges have little in common with the actual prices paid for services, prices cease to

---

[5] Tompkins, Altman, and Eilat, 2006.
[6] Hadley and Feder, 1985.
[7] American Hospital Association, 2005.

have meaning and fail to serve as market signals to guide resource allocation. Differential pricing charges those payers with the most purchasing power the lowest prices and forces self-payers, including the uninsured, to pay the inflated prices stipulated by the chargemaster. Had the one of us been uninsured when his MRI was needed, he would have been expected to pay $1,548 instead of the $416.14 actually allowed by the insurance contract. Further, it is almost certain that neither price reflects the true cost of providing the MRI.

In 2000 Congress mandated an ambulatory payment classification (APC) scheme where outpatient services are categorized into 600 distinct groupings that represent clinically similar procedures. In this arrangement, prices for outpatient services are determined by multiplying the relative weight of the APC (determined by resource use) by a monetary conversion factor.

As originally envisioned, the hospital-pricing mechanism was an elaborate system designed to subsidize the cost of medical care provided to the indigent poor by charging privately insured patients more than the cost of their care. This cost shifting was "taxation without representation," a de facto levy on those with private insurance. With insurers aggressively challenging the status quo, those with substantial market shares now wield enough power to turn hospitals effectively into classic price takers for covered patients.[8] Patients without a powerful payer backing them in the market are forced to pay significantly higher prices for services. If hospitals are to continue to provide free care to a significant portion of their constituency, they must continue to practice price discrimination; otherwise the system as we know it will have to change.

> Patients without a powerful payer backing them in the market are forced to pay significantly higher prices for services.

Physicians' Services

Prior to widespread health insurance coverage, most patients paid directly for physicians' services. Physicians, on the other hand, practiced a form of perfect monopoly, charging patients different prices based on their relative demand elasticities, using income as a proxy.

As insurance became more popular, payers' concern over rapidly increasing medical spending resulted in a pricing model that limited physicians'

---

[8] Tompkins, Altman, and Eilat, 2006.

fees to "usual, customary, and reasonable" (UCR) levels. Under UCR standards, physicians could charge the lesser of usual charge (defined as the median charged during the past year) or customary charge (defined by some percentile of the fees charged by other physicians in the area) and were allowed reasonable increases from year to year. It is easy to understand the inflationary nature of UCR.[9] If a physician's bill was paid without incident by the insurance company, next time the bill was higher. The process continued until a bill was rejected. With all physicians billing the same way, it was not long before the customary charge in the area rose, and the process continued. At no point was there a reason for a physician's usual price to be below the customary price charged by other physicians in the area. In fact, the incentive was to make sure that the charged fee was not the minimum in the formula.

As prices for physicians' services continued to escalate, payers looked for other ways to control spending. In 1986 the government took the lead and established a pricing model based on a relative value scale (RVS), a modified labor theory of value. Under RVS, physicians' fees were divided into three components: work effort, practice expense, and malpractice expense. The RVS provides an index of resources used to produce medical services and procedures across all specialty areas. RVS actually translates into a fee schedule by multiplying the relative values of over 7,000 procedure codes by a monetary conversion factor. The influence of managed care continued to grow during the 1990s and along with it so did the desire to influence the way physicians practiced medicine. Establishing a fee schedule does not control expenditures unless utilization controls are also initiated. Thus, efforts at cost control were directed at providers who determined the actual course of treatment. The managed-care approach attempted to shape physician behavior through the use of risk sharing arrangements. Instead of paying for disaggregated individual services (fee-for-service), capitation (fixed payment determined in advance) shifts the basis of payment to all services received during a specific period. Shifting risk to the provider discourages overuse of scarce resources without direct involvement in the physician-patient relationship.

Pharmaceuticals

The cost of producing a modern pharmaceutical drug is high, primarily because of the high expenditures on research and development.[10] Protection

---

[9] Frech and Ginsburg, 1975.
[10] DiMasi, Hansen, and Grabowski, 2003.

of intellectual property through the patent system establishes a mechanism whereby prices are significantly above marginal manufacturing costs. The results are quite predictable. In order to cover the fixed costs of research and development, pharmaceutical prices are high during the patent period. Once patents expire, generic competitors emerge offering chemically equivalent drugs at much lower prices.

But the prices that matter for most consumers are the prices they actually pay. Health plans including Medicare and Medicaid use benchmark prices based on average wholesale prices (AWPs) to determine how much pharmacies are paying for drugs. Many plans use pharmacy benefit managers (PBMs) to administer their plans, and PBMs often use the AWP of a drug adjusted by an estimated markup of up to 20 percent to determine how much they will pay pharmacies.

As wholesalers became more efficient, they began selling drugs to pharmacies at much smaller markups, as low as 2–3 percent, but a 20 percent markup was still commonly used as the wholesaler's drug acquisition cost (WAC). A shift to a 25 percent markup in 2002 brought the entire pricing system under attack.[11] Litigation in 2006 revealed that the survey used to determine the AWP of all drugs sold in the United States was based on information provided by a single national wholesaler and did not gather actual pricing data. The latest settlement proposed in June 2008 reduces the markup back to 20 percent of WAC on the 1,400 drugs identified in the original lawsuit; other drug pricing information in addition to AWP will also be published. PBMs and other payers are now searching for other ways to determine how much they will pay pharmacies for prescription drugs.

10.3. Restraining Prices in Theory

As the discussion thus far makes evident, medical pricing is not easy to describe. It is a combination of market-based and cost-based numbers, complicated by the addition of negotiated and administered elements. Some buyers, because of market power, exact significant discounts from published prices, whereas others pay in full billed charges that may or may not reflect the true cost of the care they received.

Rationalization of a market means removing its unreasonable features. We are

> Rationalization of a market means removing its unreasonable features.

[11] Martinez, 2006.

interested in eliminating unreasonable features from the health care market that prevent prices from reflecting cost of care. In theory, there are only three ways to restrain prices: competition (or its facsimile), countervailing market power, or administered prices.

Competition

The natural choice of a single provider of a service is to charge what the market will bear: buyers will be charged the maximum price they are willing to pay, on a-person-by-person basis if the monopoly supplier extracts as much as possible. If the buyer is covered by insurance, the monopoly response to buyers who pay fraction c of the product price is to raise the price for the initial quantity q_0 from p_0 to $\frac{1}{c}p_0$ and adjust to a different price and quantity only if profits are thereby raised further. A 20 percent co-insurance provision (common in most pharmaceutical policies), for example, results in a price that is *five times* higher at the original output level. This is discussed again in Chapter 11 in reference to pharmaceutical innovation. Appendix E provides a demonstration.

Competition is the best method known for keeping prices near marginal cost (MC). If a supplier charges a price significantly above MC (correctly calculated to include a normal operating profit margin), it creates an opportunity for competitors to take sales away by offering the product at a lower price and for buyers to search out lower prices. The advantage of competition is that it is a self-enforcing mechanism. Enough has already been written about how competition works that we do not need to elaborate here. Suffice it to say that in order for the process just described to prevent firms from charging prices greatly deviating from MC, conditions must be established for a (known) market price to exist.[12]

> The advantage of competition is that it is a self-enforcing mechanism.

---

[12] In competitive equilibrium, Profit $= q(p - AC)$ where $p = MC \geq AC$; q is quantity, p is price, MC is marginal cost, and AC is average cost. The economic meaning of average cost includes provision for normal return on investment. For example, presume that physicians incurred medical school debt and that competitive prices thereafter were too low to allow them to repay such debt. Ultimately, in that case no physicians would incur such debt (we said none could pay it off!) and the supply of physicians would fall to zero. In this environment, prices for physician services would rise, allowing some or all to incur debt that they *could* pay off, and a different equilibirum would be attained wherein competitive prices, repayment of medical school debt, and the number of practicing physicians were in balance.

As noted, medical care prices are often closely guarded, and difficult to determine. In one sense, there are too many prices; incredibly, there may be dozens of prices for every procedure imaginable – different prices for different payers. When a provider claims not to know a price, there is no reason to think otherwise. There may be too many to remember.

Countervailing Market Power

If competition (or an approximation of it) is not able to function, there are only two other ways to control prices. The first is through countervailing market power. Most medical care prices are negotiated between representatives of consumer groups and representatives of provider groups. In many countries, the government or a quasi-governmental organization represents payer groups and a medical association represents providers. In the United States, payer groups are employers, insurance companies, or an appropriate government agency, such as Medicare or Medicaid. Providers negotiate with practice groups, hospitals, and retail pharmacies. Price differences across geographic regions are reflective of competitive differences and typically not of productivity differences. Prices set by contract between insurer and provider depend on the relative bargaining strength of the two negotiating parties. Collective bargaining is possible when both buyers and sellers have similar degrees of market power. The theory used to describe this situation is the model of bilateral monopoly, a situation where a single buyer is seeking a product provided by a single seller. The negotiated outcome will result in a price somewhere between the monopoly price and the provider's reservation price, the lowest price acceptable to a willing provider that still covers marginal costs. As long as the relative bargaining positions of the two sides are similar, society stands to benefit. If one party dominates the negotiations, access problems arise, manifested by reductions in quality and quantity of services provided (Anderson, Reinhardt, Hussey, and Petrosyan, 2003).

Administered Pricing

Attempts to set administered prices based on cost make sense only under very restricted conditions. Providers must behave as neoclassical profit maximizers in perfectly competitive markets, engaging in marginal cost pricing. But in reality, medical markets are rarely perfectly competitive and prices are routinely set above marginal cost. The consequence is predictable: rent-seeking behavior by providers who control utilization at the margin.

Imperfect agency results in inefficient consumption of scarce medical resources.[13]

Absent incentives promoting the efficient use of resources, providers tend to overinvest in measurable inputs, such as technology and workers. Competition manifests itself in a technology explosion rather than a race for value creation. Attempts to cut costs *ex ante* result in reducing the budget and in turn profitability. With no incentives to use resources efficiently, the cost-based system is inherently inflationary and unsustainable. The failure of cost-based pricing paved the way for the growth of regulated pricing practices, negotiated pricing, and administered pricing.

Gardiner Means was the first economist to suggest that some prices are not set by the normal market adjustment mechanism.[14] Instead of regular price adjustments due to changing market conditions, he claimed that some prices are set by administrative fiat and remain at that level despite changes in supply and demand. In the context of medical care markets, administered prices represent rate-setting methods that ignore cost or market conditions. This price-setting behavior is largely due to market power that results from licensing, patents, reputation, or government regulation. Price differentials exist among providers largely because medical services are not easily resalable, making arbitrage incapable of eliminating price dispersion.

Much of this price setting behavior is the result of the fee schedules (DRGs and RVS) that dominate the hospital and physician services markets in the United States. Government-administered prices turn providers into price takers. Instead of adjusting prices to changing market conditions, physicians, for example, adjust the quantity of services provided by deciding how many Medicare and Medicaid patients to treat in their private practices. Hospitals, too, respond to favorable reimbursement rates by dedicating scarce resources to lucrative areas, building specialty hospitals for pediatrics, cardiology, and orthopedics. Administered prices represent a source of inefficiency in medical markets. Advances in productivity that result in cost savings are rarely translated into price decreases. When dealing with fixed-budget systems, such as Medicare and Medicaid, providers understand that voluntary price decreases in response to cost savings in one area will jeopardize their ability to provide care in less profitable areas when Congress inevitably initiates across-the-board price cuts to balance the budget.

---

[13] Wedig, 1993.
[14] Means, 1972.

10.4. Rationalization Suggestions

Controlling prices in health care requires a proper incentive structure through re-establishing *market* prices and the access to them that consumers and suppliers need to make cost-conscious decisions. Michael Porter and Elizabeth Olmsted Teisberg established price information as an essential element in creating value-based competition in health care.[15] We live in an information age and an age when travel for medical purposes is easier than ever. Most Americans live in metropolitan areas where meaningful competition is possible if given a chance. Some economists, cognizant of the dysfunctional nature of the current health care markets, conclude that because competition works differently in health care, it should be an administered sector. We argue that competition has not yet been tried. Rather than advocating radical and potentially destructive revamping of health care, wisdom suggests that a few key changes be adopted to allow competition to be tried first. Radical departures are always available, but we do not think they will ever be needed if the following simple changes, suggested by theory, are adopted.

Most Favored Customer Pricing. The term "most favored nation" treatment means that any member of the World Trade Organization (WTO) receives from another member the same treatment of its trade that the member accords the most favored of its trade partners. What is done for one is done for all. This simple principle is the bedrock of the General Agreement on Tariffs and Trade, established in 1947, and adopted by the WTO. In medical markets, a most favored customer clause should be established by law: suppliers can charge whatever price they choose, but they must, by law, charge the same price to all buyers.

Price Transparency. Second, as a condition to practice medicine, suppliers must post their prices. Government can serve a facilitating role by creating a Web-based clearinghouse where posted prices can be easily accessed. Unlike lawyers, who do not bill for every type of service they perform, but bill by the hour (and thus are ethically prevented from billing for more time in a year than can be worked), the medical sector currently charges by procedure. We believe this will change as competition is allowed to function but do not feel it is advisable nor needed for government to do more than establish guidelines that mean that whatever information is posted can be compared, like with like, to the postings of other competitors in the health care market. As a start, the prices of services represented by the most frequently used procedure codes, say

---

[15] Porter and Teisberg, 2004, p. 123.

the top 25 for each provider, could be made available on the provider's
Web site or at its office. In some cases the price for an episode of care
might be posted, much along the lines of a hospital's posting its DRG price.
Clearly, if providers do not compete on price, they do not compete on
quality either.

What about Quality Differences? We have noted that prices in health
care today reflect a strange mix of history, institutional inertia, market
forces, and illogic. For example, hospital care is billed by service diagnosis
related group. However, a given DRG may represent different levels of
severity, co-morbidity influences, need for different treatment resources,
and regional variations in the cost of inputs. How should the health plan
deal with these?

The "plan" should not. Instead, competition will lead providers to
state prices in forms that serve their needs best; inferior forms of pricing will be driven from the market and superior ones take their place.
Since quality matters to demand, suppliers will devise ways to charge
appropriately for the higher cost of resources that are needed to provide it and to inform customers of what they are getting. Lawyers do
not routinely charge by "diagnosis-related group" (product type), but
by the hours of time expended on the client's behalf. Higher-quality
lawyers are more sought after and are paid more for their time. It
would be foolish to try to predict for all time the exact form that prices
should take to reflect quality, co-morbidities, difficulty of case, effort
needed, physician reputation, and so on. The market handles difficult
issues of quality in other applications. It should be allowed to do so
again.

In addition to price, we can envision other data's being made available
(most is known to insurers now) such as how many procedures of a given
type the supplier performs each year. This information alone, along with
price, reveals a great deal to buyers. Other data might include disease-
specific outcomes data by provider (possibly appropriately adjusted for
severity of illness).

Vickrey Auctions. An option that might be useful in selected cases to help
establish a uniform market price artificially would be to allow providers
to participate in a Vickrey-type auction to create a rank-ordering of bids
within a local market area. For example, providers of a given classification
(e.g., all anesthesiologists or pathologists) might convert to billing on a per-
hour basis. (Were hospitals bidding on daily room charges, there is already

a common unit, the length of stay.)[16] Each year providers would submit a sealed bid of the price at which they would supply an hour of labor. Market size (known demand for hours of service of a given type) would be combined with the rank-ordered bids to determine an equilibrium price, and hence maximum acceptable offer price. A provider whose offer is below this price would provide service and be paid the "equilibrium price." A provider whose offer is above this price has the choice of not offering service or offering service at the price set by the auction less a penalty. For example, those bidding too high could be required for the following year to set prices at some established percentage discount below the established equilibrium price. A penalty of some form is needed as a bidding incentive.

The purpose of Vickrey-type arrangements is to induce truthful bidding in establishing a valid market price. For example, there is no winner's curse in a Vickrey auction (the original setting) because the winner pays not his or her bid, but the next highest bid, in buying the auctioned item. The penalty for bidding too low is that the bidder does not win the item. The penalty for bidding too high is that the item will have to be bought at the next highest bid. Thus the bidder has an incentive not to bid above or below his or her true value for the object. In the case of the medical version auction described, there are incentives not to bid too high (you suffer a penalty) or to bid too low (you may be required to provide service at the bid rate). No auction system is perfect, but there are ways to provide artificial aid to establishing a market in the rare cases where intervention might be needed.

10.5. Conclusions

Adopting these suggested changes to the pricing mechanism (most favored customer pricing and price transparency) is a logical, virtually mandatory, first step in rationalizing the health care market. Current pricing policies charge the uninsured the highest prices and the fully insured the lowest. The result of market pricing would be that some people would pay higher prices (for example, those who are currently fully insured) and others would pay lower prices (those currently uninsured). While any price change must favor some and disfavor others relative to the status quo, two observations are relevant – everyone in the new regime has insurance (and is able to afford it), plus the described change in pricing would be considered fair by most observers.

---

[16] Alternatively, prices based on an RVS would require physicians to submit bids on their personal monetary conversion factor. Hospitals would do likewise to price their DRGs.

Issues such as patient co-morbidities, disease severity, and service quality are undoubtedly important factors in setting prices. It is for this reason that price setting will be left up to market forces and competition. Providers will charge what they want to charge. We require only that they charge everyone the same price and that everyone know what those prices are.

There is no sound reason for prices charged to purchasers to vary across insurance companies or among insured, uninsured, and self-insured patients.[17] In contrast, there are reasons why establishing a market price is essential to establishing a market and market competition.

Most favored customer pricing and price transparency (e.g., Internet posting) would result in uniform pricing, improve the bargaining process where countervailing market power restrains prices, allow consumers to make price comparisons across providers including travel for medical reasons, and generally enhance the forces of competition – important steps toward rationalizing the market.

Given the geographic dispersion and cultural diversity of a country the size of the United States, providers should be given the opportunity to set their own prices, however. It is impossible to reflect the diversity of tastes for medical services in a single plan with administered prices.

Within the more limited context of the current prospective payment system, each hospital should be allowed to set its own monetary conversion factor. Patients would know the relative price of bundled services as defined by every DRG and APC. A single number for inpatient services and another for outpatient services would be the basis of a national fee schedule for all hospital services.[18] Physicians could be given the same opportunity to set their own monetary conversion factor within the Medicare RVS with similar results.

---

[17] Volume discounts would appear to be an exception. However, to the extent that volume discounts reflect true cost advantages, all purchasers should be able to get the same volume discounts.

[18] Reinhardt, 2006.

ELEVEN

Inducing Innovation

If we continue on our current path of trying harder and harder to shift the costs of developing new medicines to someone else, rather than paying our fair share, everyone's effort to get a free ride on new drugs will grind the development of new drugs to a halt.

Mark McClellan, Center for Medicare and Medicaid Services Commissioner, 2003

Summary: *Monopolies whose buyers pay fraction c of the product cost respond by raising their price for the initial quantity q_0 from p_0 to $\frac{1}{c} p_0$ and adjust to a different price and quantity only if profits are thereby raised further. A prescription plan that includes a 20 percent co-payment provision thus magnifies the drug patent holder's profits more than a fivefold increase in price at the original output would.*

Pharmaceutical patents are anachronistic holdovers from an era in which modern economic understanding and tax tools were unavailable. Superior mechanisms lie somewhere between a first-best pricing solution for the entire economy at one extreme and the current arrangements at the other. We discuss the economics of suggested alternatives and suggest that the intertemporal bounty is the best way to meet the multiple objectives of immediate distribution at marginal cost pricing of recently-innovated patented drugs and easily administered efficient inducement to continued innovation. The intertemporal bounty prevents the expansion of monopoly power resulting from co-pay or co-insurance provisions common to modern prescription drug plans.

11.1. Introduction

The pharmaceutical industry is characterized by large sunk costs, high fixed costs, low variable costs, segmentable markets (where sellers can distinguish consumer types and charge different prices), and strong patent protection for drug discoveries. As the likelihood of recovering research expenditures on a marketable drug is less than one in three, pharmaceutical companies maintain that they must be allowed to charge high monopoly prices to support continued innovation and an uninterrupted flow of new products.[1]

Any assessment of the pharmaceutical industry must consider the undesirable exercise of market power, the best way to reward useful innovators while spreading the benefits of their inventions quickly and widely as possible, and the size of the reward paid to the innovator. Those who believe that these problems have been solved in the current system are mistaken in their confidence. The patent system as an institution does not encourage the optimal level of innovation in a wide range of industries, including biotechnology,[2] and may even deter research and development in pharmaceuticals.[3] It impedes the delivery of health care services,[4] and needs to be modified.[5]

Patents lead to monopoly pricing with its familiar deadweight loss (unrealized social benefits) due to output levels that fall short of optimal.[6] Rewards for innovation, such as patents, that fall short of full social surplus (see Section 11.3) present a second familiar shortcoming.

Rewarding innovation involves, among other things, knowing the social surplus associated with an invention. Information on social surplus is not provided by the monopoly profits of the seller if patent rights are granted, or other immediate price and quantity observations if they are not. Most inventions are used for more than one period, so total social surplus is a stream of changing surpluses into the indefinite future, and thus depends on the timing of the invention and introduction of future substitute and competing products.

The main contribution of this chapter is to address these two issues (relating market power and the best way to reward innovators) with the intervention principle: the rule that a market intervention is efficient when targeted directly at the desired activity to be influenced.[7] We show that a program where new drugs are patented, immediately freely placed into the

---

[1] Grabowski, Vernon, and DiMasi, 2002; DiMasi, Hansen, and Grabowski, 2003.
[2] Burk and Lemley, 2003.
[3] Heller and Eisenberg, 1998.
[4] Andrews, 2002.
[5] Rai, 2003.
[6] A monopoly is defined as a good for which there is a single seller and for which there are no close substitutes. Technically, therefore, patents do not grant monopoly power per se because while patented drugs can legally be sold only by the patent holder, drugs compete with therapeutic substitutes, as well as substitutes from other types of medical care. Patents grant market power to the holder that is subject to the usual market qualifications.
[7] Grinols, 2006.

public domain, and inventors rewarded on the basis of an intertemporal bounty (ongoing payment) that is tied to market sales, is superior to traditional patents and many patent alternatives that require auctions or other devices to estimate future surplus values. Section 11.2 reviews the literature on policies toward research and development, emphasizing the static and dynamic issues. Section 11.3 is devoted to discussing practical application of, and objections to, the intertemporal bounty that is implied by the intervention principle.

11.2. Policies toward Research and Development (R&D)

Statutes tracing back to seventeenth-century Europe rewarded innovation by granting special monopoly rights. The U.S. system of patents likewise emerged as colonists in the New World recognized that rewarding individual innovators would benefit society as a whole.

Spence[8] identifies three market failures associated with large investments in R&D. First, revenues understate full social surplus, both in the aggregate and at the margin (details provided in Section 11.3). Thus there is no *a priori* reason to think that unaided market outcomes will be optimal in any sense. Secondly, because R&D is often associated with significant fixed costs (certainly true in the case of pharmaceuticals), imperfect competition and its consequences are likely to characterize the industry. Thirdly, substantial investment in R&D frequently is associated with an appropriability problem (inability to realize full benefits for the innovator); thereby reducing the firm's incentive to conduct R&D. Solving the R&D incentive problem by creating a monopoly problem merely trades one inefficiency for another.

Patents and Their Alternatives

Modern fiscal tools allow government policymakers to select more efficient public finance approaches than was true until recently. At the same time, we have broader insurance coverage of prescription drugs today that, when combined with patents, expands the monopoly power exerted by pharmaceutical companies by making consumers less price sensitive. We also enjoy a better understanding of social efficiency as it relates to the legal and institutional framework governing R&D activity. An efficient tax system

---

[8] Spence, 1984.

almost certainly would not involve creating short-lived monopolies for new inventions.[9]

The economic rationale for patents is based on the understanding that the primary product of R&D, scientific knowledge, has many of the attributes of a public good.[10] Patents create monopoly price distortions, but this defect was originally overshadowed by the absence of a need to rely on the tax system for revenues to reward inventors. On the negative side, patents create price and distribution distortions that are particularly burdensome when applied to prescription drugs. Patents also reward inventors with less than the social value of their innovations because monopoly advantages last for a limited number of years and monopoly profits are smaller than social benefits.

Once a product is produced, pharmaceutical knowledge is frequently easily reverse engineered (analyzing a drug to discover its structure). This distorts research incentives and encourages inefficient efforts by other firms to create copycat inventions in pursuit of the monopoly rents (economic profit that exceeds the normal return on an investment in a competitive market). Knowledge spillovers resulting in imperfect appropriability diminish incentives for R&D.[11]

It is unlikely that the patent system as it is traditionally envisioned can be fine-tuned to improve social welfare.[12] The number of instruments available to policymakers limits the scope of patent law to achieve the desired objectives. In addition to the length of the patent life (20 years for pharmaceuticals), policy is constrained by the breadth of protection,

---

[9]   Baumol and Bradford, 1970, provide a discussion of utility trade-offs in a tax setting where lump sum taxes are not available. The optimal tax literature goes back to the seminal work by Frank Ramsey, 1927, who asked how to raise a given amount of revenue at least loss in utility to the economic system by taxing different uses of income. The resulting system of market price plus associated tax is referred to as the "Ramsey pricing" solution. Modern treatments include income taxation, identifying circumstances in which public goods can be financed with small or no increase in distortion costs to the system. See footnote 27 in this chapter. The intervention principle asks how to induce adjustment in some action for the least loss in utility; in this chapter, the action is innovation of patentable drugs followed by widespread dissemination. The three questions are related because innovation has public good aspects, an intertemporal bounty of the type described here satisfies the intervention principle, and taxes are needed to finance the bounties paid.

[10] Levin, 1986; Waterson, 1990.

[11] The term "knowledge spillovers" refers to the situation where the benefits derived from one party's creation of knowledge are used without compensation by a second party. In many cases knowledge can be protected from unwanted dissemination, but the full protection of trade secrets is not accomplished in all cases, even with patents and other legal intellectual property protections in place.

[12] Scotchmer, 1991.

which connects to the likelihood that second-generation technology will infringe on the patent. Whether the patent is awarded to the first to invent (U.S./Canada priority rule) or to the first to apply (rest of the world), it remains a limited instrument.[13]

Government subsidized research has been suggested as one alternative to patents. This addresses the problem of monopoly, but has the overwhelming disadvantage that the government is targeting *inputs* with the subsidies rather than *outputs*. This creates an incentive for research, but not necessarily for socially desirable research. Also, government may not be able to conceive of some inventions in advance and may not know the expected benefits and costs of research.

Prizes for inventions have been tried with success in cases where the government or other prize-granting body can specify in advance what it wants. In many cases, however, the government does not know in advance what to support and cannot envision the direction that research should take.

Kremer[14] suggested patent buyouts via auction as a way to eliminate monopoly patent rents. A related process is buyouts through eminent domain, where judges would determine buyout value.[15] An auction has a number of advantages, including the advantage of determining value through a market mechanism. Removing monopoly rents that result from awarding a patent, as auctions do, eliminates a distorting incentive for pharmaceutical firms to expend efforts to find new uses for under-patent drugs rather than developing new uses for out-of-patent drugs.

Auctions have the disadvantage that to maintain auction feasibility randomly selected patents would be sold to the highest bidder. In these cases the monopoly inefficiencies remain. Auctions are also potentially vulnerable to collusion, although it is unclear to what degree this would be a problem in practice. Auctions have the potential to create bidding problems if inventors have private information or hold special positions in the market such as being the lowest cost producer and can decide to retain or sell their patents. Ideally, all patents should enter the public domain and the inventor should be in the same position as other users once the product is invented. The inventor would hold a special position only as regards payment for the invention.

The use of a reward system where innovators receive direct payment for their discoveries has also received a degree of attention in the literature.

[13] Grabowski and Vernon, 1986.
[14] Kremer, 1998.
[15] Guell and Fischbaum, 1995.

Polanvyi[16] informally introduced the concept in 1943, although it took 40 years before Wright[17] developed a formal model of innovation showing that, under appropriate circumstances, rewards were superior to patents. Shavell and van Ypersele[18] formalized the superiority of an optional reward system over patents.

Implications of the Intervention Principle

The approach that we take in this chapter is to address the issue of the most appropriate way to reward innovation consistent with the intervention principle. According to the intervention principle, the most efficient way to accomplish a desired objective is to identify the activity to be influenced and apply a tax or subsidy directly to that activity at the minimal level needed to accomplish the objective. Patenting prescription drugs violates this principle, as do subsidies to research, and most other alternatives. In the case of prescription drugs, the desired social objectives are that research and development create useful new drugs that are then patentable (as a method of certification of the product), followed by their dissemination as quickly and widely as possible. The latter requires marginal cost pricing (setting the selling price at the cost of producing the unit sold, plus standard business markup for economic profit) or, if there are increasing returns to scale in production, as large a scale as possible until those returns are exhausted. The application of the intervention principle suggests that the government announce a reward that will be paid on the sales of newly invented and patented drugs that are licensed without restraint and sold. The reward will be a specified subsidy on freely (competitively) licensed drugs based on all sales, whether by the innovating firm or by others.

Margins at which the reward could be adjusted include the specified rate and the number of years (which could be indefinite) for which the payment applies. Because payment is based on past sales, there is no need to foresee at one moment the full future and its present discounted value as there would be if an eminent domain action, patent buyout, or subsidy to research were to be employed.[19] No monopoly rights are issued, so market equilibrium mimics competitive results with price equal to marginal cost at socially optimal output levels.

---

[16] Polanvyi, 1943.
[17] Wright, 1983.
[18] Shavell and van Ypersele, 2001.
[19] The two-part pricing contract envisioned by Lakdawalla and Sood, 2005, leads to perfect innovation and utilization but requires accurate *ex ante* estimation of all future benefits.

11.3. The Intertemporal Bounty

The intertemporal bounty fulfills the threefold objectives assigned to the intervention principle: it creates incentives that reward innovation, patentability, and sales. For continuing innovation at the socially desired level, bounty payments should reflect both the timing and the size of the social value created by the invention through time. One-time fixed prizes, subsidized research, buyouts via eminent domain or auction, as well as static bounties all suffer from the need to estimate an imperfectly known collection of future magnitudes, and, in the case of auctions, leave monopoly losses in place for some auctions.

Details

Figure 11.1 displays a standard demand diagram measuring quantity demanded on the horizontal axis and price on the vertical axis. Areas A, B, and C under the demand curve sum to the full social surplus of the drug when quantity q_0 is supplied at marginal cost p_0. Areas D and E combine to equal total revenue from sales. The figure represents a single time period. A similar diagram applies for succeeding time periods into the future. Because the profit maximizing monopolist produces quantity q_1 and charges price p_1, monopoly rights provide profit equal to area B to the patent holder for a limited number of years, clearly an understatement of the true value of full social surplus, the true value of a new innovation.[20]

Under monopoly pricing the social surplus shrinks to area A, and society loses the benefits of area C, the unrealized social value that potentially could accrue to users of the drug, but in the patent regime goes neither to the manufacturer nor to the public. For example, at quantity q_1 consider the effect of supplying one more prescription: the user would be willing to pay price p_1, which exceeds the marginal cost of providing the additional product. The difference is a social benefit; the sum of all such is area C. An auction uses *ex ante* market information and projections by bidders of area B over future periods to estimate area $(A + B + C)$ over such periods. Note that unless the innovated product has been marketed, all such values are prospective, and estimates of values far distant into the future become more difficult to make

---

[20] It is important to keep in mind that area B profits refer to what economists call economic profits. These are profits above and beyond the usual or standard rate of business profit. As such, economic profits could be set to zero (as they should in a first-best world) and not harm the ability of the manufacturer in question to continue operations. Full social surplus, area $A + B + C$ should accrue to someone in society.

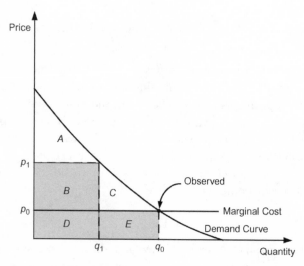

Figure 11.1. Product Social Values. Standard demand curve illustrating the relationship between quantity demanded and price. Social value of innovation and willingnness to pay are shown in areas *A–E*. See Section 11.3.

because of changing market conditions, such as unforeseen creation of replacement drugs and changing needs of the public. However, matching the timing of payments to the timing of social benefits removes the intertemporal problem. In the case of an intertemporal bounty, the price-quantity pairs (p_0, q_0) are observed through time. They do not need to be predicted for future periods.[21] A program that provides \$0.30 in bounty for every dollar in sales, for example, could be evaluated periodically to see if the bounty reflected the average value of social surplus generated by innovations over time. Adjustments could be made as desired.

In the simplest implementation, the bounty could represent an industry average over all prescription drugs, similar to the compulsory-licensing arrangement in the music industry.[22] Based on a simulation using industry information for 2004, a bounty of 10 percent of sales would be adequate

---

[21] There are good ways to identify $(A + B + C)$. Kremer, 1998, used U.S. Current Population Survey household income data to conclude that the social value of new pharmaceuticals, area $(A + B + C)$, is 2.7 times the profits that would be achieved by a monopolist, area B, and the deadweight loss, area C, is 25 percent of the sum of profits and consumer surplus (area $A + B$). Others (Danzon, 1997) have used information about the marginal cost of manufacturing combined with estimates of demand elasticity.

[22] We thank Christopher Bradstreet for suggesting this connection. For references see Krasilovsky and Shemel, 2003, Passman, 2000.

to generate payments exceeding the current domestic R&D spending by U.S. firms of $29.6 billion.[23] A bounty of 28 cents per dollar of sales would transfer full social surplus (area $A + B + C = \$92b$) to innovating firms.[24] It is not possible to state with great confidence the precise consequences of bounty incentives of this size (one of the advantages of the intertemporal bounty is its ability to be adjusted) but it is likely to result in greater innovation than at present.

The cost of innovating a new drug is $909 million (year 2005 values),[25] implying that a bounty between 10 and 28 cents per sales dollar would finance 32–100 new drugs per year. Actual approvals per year by the FDA between 1995 and 2005 varied between 17 and 53 (average 30). However, in recent years, the cost per new introduction appears to be rising (declining returns to R&D resources), so the figure of 100 is probably optimistic. If more product-specific detail is possible based on pre-announced procedures (for example, firms might be allowed to generate test marketing data that demonstrate the shape and elevation of the demand curve), the bounty could be made more product-specific. The more popular the drug among consumers (i.e., the more valuable the drug can be demonstrated to be to society) the more money the innovator would make.[26]

---

[23] Congressional Budget Office, 2006, p. 7, reports that 2003 domestic spending for R&D by U.S. firms was $29.6 billion in 2005 dollars.

[24] Combining estimates from Kremer, 1998 (see footnote 21), profit as a fraction of industry sales of 0.18, and Centers for Medicare and Medicaid Services (CMS) information on U.S. prescription drug expenditures in 2004 of $189.7 billion is sufficient to solve for area $(A + B + C)$, $92.2 billion, and area $(D + E)$, $323.6 billion, of which unrealized social surplus, area C, is $18.4 billion, and industry profit, area B, is $34.1 billion. If these numbers are representative of steady state, a bounty per sales dollar of $0.092 would generate $29.6 billion, equal to the current domestic R&D spending by U.S. firms (footnote 23), and setting the bounty at $0.285 per sales dollar would transfer full social surplus (area $A + B + C$) to innovating firms.

Applying the same analysis to Pfizer (22 percent profit in 2004), Lipitor sales of $7.1 billion annually implies induced sales of $11.5 billion, a rise in social surplus of $2.405 billion, and a bounty payment of $3.28 billion to Pfizer. This is less than Lipitor actually earns, of course, because it is Pfizer's most successful drug and 22 percent is Pfizer's average profit rate on all sales.

[25] Congressional Budget Office, 2006, p. 19; $909 million in year 2000 values is $802 million.

[26] Implementation issues include other questions such as how to treat the bounty paid on faulty or recalled drugs such as Vioxx. In the present patent system, already-earned patent profits are not rescinded. The relevant principle is that the chosen arrangements should be best suited to induce creation and dissemination of non-faulty drugs. If negligence or lack of due diligence is the cause of recalled drugs, then the bounty paid to time of recall should be returned. If recall is more often the result of error that prior effort is unlikely to be effective in avoiding and the recall itself costly, then the intertemporal bounty should be implemented more along the lines of the current patent system: bounty paid to time of recall is retained by the firm. Other implementation details can be similarly evaluated.

The issues just discussed involve the need to estimate social value over time, for which the intertemporal bounty has advantages, and the need to replace an imperfect system of patents that creates deadweight loss. Improvements are possible because monopoly is replaced by an intervention that is supported by more efficient taxes that have lower social cost.[27]

Questions

Any proposal to replace patents will likely be viewed with apprehension by those accustomed to current arrangements, and especially by those who have learned how to prosper under them. Two points are worth considering.

First, replacing patents can be a Pareto-improving change as we have described, meaning that every stakeholder receives a positive increment of gain. It is feasible to distribute from a larger pool of social benefits so that innovators are rewarded more generously than now while consumers have lower-priced access to a greater range of drugs compared with a patent regime. Second, the relevant incentives themselves provide guidance about many of the implementation choices and details. For example, should the new system be phased in or introduced immediately? Should the change be mandatory or optional? Should existing drugs be grandfathered (i.e., exempted) or should the changes apply to all drugs equally?

Because the arrangements we care about are forward-looking, the new system can and should be implemented immediately. Phasing in is also an acceptable option, but postpones reaping any potential gains. Allowing time for learning and education about the new process is presumably the compensating benefit of a phased approach. Even if the reward system were optional, innovators would soon realize its superiority. With respect to grandfathering existing patented drugs, because existing innovation is a sunk cost, only static considerations are relevant for this decision: grandfathering causes no loss compared to the status quo and honors expectations

---

[27] When taxes are not an issue, rewards to innovators in the form of intertemporal bounties are unambiguously superior to intellectual property rights because government uses *ex post* sales-related observations and therefore has information about demand at least as good as the *ex ante* information of innovators. (See Shavell and van Ypersele, 2001, pp. 542, 544–545.) When funds for the bounty must be raised by taxation, incentives for production, investment, and innovation can be distorted, for example. However, in this case, under standard simplifying assumptions, the bounty can be financed in a manner that results in no additional distortion. The *ex ante* benefits of drug innovation are of equal value to everyone so the uniform case described by Kaplow, 1996, p. 516, is most relevant.

of innovators under patents. For these reasons it is probably preferred. Not grandfathering allows area C in Figure 11.1 to be gained for the grandfathered drugs in question, but at the same time alters the pattern of social gains reaped and introduces the transactions costs of administration.

Credibility and time-consistency are obviously concerns. The patent system, for all its faults, leaves future rewards largely in the hands of the innovator. The patent system is also subject to time inconsistencies (anticipated court protections today may be re-interpreted or no longer in the public's interest to provide in the future) but patent law has tended to be enforced with reasonably predictable intensity through time.[28] In the present case, simplicity is a virtue. Only a single number (the bounty paid per sales dollar) need be defined. A single number can be credibly announced, grandfathered when needed, and adhered to. The size of the ultimate payment is then largely in the hands of the producer based on *ex post* market sales. However, if government commitments to the premium rate cannot be trusted, then the system breaks down.

Supporting pharmaceutical R&D involves incentives that reach beyond the borders of a single country. Global joint cost, i.e. cost that remains the same regardless of the number of worldwide consumers that benefit or their location, creates a cost allocation problem. R&D expenditures are quasi-fixed,[29] no matter how many consumers or how many countries receive access to the drug. In most countries, drug spending is reimbursed through government-run programs at regulated prices and regulators tend to focus on country-specific costs in setting prices. The challenge in implementing a bounty program is determining how much each country should contribute to the innovator for use of the patented drug. Equitable cost sharing across countries should be aimed at estimating the value of the drug to residents of each country. Much of the reason why non-innovating countries have an incentive to "cheat" on current patents is that innovating firms are trying to enforce prices higher than marginal cost which appear to "rip off" the buyers. With an intertemporal bounty the "rip-off" effect disappears. That is, the bounty paid in the United States should reflect the benefits accruing to U.S. citizens only and likewise in other countries. If other countries participate, then it creates an incentive for U.S. innovators to include their interests in their innovating decisions.

---

[28] Patent law is subject to variability and vagaries, too, based on how firmly patent rights are enforced by the courts, and how much courts change their interpretations of law.

[29] Fixed costs are costs for fixed inputs that must be paid by the firm independently of output level. Quasi-fixed costs are fixed costs for positive levels of output, but equal zero if zero output is selected by the firm.

If all countries, by treaty or other agreement, provide payments that reflect the value of drugs to their citizens, there is no unaccounted spillover of externalities to other countries. The innovating country (e.g. the United States) and the non-innovator are in positions similar to that of any creator and user of a product that has spillover benefits. The inefficiency from the rest of the world's perspective is that U.S. innovators will take no account of the benefits the rest of the world receives from U.S. innovation and therefore innovate too little or focus innovation on U.S. priorities, and that the U.S. firms will sell drugs at high patent prices. However, the incentives under the proposed bounty program are perfectly aligned to the proposed solution. The rest of the world provides a payment (in this case a bounty tied to sales of a drug in their market) in an amount that reflects the size of those benefits. The incentive to do so is the same incentive that the United States has to adopt the improved system. If a foreign country refuses to participate, the firm would retain the rights to the innovated drug in that country and exercise its monopoly rights to establish a mutually agreed upon price. The country pays higher prices for its drugs compared to marginal cost pricing and risks reduced access to drugs innovated with its needs in mind. In fact, Grinols and Lin[30] show that there are strong incentives for non-developer countries to cooperate with innovating regions of the world for exactly these reasons. Shifting from a patent regime to an intertemporal bounty therefore contains within it the incentives for countries to cooperate, and the "penalties" if they do not. The global solution requiring least oversight is to allow the innovator to charge market prices in each country.

The resulting bounty paid by each country in return for free licensing would reflect its social surplus.

Undoubtedly this will challenge, in a beneficial way, the regulatory culture of many national health systems and getting them to participate will be a departure from business as usual. If countries nevertheless steal intellectual property and/or free ride on the innovation of others, there will be lamentable loss in potential world benefits. Even so, the intertemporal bounty would continue to create net social benefits relative to patents when considering internal, U.S.-only implications and remains a superior mechanism.

Re-importation ceases to be a problem for the host (innovating country) because production at home is at marginal cost and therefore lower-priced than in the nonparticipating country. The flow of drugs in the reverse direction is controlled by the seller who, as noted, exercises monopoly rights and

[30] Grinols and Lin, 2006.

so sells only if he deems it worthwhile. However, no system is perfect and incentives to smuggle (an illegal activity) will continue to exist as they do now. Countries that wish to make the drug available at marginal cost have a means to cooperatively share in the cost of developing innovative drugs that provide value to their residents by establishing and paying the appropriate bounty.

11.4. Conclusion

The social objective is to induce the creation of new products that are then patented and competitively sold. The efficient outcome involves the competitive sale of patented products following what is the first best inducement to R&D, a subsidy to invention funded by lump sum taxes.

Presuming lump sum taxes are infeasible, second best involves a subsidy to invention financed by optimal taxes and Ramsey pricing. Economy-wide implementation of Ramsey pricing is also infeasible. Thus, among feasible alternatives the intertemporal bounty meets the social objective most efficiently. It relieves much of the burden of estimating future values because it is applied intertemporally and is tied to current sales. The result is that a newly patented product is available to all producers, the patent holder documents and is paid a bounty as a multiple of current sales, and the bounty is set to reflect the social value provided by the product's (competitive) provision. Other policies toward research and development including subsidies to research, prizes, and auction buyouts also have desirable features relative to patents. While no single tool is perfect, the case is strong that intertemporal bounties incorporate properties that push them further in the direction of capturing social efficiency.

TWELVE

Summary

There is nothing so adamant against change, nothing that excites such indignation when attacked, as a wrong way of doing things that people have got used to.
Gifford Pinchot, American Conservationist, 1947

Summary: *We have referenced the founders of the American republic several times in this volume. Why did their work survive? Why did it do so well? To understand their choices, you must understand their reasons and their principles. At heart, they were "idea politicians" who applied principles to the task of establishing right incentives for government. There is a lesson here. Without referencing principles, the debate over health care degenerates into nothing more than a jumble of conflicting attitudes and opinions.*

Variation regarding flexible implementation details notwithstanding, there is a virtually unique way to influence the economy to accomplish universal health insurance coverage that satisfies the objectives of Chapter 2, avoids the pitfalls of Chapter 3, and applies the principles of Chapter 3. Collected from the work of many others, with additions of our own, the implied structures incorporate and align incentives for an effective, sustainable health care system.

We are not the first to note that American health care has drifted into a wrong way of doing things that increasingly ignores economic principles. It needs answers to get back on track, but to get the right answers one needs to ask the right questions. There are three problems connected to American health care: Some people choose not to buy health insurance (too little insurance); some people do not have enough income for their needs, including health insurance (too little income); and the health care sector and health insurance sector contain features that prevent them from functioning rationally (too little market). We want these issues resolved in a way that satisfies the wants listed at the beginning of Chapter 8. The implied questions, therefore, are:

1. How do we induce people to buy health insurance most efficiently?

2. How do we increase incomes most efficiently?
3. How do we rationalize the health care market and its insurance?

Three policies address three problems. Why risk doing well in none by failing to use the best policies for each? Without much elaboration, we here lay out the implications of the main body of this book, in some cases reproducing conclusions reached in earlier chapters.

Too Little Insurance

If we want a health care system with universal access, we must encourage individuals to purchase health insurance who do not do so now. The argument for insurance relates to the benefits of risk pooling, but in the absence of counter-incentives, the incentive to free ride dominates for many. Partly this is because they have been given a poor choice: the insurance they are being asked to buy costs more than it should and more than its value, as far as they are concerned. This particular problem will disappear in a properly functioning insurance market, however, and is addressed later. Being able to afford health insurance is a separate problem, also addressed later. Thus, presuming the rest of the policy – everyone can afford insurance, and insurance is actuarially fair and covers wanted benefits – what is the economically justified (most efficient) way to induce insurance purchase?

The intervention principle says that the best way to reach the targeted state where everyone buys health insurance is to subsidize the health insurance purchases of those who do not now purchase it, at a level just sufficient to induce purchase. We do not want to subsidize the entire nation inefficiently just to affect the few, however. A subsidy requires budget outlays, and once all individuals' insurance purchases are subsidized, it is not possible in subsequent periods to distinguish those who would have bought insurance without government help. There is a remedy. By incentive symmetry (see Appendix C), the efficient intervention is equivalent to *taxing* the purchases of everything else (i.e., non-insurance purchases) of those who do not have health insurance. The non-buyers self-identify and the program collects revenues, rather than pays them out. This version, again using incentive symmetry, can be applied in a way that requires no net budget outlays and resembles a subsidy: a price differential is created whereby those with health insurance are rewarded with lower prices for all of their non-health-insurance purchases (see "The Subsidy Version" in Section 8.1).

The incentive can be made as large as needed to accomplish its objective because the intervention is "self-eliminating" when everyone buys health insurance in the sense that it collects no net revenues, makes no net out-lays, and leaves net prices unchanged for everyone who buys insurance. For this reason, and because we prefer positive incentives to negative ones, the subsidy version of the tax alternative is our preference among the different ways that an efficient intervention could be implemented.

Using the tax alternative of the best incentive in its subsidy form has a number of advantages. The price differential can be altered as needed, providing an easy-to-adjust point of flexibility, and it creates a constant reminder to buy insurance. Other incentives operating through annual tax filing do not, because losing tax credits, tax deductions, or personal exemp-tions occurs too infrequently to have the same impact as a daily reminder. For the targeted group of individuals a daily reminder is better.

Further, this incentive does not affect those who have insurance. They simply provide proof of coverage to collect their price advantage, which can be done by a credit card, ID card, or similar means. Purchasers al-ready provide "proof" of ability to pay so little is altered in the exchange. Compared to the costs associated with establishing permanent federal pro-grams to cover insurance purchases for the entire nation, this approach is modest. The incentive also does not create the false impression that it is the responsibility of government to publicly provide a private good (health care).

To the extent that the American public does not want its health care determined by the choices of politicians and offered in a Department of Motor Vehicles–type setting, this approach removes health care from the immediate attention of politicians and provides a measure of restraint to polittroughing.

Too Little Income

Successfully incentivizing everyone to buy health insurance requires that everyone have sufficient income to buy health insurance. That some may have too little income is a separate problem that should be dealt with separately.

For those who cannot afford to purchase insurance, some form of in-come assistance is needed to allow the recipient to use the money, combined with his or her own resources, to buy the needed insurance. The amount of aid provided can be calculated as an internal program consideration. It is not earmarked, but when combined with the recipient's own income, the aid enables the recipient to purchase the targeted level of insurance. The aid itself should take the form of cash income associated with work effort for those capable of work effort. Consistently with the intervention principle discussed earlier, vouchers are an unnecessary and economically inferior tool.

Refundable tax credits for everyone – an often suggested means of financing health insurance purchase – create a tax-financed program for everyone, when the goal is to influence the behavior of only a few. The larger the government program, the greater its excess cost to the private sector in the form of tax deadweight loss; the mid-range figure reported in this book is a 51 percent "excess cost." A focused program avoids excess cost. Income assistance should be offered in the manner that supports the correct incentives, both for individuals and for politicians. For the capable needy (those able to work and earn) the Earned Income Tax Credit (EITC) is an already-available tool to augment the income of those who are working but unable to earn enough income to afford adequate health insurance. The EITC can be enhanced in such a way that it provides appropriate incentives to work effort and leads to total available income that allows the purchase of health insurance (induced as described).

The incapable needy are distinguished from the capable needy (see Chapter 6). Because the incapable needy are not susceptible to incentives (they are unable to work, unemployable, disabled, or otherwise physically or mentally incapable), they present a different problem. Providing assistance to these individuals necessitates some form of direct welfare payment. As a social insurance matter, we believe that Americans, in general, would want the needs of the incapable needy to be met.

Regardless of the level of program chosen, there are likely to be some Americans who want more to be done. The considerations in Section 5.3, "Summary of Public Provision of Private Goods and Cautions," apply. Therefore, income tax filers should be given the opportunity to use a check-off box (similar to the private, voluntary programs sponsored by utility companies that provide assistance to low-income households) to contribute to the pool from which aid is given toward the health care needs of the capable and incapable needy. For taxpayers, the checked-off amount would increase such individuals' tax payments but be counted toward their charitable contributions and would be used to augment the Earned Income Tax Credit program and program for incapable needy.

Charitable foundations also have a larger role to play in contributing to the furtherance of the health care needs of the capable and incapable needy. Their contributions could be added to the government budget devoted to the program or administered as separate charitable programs. As discussed in Chapter 6, collective action through these forms is still voluntary and private but facilitated through the most efficient means, the current federal income tax filing system and the work of foundations.

Too Little Market

Respect for the market means that we recognize the role of incentives in consumer decision making, in insurance underwriting, and in the provision of health care: Increasing the reliance on voluntary interactions in markets promotes quality, improves efficiency, and fosters innovation, all of which are essential in getting the most from our health care investment.

Creating a fully functioning market would ideally mean price-taking behavior by providers, a standardized product, contestability, and full information. We have talked in this book about a number of market rationalizations that would take the medical care market closer to this ideal.

The most important of these rationalizations is the re-establishment of prices to health care. At a minimum, this means:

1. Most favored customer pricing. Providers can negotiate and charge whatever price they want, but their charges must be the same to all users of the product. Everyone is treated as well as providers treat the "most favored customer."

2. Price transparency. Prices must be posted. Health care currently tends to charge by procedure code. If this is the best approach, such prices should be posted. If, as with legal services where the attorney bases charges on an hourly rate and the number of billed hours, portions of the health care sector would do better to bill at an hourly rate, these rates should be posted. The Internet is an easily accessible forum for prices that can be facilitated by government. Let the market determine the appropriate billing base and prices.

3. The consumer needs to know something about service availability and quality. At a minimum, procedures performed by a given provider and their frequency would offer the customer a great deal of information. Other quality measures can be devised as circumstances dictate, facilitated by government as an information arbiter.

These requirements on health care providers are aimed primarily at allowing a market to function. In the Targeted Intervention Plan, providers would also be subject to a revenue tax, but it is expected to be small (3–4 percent). Apart from this, health care providers are free to practice medicine in the best fashion they know and to earn the rewards from their own innovations and improvements without interference of government.

Rationalizing the market in health care also requires changes to health care insurance that we have treated in Chapter 7. A consumer risks the occurrence of a medical event, but also the event that he or she enters a higher risk class ("reclassification risk"). Both risks are insurable at actuarially fair premiums. Basic insurance coverage should provide equal access to covered services, and individuals should be allowed to supplement their coverage with their own money. Insurance financing should be tax neutral regardless of the source of the insurance – whether purchased individually, through an employer, or through an insurance exchange (along the lines of the connector under the Massachusetts plan). Rationalizing the market in health care insurance implies at a minimum:

1. Guaranteed renewability. Every holder of a health insurance policy may renew the policy at the same premium rate as others of the same age, sex, and location of residence. This is nothing more than the statement that an insured reclassification risk, once it has occurred, must be honored by the insurer. The onset of an illness will not affect insurance status.

2. Source tax neutrality. Individual purchase of insurance should receive the same tax advantages as employer-offered insurance. Competition and efficiency will dictate the forms and groups that result in offering good insurance coverage.

3. Actuarially fair insurance. Insurance premiums should be based on actuarially fair prices. Actuarially fair insurance pricing requires pooling like risks with like risks. Community rating or group rating does not do this.

   Actuarially fair insurance is not charity. Actuarially fair insurance means that every individual through life will pay for the true expected insurance benefits that he or she receives from insurance. If an individual does not have the needed income to buy actuarially fair insurance (rated for his or her age, sex, and location of residence), then that individual will have his or her income augmented separately through the best means. All who need more income will have their needs met through participation in one of the programs designed to provide income aid efficiently (see earlier discussion.) Actuarially fair insurance offered in the fashion described here is cheap insurance for which innovations and incentives to good health can be attached that reward those who implement them.

4. Closely related to actuarially fair pricing is freedom of sourcing. Individuals may voluntarily pool with whomever they wish, but if a place of employment offers a medical benefit, employees will have the right to take the dollar amount of the medical benefit and apply it to the purchase of health insurance in the private market.

5. Portability. Insurance policies are the property of the individuals holding them. We discussed in Chapter 7 suggestions for how portability
may be supported. Implementation details can be worked out as circumstances arise in the future.

6. No utilization gatekeeping (often referred to as prior authorization or
utilization review). In a market, the consumer sees the price for a product, decides to buy or not, and pays the price for a purchase. The same
applies to health insurance. Once a policy is purchased, the consumer
knows the prices that he or she will have to pay for a covered procedure
and can make the choice to buy the procedure without second guess-
ing by the insurance company. For example, if a medical consultation
is a covered benefit, and the patient is willing to pay the co-insurance
payment for a consultation, he or she is able to get a second opinion, paying the co-insurance rate without input from the insurer. The
only question relevant to the insurer is whether the service took place
or not. Anticipating this, policies will be designed to deal better with
moral hazard.[1]

7. Health insurance that meets the minimum standard of coverage (deductible, co-insurance rate, out-of-pocket limit, and list of covered
benefits that are designed to be "moral-hazard-aware") should be selected to include only necessary coverage and vary by the age group
and sex involved.[2] For example, elective cosmetic surgery would not
be part of the basic plan. If individuals want additional coverages, these
can be offered but should require additional premiums at actuarially
fair rates for those selecting more than the minimal coverage.

8. Pre-paid care should be kept to a minimum (to procedures only that
are premium-reducing) or be absent entirely from the required insurance product, which may vary by the age and sex cohort for which it
is written. The reason is that insurance involves a "handling charge"
(typically in the 10–20 percent range) to pre-paid care, raising the cost
of a routine physical. This cost escalation, coupled with mandating

---

[1] Under this arrangement individuals will demand medical care until the marginal benefit of
the care received is equal to the co-pay. There is nothing to prevent insurance companies
from selling policies (at lower premiums) that include a form of gatekeeping, assuming of
course that individuals want to purchase such policies. The point is that spending should
not be controlled by gatekeeping, but by the structure of the insurance policy.

[2] Determining the essential coverage of a standard policy is a decision that is best left to
the market. However, if the goal is to encourage everyone to purchase a standard policy,
standards must apply. Supplementary plans may be offered that include benefits that go
beyond those in the basic plan.

multiple pre-paid care coverages that insureds do not want, is a "deal breaker" for effective, cheap insurance.

9. Finally, there should be freedom of underwriting to encourage competition, price transparency for insurance products, and an "insurance connector" or insurance exchange to facilitate purchase.

Health insurers are subject to a tax on the revenues of their health insurance policies. Apart from this, however, and the fact that base policies are rated on age, sex, and geographic location only,[3] there are virtually no restrictions on their ability to underwrite, innovate insurance products, or compete for customers. Access to affordable insurance (with income assistance to some) and knowledge of all prices will foster competition and go a long way toward creating a fully functioning market.

What would the life of an American look like under the Targeted Intervention Plan? Every child would have a health insurance policy that begins at birth. Its price would be low because it would cover only needed and wanted benefits, and all base insurance policies would be bought and sold on an actuarially fair basis. The child's parents would be able to afford the policy, and if they could not, their Earned Income Tax Credit would reflect the need to purchase insurance and would guarantee that they had enough total income including their own resources to buy the policy for their child. The child would carry the policy, or shift to other policies, through life much as is possible now. Policies' guaranteed renewability feature allows them to be personal and portable if desired, or to be replaced with other coverage. If the child as a young adult wants more coverage than the base plan, he or she is able to buy it at actuarially fair rates. No restrictions limit how the child, later an adult, chooses to carry coverage or pay for it or from which provider. For example, term coverage or level premium coverage could be contracted for as desired. If a worker who is an employee believes he or she has better coverage than the employer's plan, that worker has the ability to take the dollars the employer contributes on his or her behalf to the company plan and apply it to private coverage with the same tax advantages.

The effects of the plan are even simpler to describe for insurers and providers. They are subject to a small revenue tax but in all other respects are free to offer insurance and health care as they wish. They must adhere to certain market features such as making their prices known and offering most favored customer pricing, but very little else limits their freedom.

---

[3] This oversimplifies somewhat: it may be desirable to allow rating on verifiable lifestyle choices such as smoking, overweight, hang gliding, et cetera.

The military sometimes talks about "surgical strikes," operations designed to accomplish precise objectives as finely as possible. As authors, we find it hard to envision a less intrusive means to accomplish the surgical strike objectives of encouraging – not forcing – everyone to buy health insurance and seeing that he or she has the means to do it. At the same time, we – and many other health care economists – suggest that a market be re-established in health care.

Universal insurance coverage does not mean free medical care or even first-dollar coverage. It means equipping the capable needy with the means of independent survival and providing for the incapable needy through social insurance. The prudent use of deductibles, co-insurance, and co-payments provides a useful way of dealing with moral hazard without adversely affecting health. Everyone pays something for medical care; no one gets a free ride. The details are an implementation choice, but we envision that those capable of working who must spend more than an allowable threshold for basic coverage will be eligible for a subsidy through the EITC. The application of a subsidy, or preferably the application of its incentive-symmetric equivalent tax, would further encourage the desired behavior.

The government has an important role in a market-oriented system. Most importantly government policy must establish rules to guard against fraud and abuse, facilitate information flows to ensure transparency, decide how much taxpayer money to spend on the subsidy program, and spend no more. Thus, it is not necessary to nationalize an entire sector.

When everyone has insurance, there will be no need to shift costs to the insured to cover the uninsured. To the extent that there is a remnant of uninsured, they will be paying the consumption tax that approximately covers their medical care needs.

Ultimately, American health care must treat individuals with respect and dignity. This requires that the insured individual be the decision-making center of the system. If the system following the principles outlined in this book is established, we can avoid the pitfalls and sustainably enjoy access to high-quality medical care at affordable prices.

Appendix A

Top Ten Goals for the American Health Care System

Many documents describe Americans' desires and goals for their health care. Interested parties include users, providers, and government. Insurance companies also have a critically large role in a sustainable well-functioning system. Referencing only a handful of documents is sufficient to reveal that a great degree of commonality exists in the themes that emerge. This appendix produces an unscientific "Top Ten List" that is reduced by policy triage to three points of policy focus that, when addressed, accomplish the five objectives in Chapter 2. With one exception, all of those objectives are themselves points of policy interest. The exception is the objective of patient-centered coverage. Patient-centered coverage is achieved as a consequence of making sure that everyone has enough income to buy health insurance coverage and is covered by adequate health insurance of the right kind. Coupled with market provision of health care, this makes the patient the key decision-making unit. Patient-centered coverage was listed as a stand-alone objective to emphasize its importance. Generally, the meaning of the items on the list needs no explanation. A summary of objectives by organization follows. Table A.1 distributes the ten goals into the policy triage groups based on the description of the Preface. Columns (2) and (4) are not objects of policy for the reasons described in the first row of the table. Column (3) lists goals that should be addressed and solved.

The Top Ten Goals

1. **Achieve universal coverage.** (American Hospital Association (2002), Deloitte Center for Health Solutions (2008), Citizens' Health Care Working Group (2005), Gauthier (2005), Kling (2006), Mayo Clinic

215

Table A.1. *Policy Triage Applied to Top Ten Goals List*

Explanation (1)	Not policy domain (intrinsic problem not susceptible to policy) (2)	Policy domain (can be addressed and solved) (3)	Not policy domain (solved by meeting Chapter 2 objective listed in column (1)) (4)
Cannot set prices below true cost of provision[a]	Maintain affordability		
Goal 1: Universal coverage		Achieve universal coverage	Empower the patient
Goal 3: Respect for market, incentives, efficiency[b]		Rely on prices and the market	Provide high-quality care Encourage efficiency Provide better information and information transparency Integrate best technologies and practices Preventive, continuous, rather than just episodic care
Objectives 4 and 5: Cost containment, sustainability		Sustainable stable system[c]	

[a] However, competition will maintain prices close to marginal cost.

[b] Goal 2 (Patient-centered coverage) is met as a consequence of Goals 1 and 3.

[c] Sustainability is met as a consequence of sound financial Principles 3 and 6 of Chapter 3.

(2007), National Academy of Sciences (2003), Pauly et al. (1991), Ryan (2000), White House (2006))

2. **Empower the patient.** (American Hospital Association (2002), Deloitte Center for Health Solutions (2008), Institute of Medicine (2001), Gauthier (2005), Mayo Clinic (2007), National Academy of Sciences (2003), National Governors Association (2005), National

Partnership for Women and Families (2006), Pauly et al. (1991), White House (2006))

3. **Rely on prices and the market.** (American Medical Association (2002), Deloitte Center for Health Solutions (2008), Goodman (2001), Pauly et al. (1991))

4. **Provide high-quality care.** (Deloitte Center for Health Solutions (2008), Citizens' Health Care Working Group (2005), Hellander (2001), Institute of Medicine (2001), Gauthier (2005), Kindig (1993), Mayo Clinic (2007), Shortell (2006))

5. **Encourage efficiency.** (American Hospital Association (2002), American Medical Association (2002), Citizens' Health Care Working Group (2005), Gauthier (2005), Gilmer and Kronick (2005), Hellander (2001), Institute of Medicine (2001), Mayo Clinic (2007), National Academy of Sciences (2003), National Governors Association (2005), Pauly et al. (1991), Reinhardt et al. (2004))

6. **Sustainable stable system.** (American Hospital Association (2002), American Medical Association (2002), National Academy of Sciences (2003), others by implication have same goal)

7. **Provide better information and information transparency.** (American Hospital Association (2002), Deloitte Center for Health Solutions (2008), Gauthier (2005), Institute of Medicine (2001), National Partnership for Women and Families (2006))

8. **Maintain affordability.** (American Hospital Association (2002), Deloitte Center for Health Solutions (2008), Citizens' Health Care Working Group (2005), National Academy of Sciences (2003), Gilmer and Kronick (2005), White House (2006))

9. **Integrate the best technologies and practices.** (American Hospital Association (2002), Deloitte Center for Health Solutions (2008), Chappell (2006), Citizens' Health Care Working Group (2005), Lohr (2004), Mayo Clinic (2007))

10. **Preventive, continuous, rather than just episodic care.** (American Medical Association (2002), Landro (2005), National Academy of Sciences (2003))

American Hospital Association[1]

1. Basic health services for all.
2. Timely accessibility for all.

---

[1] American Hospital Association, 2005.

3. High-quality, safe, technologically innovative care.
4. Responsive, accountable care. The system should be patient-centered
   and responsive to individual needs, preferences, culture, and values. . . .
   The system should be equitable, so that care does not vary in quality
   solely because of personal characteristics.
5. Affordable care. . . . Keeping care affordable means delivering care efficiently by avoiding waste and duplication of service among providers.
   Keeping care affordable also means mitigating cost shifting by adequately and fairly financing the system to bear the full cost of services
   promised.
6. Personal responsibility. . . . Consumers should be given incentives
   to [maintain healthy lifestyles] where possible. Consumers should
   also be given an incentive for responsible use of health care services
   through cost sharing, focused especially where consumers' judgment
   on whether, where, and when to seek services plays an important role
   in appropriate utilization.
7. The consensus description was modified in 2004. It specifically included the objective that care

   (a) "be structured to provide more coordinated continuity of care,"
   (b) "be transparent in sharing information with consumers and clini-
       cians," and
   (c) "be sufficiently financed to meet long term responsibilities."

American Medical Association[2]

1. How does the proposed system confront scarcity?. . . No system, public or private, can meet the demands for medical care in the quantities
   that are generated when patients view it as free or nearly so.
2. Is the system an equilibrium or disequilibrium system? A health care
   system that tries to insulate medical care from scarcity will be unstable
   from both the economic and political standpoints.
3. What is the role of prices in the system?. . . Most of our health care
   problems related to rapid expenditure growth are due to the absence
   of a proper price system.
4. Are incentives facing producers and consumers consistent with
   reform goals? Without cost conscious consumers on the demand
   side of the market, there will be no incentive for serious market price
   competition, efficient production, or consumer-oriented service on
   the supply side.

---

[2] Hixson, 2002.

5. Who determines what health care is produced and who gets it? If our politicians' differences. . . persist, we will never solve our health system problems. The mistrust of the market to solve health system problems by many of our politicians is profound, while many others recognize the inability of government to effectively perform the functions that have to be performed if government, rather than the market, is relied upon to run the system.

6. How will they know if it is working?. . . A better alternative, however, is to rely on the market with correctly structured incentives and pricing mechanisms to guide both public and private systems automatically toward their goals.

Deloitte Center for Health Solutions[3]

1. Affordability is an issue, but both [the insured and uninsured] perceive quality differences, want more information, and are looking for access to online tools.

2. Insured consumers, including those covered by Medicare, are generally satisfied with their health plan.

3. Consumers want to customize their health plan. Gen Y, Gen X, and Boomers are especially interested in policies that are customized to their needs.

4. Thirty percent of consumers anticipate switching insurance companies or health plans in the future. Even higher percentages anticipate switching physicians and medications.

5. Health plan Web sites are a critical source of information for enrollees. Most want their plan's Web site to expand its Web offering to provide more information about provider quality and pricing, treatment options, and claims status.

6. Insured consumers want plans to address their questions and concerns about coverage, claims, and health care experiences. Many also seek advice from their plan about health problems and needs.

7. Consumers use health plan Web sites for information about prices and coverage of doctors, hospitals, and medications. They are interested in accessing additional information about the quality of these services. However, for clinical information, consumers turn to providers and online health sites more than health plans.

[3] Deloitte Center for Health Solutions, 2008. Most of this very informative survey records attitudes and behavior, but much of it also reveals unmet needs. This synopsis reflects needs from sections entitled "Behaviors, Attitudes and Unmet Needs Related to Health Insurance" and "Conclusions."

8. Consumers want to make their own decisions and they want tools to help them do this. The source for these tools is up for grabs.

9. Consumers are embracing innovations that are "disruptive" to stakeholders who provide traditional health services and health plans. The majority of consumers see a need for better value, better service, increased transparency, and personalization of services from doctors, hospitals, and health plans. They are receptive to innovations in how services are delivered and paid for.

10. Nearly 30 percent would be in favor of increasing taxes to help provide coverage for the uninsured; another third are not sure; only 37 percent oppose.

Among the behaviors recorded, the following are particularly relevant to a national health care framework.

1. Consumers see distinctions in quality: They are paying attention to differences and want more information to make comparisons.

2. Consumers are paying attention to prices for their prescriptions, office visits, hospital services, and insurance premiums: They want tools to help them know in advance what those costs will be.

3. Both the uninsured and insured desire improved service, greater access to clinical information and tools to compare costs and quality, and performance-based payments to providers.

4. Consumers will travel across state lines or country borders to save money or get better quality: They recognize that close at home may not mean "best at home."

Citizens' Health Care Working Group[4]

1. Make affordable health care public policy. Comprehensive and high-quality care should be available to everybody regardless of health and without threat to the financial security of the individual or his or her family.

2. Establish a group to recommend what would be covered under high-cost protection and benefits. Members of an independent, nonpartisan group, including patients and health care providers, will define a set of core benefits that encompass physical, mental, and dental health throughout an indvidual's lifetime.

3. Guarantee financial protection against high health care costs. A public or private national program should provide coverage for everyone,

---

[4] The Citizens' Health Care Working Group (created by Congress in Medicare legislation of 2003), 2006.

protect against high out-of-pocket costs, and ensure financial protection for low-income people.

4. Support integrated community health care networks. High-quality care should be provided to low-income people, the uninsured, and people in rural and under served areas. The federal governnment should coordinate efforts to help strengthen the infrastructure at the local level.

5. Promote improved quality of care and efficiency. The federal government should promote integrated health systems built on evidence-based best practices, emerging information technologies with emphasis on teaching hospitals and clinics, fraud and waste reduction, patient education, and consumer-friendly resources.

6. Restructure end-of-life services to increase access. Individuals nearing death and their families should clearly understand their options and have their choices carried out accordingly. Communication among providers, patients, and their families is vital. Funding, at the community level, should be available to help individuals and families gain access to care.

National Center for Policy Analysis[5]

1. We should subsidize those who insure and penalize those who do not.
2. The subsidy for private insurance should equal the value society places on insuring individuals, at the margin.
3. The revealed social value of insurance is the amount we spend on free care for the uninsured.
4. The penalties paid by the uninsured should be used to compensate those who provide safety net care.
5. The subsidy for each newly insured should be funded by reducing the expected amount of spending on free care for that person.
6. Subsidies for being insured should be independent of how the insurance is purchased.
7. The optimal number of uninsured is not zero.
8. The principles of reform apply with equal force to all citizens, regardless of income.
9. Health insurance subsidies need not add to budgetary outlays.
10. The federal government's role should remain strictly financial.

[5] Goodman, 2001.

Institute of Medicine[6]

1. Effective: providing services based on scientific knowledge to all who could benefit.
2. Patient-centered: providing care that is respectful of and responsive to individual patient preferences, needs, and values, and ensuring that patient values guide all clinical decisions.
3. Timely: reducing waits and sometimes harmful delays.
4. Efficient.
5. Equitable: providing care that does not vary in quality because of personal characteristics.
6. The Institute goes on to provide ten rules for health care system design.

   (a) Care is based on continuous healing relationships.
   (b) Care is customized according to patient needs and values.
   (c) The patient is the source of control.
   (d) Knowledge is shared and information flows freely.
   (e) Decision making is evidence-based.
   (f) Safety is a system property.
   (g) Transparency is necessary.
   (h) Needs are anticipated.
   (i) Waste is continuously decreased.
   (j) Cooperation among clinicians is a priority.

Mayo Clinic[7]

1. Require adults to purchase private health insurance for themselves and for their families.
2. Move from employer-based insurance to portable, individual-based coverage.
3. Create a simple mechanism (similar to Federal Employees Health Benefit Plan) to offer private insurance packages to buyers.
4. Require individual ownership of health insurance, with sliding-scale subsidies for people with lower incomes.
5. Appoint an independent health board (similar to Federal Reserve) to define essential health care services. Allow people to purchase more services or insurance, if desired.
6. Center care around the patient.

[6] Institute of Medicine, 2001.
[7] Mayo Clinic, 2007.

7. Realign the health care system toward improving health rather than treating disease.
8. Form coordinated systems to deliver effective and appropriate care to patients.
9. Develop a "portfolio of incentive" to encourage teamwork.
10. Increase support for health care delivery of science.
11. Provide complete and accurate information so patients can make informed decisions about their care.
12. Develop a definition of value based upon the needs and preferences of patients, measurable outcomes, safety, and service, compared to the cost of care over time.
13. Measure and publicly display outcomes, patient satisfaction scores, and costs as a whole. Create competition around results through pricing and quality transparency.
14. Create a trusted mechanism to synthesize scientific, clinical, and medical information for both patients and providers.
15. Reward consumers for choosing high-quality health plans and providers.
16. Hold all sectors in health care accountable for reducing waste and inefficiencies.
17. Design payment systems to provide patients with no less than the care they need and no more than fully informed, cost-conscious patients would want.
18. Create payment systems that provide incentives for colleagues (physicians, hospitals) to coordinate care for patients, improve care, and support informed patient decision making.
19. Pay providers based on value. (See item 18.)
20. Further develop and test models of payment based on chronic care coordination, shared decision making, and mini-capitation (i.e., one bundled fee for the physicians and hospital delivering acute care).

National Academy of Sciences[8]

1. Health care coverage should be universal.
2. Health care coverage should be continuous.
3. Health care coverage should be affordable to individuals and families.
4. The health insurance strategy should be affordable and sustainable for society.

[8] National Academy of Sciences, 2003.

5. Health insurance should enhance health and well-being by promoting access to high-quality care that is effective, efficient, safe, timely, patient-centered, and equitable.

National Governors Association[9]

1. Effectively use information technology, encourage efficiency.
2. Emphasize quality and effectiveness of care.
3. Permit the consumers to make informed decisions on the cost and quality of the services they receive.
4. Encourage innovative approaches for extending coverage to the uninsured.

Mark Pauly, Patricia Danzon, Paul Feldstein, John Hoff[10]

1. Provide universal access to medical care to all Americans at a politically acceptable cost.
2. Promote "appropriate equity in the health care system."
3. "Allocation of resources to health care should rest on individuals' choice of insurance, in light of their different needs and desires" (p. 5). Enable "all persons to act on their quite different desires for health care and their willingness to forgo other goods and services for health care" (p. 6).
4. Establish setting that "will drive a comprehensive market and improve the efficiency of the health care system" (p. 5) and establishes "an institutional framework that encourages a vigorously competitive market" (p. 6).
5. Limit governmental rules and incentives to the extent necessary to achieve the objectives.

White House[11]

1. Empower the patients.
2. Create a system that helps control rising costs in health care.

---

[9] National Governors Association (NGA), 2005. The NGA document includes an analysis of the failings of the present system, the negation of which is the list provided.
[10] Pauly et al., 1991.
[11] White House, 2006.

Appendix B

Badly Done Insurance Programs Can be Worse Than No Insurance

A frequently encountered – but invalid – perspective on health care and health insurance is that if a well-designed framework is not adopted, then, at a minimum, insuring everyone through some government plan would be better than no insurance. This appendix provides an example demonstrating that this perspective is false.[1]

There are four elements that interact to determine whether health insurance will improve the well-being of the insured:

1. risk aversion,
2. moral hazard,
3. handling costs, and
4. market power response to insured customers.

Each of these has been discussed in the text in Chapters 7, (Section 7.2, "Essential Insurance") and 11.[2] Here we provide a small equilibrium model incorporating all four elements that shows that it is possible for everyone to be worse off with insurance compared to the alternative where no one has it. In this example, it is the case that when everyone is insured, an individual is better off to buy insurance (showing that the insurance equilibrium is stable), even though all would be better uninsured. The reason is that being outside the insurance pool when prices have been made higher as a result of the presence of insurance makes it harder to pay for medical treatment. Before describing the model, we explain briefly the relevant factors.

---

[1] We draw on and expand the model of Bernhardt and Zabojnik, 2006, to include the four elements of risk aversion, moral hazard, handling costs, and market power response to insured customers.

[2] Adverse selection is primarily a concern to insurance providers that is dealt with in the Targeted Intervention Plan framework and need not concern us in the example here because all consumers are insured alike.

Risk management through insurance is, in and of itself, welfare-enhancing to risk averse individuals. If being insured, however, induces an inefficiently large increase in the need for and usage of the insured product – in this case, health care – and/or coverage extends inappropriately to benefits that should not be part of the benefits package, then we can be in a position similar to the lunch club participants described in Chapter 3. All are forced by the choices available to them in the insurance regime to spend more than they want and more than is efficient. An insurance plan that made all health care costless to the insured once an event has occurred, for example, would cause the insured to treat health care as if it were a free good, even though it costs the insurance plan to provide it. The insurance premiums that everyone pays would be higher, but de-coupled from any decision that the individual could make to reduce premiums. In addition, dollars run through an insurance plan – whether it is government administered or privately administered – incur a handling cost that the insured must pay, also inflating expenditures. Last, when suppliers of the insured product have market power, meaning the ability to charge prices above their cost of provision, their response to buyers who have some or all of their charges covered by insurance is to raise prices. Combining the harmful consequences of moral hazard, handling costs, and market-power-induced higher prices may lead to lower welfare for everyone compared to the alternative where no one is insured.

As we have emphasized, to avoid this outcome, health insurance must

- keep handling costs low by insuring only for essential and wanted benefits,
- take care not to insure for routine, non-risky, and predictable care (though, of course, these features can be offered as add-ons for those who want such policies), and
- tailor the list of covered benefits, deductibles, co-insurance rates, and out-of-pocket limits to avoid moral hazard. For example, this implies adopting low co-insurance provisions only for types of care that are not subject to large adverse choice incentives to the insured.

The health care market must

- control prices through competition or competition substitutes (see Section 10.3, "Restraining Prices in Theory"). This last condition involves features that require specific government interventions and oversight compared to the present, as we have described.

We now turn to the example. Consider an economy of P risk-averse individuals with utility described by

$$Utility = E[y] - \rho Var[y]$$

where y is income, $\rho > 0$ is a coefficient of risk aversion, $E[y]$, $Var[y]$ are mean and variance of income, respectively. Each individual has income y but faces the chance that he or she might suffer a medical event leading to damage equal to V_2 and another event with damage V_1. For simplicity, we assume that both events occur together with probability p. Medical treatment is available at cost d per unit of treatment, where $y > V_2 > d > V_1$. For each condition, the purchase of one unit of treatment cures the condition, fully eliminating the cost of the condition, V_2 or V_1.

Figure B.1 depicts the costs and benefits just described. The vertical axis measures the benefits to the patient from medical treatment, and the horizontal axis measures treatment levels. We have arranged the two conditions side by side; if one unit of treatment ($t = 1$) is selected, V_2 is avoided, so the benefit is shown as V_2. If two units of care are selected ($t = 2$), the benefit is $V_2 + V_1$. The cost of providing treatment is d per unit. In the absence of insurance, the individual's maximum willingness to pay for treating the first condition is V_2. The cost of treatment exceeds V_1, so the individual would rather not treat the second condition.

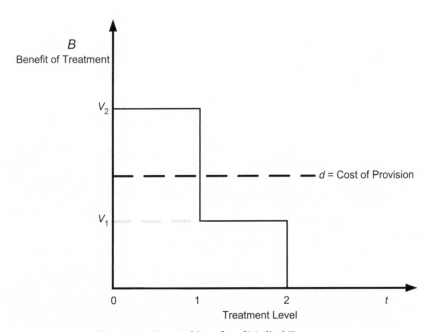

Figure B.1. Cost and Benefits of Medical Treatment

Providers of medical care charge price $P_{No\,Ins}$ (not shown on Figure B.1) per course of treatment, where $P_{No\,Ins}$ lies between d and V_2. Attempting to charge a price outside these bounds produces zero or negative profits to the supplier based on the way the non-insured individuals would respond. Let $m = 0$ be the degree of market power,

$$P_{No\,Ins} = mV_2 + (1 - m)d$$

where $0 \leq m \leq 1$, $m = 0$ corresponds to no market power ($P_{No\,Ins} = d = $ marginal cost of care), and $m = 1$ is the opposite extreme where the supplier charges the maximum price the market will bear.[3] In the absence of insurance, the individual will pay for treatment out to level $t = 1$. In this case

$$y = \begin{cases} Y & \text{with probability } (1 - p) \\ \\ Y - V_1 - P_{No\,Ins} & \text{with probability } p \end{cases} \tag{B.1}$$

If the individual is insured, he or she will pay a premium and receive benefits of 0, V_2, or $V_2 + V_1$ depending on whether $t = 0, 1$, or 2, respectively. The amount paid for care will depend on the care price prevailing in the insurance market regime (P_{Ins}), less what the insurance policy covers. With insurance,

$$y = \begin{cases} Y - Premium & \text{with probability } (1 - p) \\ \\ Y - Premium - (V_2 + V_1) \\ \quad + Min[t, 1]V_2 + Max[t - 1, 0]V_1 \\ \quad - tP_{Ins} + tP_{Ins}n & \text{with probability } p \end{cases} \tag{B.2}$$

for choice of $t = 0, 1, 2$, where $n \, \varepsilon \, [0, 1]$ is the co-insurance rate and $tP_{Ins}n$, therefore, is the insurance benefit payout. In the insurance regime, the insured's maximum willingness to pay is no longer V_2, but $\frac{V_2}{1-n}$. That is, if I am willing to pay \$10 for a treatment, I would be willing to pay \$50 for treatment if my insurance covers 80 percent of the cost. Thus

$$P_{Ins} = m\frac{V_2}{1 - n} + (1 - m)d.$$

---

[3] Variable m is an exogenous placeholder for degree of market power. For an example of how it, too, could be endogenized without changing the conclusions, see Bernhardt and Zabojnik, 2006.

Table B.1. *No Insurance Is Better Than Poorly Designed Insurance*

Regime	Consumer utility	Market price for treatment	Price paid by consumer
No insurance			
$t = 1$	932.2[a]	243.0	243.0
Insurance			
$t = 2$	923.0	711.0	142.2
Insurance			
$t = 1$	921.3	711.0	142.2
Insurance			
No insurance bought	853.3	711.0	711.0

[a] If $t = 2$, utility falls to 910.9. Economy parameters are $(P, Y, V_2, V_1, d, m, c, \rho, n, p) = (1,000, 1,000, 390, 150, 180, 0.3, 0.02, 0.0025, 0.8, 0.1)$.

In the equilibrium we are about to complete, it will be the case that the insured individual optimally chooses $t = 2$ when insurance is present and $t = 1$ when he or she has no insurance. Thus, the expected benefit payout in the insurance regime is $2P_{Ins}np$, implying that the policy premium in a competitive insurance market is $Premium = 2P_{Ins}np(1 + c)$ where c is the handling charge.

In equilibrium, profits earned by suppliers of medical care accrue to someone in the economy. In our example, all consumers are alike. Therefore, each one receives his or her share of endogenously determined supplier profits, equal to $2p(P_{Ins} - d)$ in the equilibrium computed here.

Table B.1 provides the relevant comparisons. Several things should be noted. First, when no one is insured, the first row of the table shows that the price of one unit of treatment is \$243. If the medical event occurs, consumers buy one course of treatment because the benefits of treatment ($V_2 = \$390$) exceed the cost to them. They do not select $t = 2$ because the second treatment is not worth undertaking (\$243 > $V_1 = \$150$). This is also the socially appropriate outcome because the true cost of providing care, $d = \$180$, also implies that only one course of treatment is worth undertaking. Treatment demanded is pPt (number of people needing care, pP, times t treatments each). Suppliers, therefore, make profits of $pPt(P_{NoIns} - d) = 0.1 \cdot 1,000 \cdot 1(\$243 - \$180) = \$6,300$ on the 100 individuals receiving treatment.

In contrast, when everyone is insured, his or her co-insurance rate (20 percent in this example) means that the price to the insured of a course of treatment is \$142.2. This makes it worthwile for everyone to select treatment $t = 2$ ($V_2 > V_1 > \$142.2$). The extra care is socially inefficient because the true cost of care is \$180, as already noted. Moreover, because everyone is insured, the suppliers of care are able to raise their price to \$711, implying profits of $pPt(P_{Ins} - d) = 0.1 \cdot 1{,}000 \cdot 2(\$711 - \$180) = \$106{,}200$ on the 200 treatments provided. Even though this money is returned to the individuals in their role as owners of the supplying firms, the net effect of the greater inefficiency is that utility for every individual in society falls from 932.2 in the no-insurance regime to 923.0 when everyone is insured. Moreover, in the insurance regime, the hapless individual who might want to go without insurance now finds himself or herself paying so much for care that attempting to pay for one course of treatment out of pocket, as before, would lead to utility of 853.3. The person has little choice but to pay for the insurance along with everyone else and select $t = 2$ if a medical event occurs.

Other examples could be constructed to show the effects of moral hazard, market power, and handling overhead costs, but the moral is the same: A single-payer system that forces everyone to buy coverage, runs too many dollars through the system, and covers too much can harm everyone and leave the individual no room for escape. In the economy described here, we did not have the insurance provide first-dollar coverage for routine (non-random) care, but had we done so, the utility from insurance would have fallen even further. In constrast, had we crafted coverage differently (not including the V_1 event in the policy comes to mind as one change), reduced market power of the suppliers and selected the policy better (in the example this would include selecting the co-insurance rate), it would be possible to insure everyone to everyone's advantage.

Appendix C

Incentive Symmetry and Intervention Principle

The decision-making units of an economy consist of firms, households, and government. If an economic equilibrium does not achieve a desired outcome, then an outside influence in the form of changed incentives is needed to move the equilibrium to accomplish the outcome. In most cases, there are different ways to do this, implying that there is a *best* way. "Best" means accomplishing the altered outcome in a fashion with highest utility for the people that make up the economy, so why not do it in the best (i.e., most efficient) way? Otherwise, you are saying that the same objective could be accomplished, raising the well-being of one or more individuals without harming others, but you are choosing not to do so. This is the basic meaning of efficiency. Rather than merely "order people about," economic theory has something to say about the way to intervene in an economy using the tax system to create incentives that *encourage* people to take the coordinated steps they need to take. Tax tools must be used in the right way for these methods to work, but, then, that is the message of this book. This appendix demonstrates in more detail for a technical audience two of the principles that lead us to conclude that there is a virtually unique way to accomplish national health care objectives best.[1]

We first demonstrate *incentive symmetry*. Firms, consumers, and government might face different prices according to which taxes and circumstances apply to each. Given world prices, if all prices for producers were

---

[1] We recognize that the treatment here, unfortunately, is necessarily limited relative to the relevant public finance literature on taxes and their interactions with the economy. We have selected two demonstrations best to explain the nature of the two principles. As an introduction to that literature the reader is referred to Guesnerie and Roberts, 1984; Dixit, 1985; Kaplow, 1996, 1998; Grinols, 2006; and references cited there. Kaplow is concerned with ways to de-couple the called-for intervention incentives from existing taxes to support the intervention principle in more general circumstances.

multiplied by the same non-negative number, producer choices would be unchanged. For example, if prices were measured in quarters (coins of value $0.25) rather than dollars, all costs and revenues would be multiplied by 4. Choices that were profit maximizing when profit was measured in dollars would also be profit maximizing when profit is measured in quarters.

A similar result applies to international trade (a form of production) and to consumers. This leaves us with the interesting conclusion that all quantities continue to prevail in the economy as prevailed before the multiplications were done. We would need to verify that government can collect enough from the tax system with the altered prices in place to hold its quantities constant, but this too can be shown. In other words, if an equilibrium set of prices for domestic consumers, producers, government, and the world $\{p_x, p_y, p_g, p_w\}$ is found, then $\{\lambda_x p_x, \lambda_y p_y, \lambda_g p_g, p_w\}$ is also an equilibrium set of prices for the *identical equilibrium*, where $\lambda_x, \lambda_y, \lambda_g$ are positive scalar numbers and p_x, p_y, p_g, p_w are lists of prices (price vectors). We require a minimal amount of notation to demonstrate this result. Its implication is the *incentive symmetry principle* of Chapter 3 that says that a subsidy (tax) is equivalent in its effect to a tax (subsidy) on all other goods.

We also demonstrate the *intervention principle*, which states that the efficient (least-cost) way to accomplish an economic objective is through a tax/subsidy narrowly directed to the margin to be influenced and applied at the minimal level to accomplish the objective. The main application of this principle (see Chapter 8) is to reach the conclusion that to induce individuals to buy insurance, a subsidy to insurance purchase (or its incentive-symmetric equivalent tax form) is the implied tool.

C.1. Notation

Let K be the number of goods, and let $x_i \epsilon \mathcal{R}^{\mathcal{K}}$ ($\mathcal{R}^{\mathcal{K}}$ is K-dimensional Euclidean space) be household i's vector of consumption.[2] The kth component, x_{ik}, is the household's consumption of good k. The consumption of all households in the economy is $\sum_{i=1}^{I} x_i = x$. By convention, a positive element of x_i is a good consumed by the household, while a negative element (such as hours of labor supply) is a good or service that is supplied.

Production follows a similar nomenclature. $y_j \epsilon \mathcal{R}^{\mathcal{K}}$ is the production of firm j, the kth component of which is y_{jk}. For production vectors, positive elements are outputs and negative elements are inputs. $y = \sum_{j=1}^{J} y_j$ is the vector of country production.

---

[2] The description of notation follows Grinols, 2006.

The vector of real resources used by government as inputs, for the production of public goods as well as directly consumed in the operations of government, is $r \epsilon \mathcal{R}^{\mathcal{K}}$.

In conformity with the production conventions, vector $z \epsilon \mathcal{R}^{\mathcal{K}}$ denotes the excess demands, that is, international trade, of the economy. An element of z with a positive sign represents an imported good and a component with a negative sign is an exported good. Zero components are non-traded goods.

Endowments (nonproduced goods inherited from nature or the past) are denoted by $w \epsilon \mathcal{R}^{\mathcal{K}}$. Endowments owned by firm j are w_j. Firms, in turn, are owned by households. The share of firm j owned by household i is given by scalar θ_{ij}, where $\sum_i \theta_{ij} = 1$. Indirectly, therefore, the household owns $\theta_{ij} w_j$ of firm j's endowment and is entitled to θ_{ij} of firm j's profits and earnings from the sale of its endowments.

The vector of home-country domestic prices is $p_g \epsilon \mathcal{R}^{\mathcal{K}}$, although these prices are somewhat artificial in the sense that it is possible no agent (other than government, which does not pay taxes to itself) actually trades at them. World prices p_w can be thought of as the prices prevailing just outside the port location of the home country. They differ from home-country prices by duties γ, $p_g = p_w + \gamma$. The elements of p_w corresponding to non-traded goods are irrelevant since they appear opposite markets with zero quantities. Without loss of generality, therefore, we set them equal to domestic prices. To maintain the relation between p_g and p_w, of course, this implies that components of γ corresponding to non-traded goods are zero. Firms and households may also be subject to taxation. Their prices differ from domestic prices by tax wedges $p = p_g + t$, $p_y = p_g - \tau$. In each case the levy on good k is a *tax* if it collects positive revenue, $t_k x_k > 0, \tau_k y_k > 0$, or $\gamma_k z_k > 0$, as the case may be, and a *subsidy* if the signs are reversed, implying that collected revenue is negative.

An *allocation* $a = \{(x_i), (y_j), r, z\} \epsilon R^{(I+J+1)K}$ is defined as the list of all quantities of households, firms, government, and international trade. These definitions are, for the most part, standard and agree with general equilibrium conventions. When we compare discrete equilibria, we will reserve superscripts 0, 1 to refer to the alternative periods or situations being compared. Generally 0 refers to the initial or pre-policy situation and 1 to the final or post-policy situation.

C.2. Incentive Symmetry

Presume that an equilibrium obtains at prices $\{p_x^0, p_y^0, p_g^0, p_w^0\}$ where all markets clear

$$x^0 + r^0 = y^0 + w + z^0$$

$x^0 = x[p_x^0, I_x^0]$, $y^0 = y[p_y^0]$, the government's choices are r^0, and international trade is $z = z^0$. Household i's budget constraint is

$$p_x x_i^0 = I_i^0 = \sum_j p_y(y_j^0 + \omega_j) + T_i^0$$

where T_i^0 is transfers, if any, from government to individual i. Government revenues equal expenditures,

$$p_g^0 r^0 + \sum_i T_i^0 = \sum_i t_i^0 x_i^0 + \sum_j \tau_j^0(y_j^0 + \omega_j) + p_g^0 z^0.$$

Now presume that prices are altered to $\{\lambda_x p_x^0, \lambda_y p_y^0, \lambda_g p_g^0, p_w^0\}$ for positive scalars $\lambda_x, \lambda_y, \lambda_g$. Direct calculation shows that the implied taxes, $\gamma^1 = \lambda_g p_g^0 - p_w^0$, $t^1 = \lambda_x p_x^0 - \lambda p_g^0$, $\tau^1 = \lambda_g p_g^0 - \lambda_y p_y^0$, $T_i^1 = \lambda_x p_x^0 x_i^0 - \lambda_y p_y^0 (\sum_j \theta_{ij}(y_j^0 + \omega_j))$ satisfy the households' and government's budget constraint at the original allocation $a^0 = \{(x_i^0), (y_j^0), r^0, z^0\}$ and $I_x^1 = \lambda_x I_x^0$. The functions $x[\cdot, \cdot]$ and $y = y[\cdot]$ are homogeneous of degree 0, meaning that multiplying their arguments by a positive scalar does not alter the value taken by the function. For example, doubling all prices and income does not change the choices of individuals, neither does doubling all prices change the choices of firms. By homogeneity, therefore, firm choices have not changed, and because prices and income for the household are altered proportionally by λ_x, they are unchanged as well.

Scalars $\lambda_x, \lambda_y, \lambda_g$ can always be chosen so that good k is untaxed to a household or firm in the equilibrium 1 equivalent, $(p_{xk}^1 = p_{gk}^1, p_{yk}^1 = p_{gk}^1)$. We conclude that any equilibrium reached with a subsidy (tax) present on purchase of good k is reached by employing a tax (subsidy) on all other goods where the good k is unsubsidized (untaxed).

C.3. Intervention Principle

If the social goal is to increase the purchase of a given good, a specified quantity change is equivalent to a compensated change in the price of the good in question to the targeted economic agent sufficient to induce demand for the good at the new level (Guesnerie and Roberts, 1984). In our application an income adjustment to the selected agents is available through a mechanism such as the Earned Income Tax Credit. If society decides that it is desirable to raise the purchase of a given commodity by a specified list of agents, under a wide range of conditions a targeted intervention can accomplish the objective with increase in social well-being.

Proof that a targeted intervention is also part of an efficient policy is not difficult to demonstrate. The always-available ability to implement the tax-equivalent form of a subsidy was just shown. We now provide a demonstration of the result that the efficient remedy for underpurchase of a socially valuable commodity is a subsidy to its purchase. We do this in a simplified framework consisting of a representative consumer, no government (other than intervention to affect purchase of commodity 1), and a closed economy.[3] Thus $p_y = p_g \equiv p$, though $p_x = p - s$ differs from either by the (soon-to-be-shown-efficient) subsidy to purchase of the first good. s is a vector of zeroes except for its first element, which is $s_1 > 0$.

Let $e[p_x, u]$ be the expenditure function of the representative consumer, where $u = u[x]$ and x is the K-dimensional vector of consumption defined previously. Expenditure equal in value to $e[p_x, u]$ is the least that is capable of generating utility u to the consumer when prices are p_x. $e[p_x, u] = p_x \cdot x$ by construction of e. Market clearing is $x = y + \omega$.

Define the change in welfare by $\Delta \overset{o}{W} \equiv e[p_x^0, u^1] - e[p_x^0, u^0]$. Because the expenditure function is monotonic in utility for fixed prices, $\Delta \overset{o}{W}$ is positive if and only if $\Delta u = u^1 - u^0 > 0$. Now make use of the fact that if state 0 with the desired quantity of good 1 has been obtained in the best possible fashion, the move from it to any other state 1 with the desired provision attained by alternative means must *lower* utility. Showing that attaining the desired level of purchase of good 1 by any other means than a subsidy (or its tax equivalent) lowers u proves the result. Superscript 0 represents the initial situation where the subsidy has been used, and 1 the alternative situation, respectively. By direct computation,

$$\Delta \overset{o}{W} = -(p_x^0 \cdot x^1 - e[p_x^0, u^1]) - p_x^0 \cdot (x^0 - x^1)$$

$$= -(p_x^0 \cdot x^1 - e[p_x^0, u^1]) - (p^0 - s) \cdot (x^0 - x^1)$$

$$= -(p_x^0 \cdot x^1 - e[p_x^0, u^1])$$

$$-p^0 \cdot (y^0 - y^1) + s_1 \cdot (x_1^0 - x_1^1). \tag{C.1}$$

Since the targeted purchase of commodity 1 has been achieved at the minimally acceptable level in the initial equilibrium using positive subsidy s_1 and is also achieved in the alternative equilibrium, we have $x_1^1 \geq x_1^0$ and $s_1(x_1^0 - x_1^1) \leq 0$. However, we also know that the first two terms on the right-hand side of the last equation in (C.1) are nonpositive. The first term is nonpositive because of the fact that $e[p_x^0, u^1]$ is the least cost of attaining utility u^1 and therefore is less than or equal to $p_x^0 \cdot x^1$ (bundle x^1 also achieves

---

[3] The result is treated in more generality in Grinols, 2006.

utility $u^1 = u[x^1]$). The second is nonpositive because of the fact that firms maximize profits at market prices and hence $p^0 \cdot y^0 \geq p^0 \cdot y^1$. Thus, if the desired level of purchase of the first good is achieved through the application of a subsidy to its purchase, *any other policy that achieves the same objective lowers welfare when compared to the subsidy policy equilibrium.* We have shown that the intervention-principle-determined intervention does better than (or at least no worse than) any other intervention that accomplishes the targeted objective.

Appendix D

Plan Workability

In April 2006, Baylor University graduate students traveled to Washington, D.C., in fulfillment of the final requirement of their M.B.A.-based project. There they presented their carefully researched plan for universal health coverage, crafted on principles comparable to those in this book. Their research used Medical Expenditure Panel Survey data (MEPS, the gold standard for U.S. medical expenditures data), other sources, and their own statistical input to "price-out" what a national plan might cost. Their independently worked proposal had features in common with the Massachusetts plan (Section 9.2), which was publicly announced the day before their own presentation in the Russell Senate Building (arranged by Texas senator Kay Bailey Hutchison's office) before an audience of representives of Washington think tanks, the Council of Economic Advisers, and senatorial staff.

This appendix reproduces abbreviated highlights, edited for length. Within the normal range of uncertainties, their numbers parallel those from careful work by others and provide confidence in plan feasibility. For example, Jack Hadley and John Holahan (2003) report that it would cost $33.9–$68.7 billion (2001 dollars) in additional medical care if the uninsured were insured, versus $47 billion here. Our editorial comments are appended at the end.

D.1. Data

The Medical Expenditure Panel Survey (MEPS) for 2003, compiled and edited by the Centers for Medicare and Medicaid Services (CMS) at the U.S. Department of Health and Human Services, served as our primary data source for personal care expenditures. All data used in the model of the plan were 2003 data. To ensure comparability, MEPS aggregate data were reconciled to 2003 Personal Care Expenditures provided by the National

237

Health Expenditure Accounts (NHA) also compiled by the CMS. The NHA is prepared annually from a sample of hospitals, physician and clinical offices, and other sources. It is by far the most visible measure of national health expenditures. The aggregate personal health care figures from these two sources are remarkably compatible when put on the same definitional basis.[1]

D.2. Assessing the Targeted Intervention Plan

According to the MEPS data set, 2003 personal health care expenditures total $1.446 trillion. Non-reimbursed care is $40 billion; net of out-of-pocket payments from the uninsured are $34 billion.[2]

Impact of Insuring the Uninsured

Upon the purchase of insurance, we assume that a previously uninsured person will spend as much as a demographically comparable insured person. To simulate new expenditures of the uninsured, health expenditures were regressed on demographic characteristics including age, the number of children of selected ages, the number of adults in the family, household income, the number of family members in the household, race dummies, and sex, as well as zero-one indicators of insurance coverage and public insurance coverage (publicly insured consumers spend more, on average, than those with other sources, MEPS). Some of these variables were deemed critical determinants of health expenditures by both outside sources (MEPS, ehealthinsurance.com) as well as the regression.[3] The resulting regression equation was used to assign more accurate expenditures to the previously uninsured. Expenditures for currently insured people were assumed to remain the same.

Government Subsidies

Government aid was administered through the MEPS simulation by determining the household's health expenditures as a percentage of household income (HEPHHI). If the household's HEPHHI exceeded an income-dependent threshhold, the household received government aid covering spending beyond the threshhold. For instance, if a family had a HEPHHI

---

[1] A reconciliation of aggregate MEPS personal care expenditure figures to personal care expenditure figures in the NHA for 2003 was provided in the report.

[2] Explanation of how these numbers were derived is omitted in this appendix.

[3] Regression details omitted in this appendix.

Table D.1. *Maximal Household Spending as Percentage of Own Income Before Program Aid Is Given*

Household income	Percentage of household income
$0	Full aid
$3 to $9,277	1%
$9,278 to $19,348	1.5%
$19,349 to $24,999	2%
$25,000 to $35,455	5%
$35,456 to $44,999	7%
$45,000 to $54,999	10%
$55,000+	Little or no aid

of 10 percent and their income group's threshhold was 2 percent, they received aid for health expenditures equal to 10 percent − 2 percent = 8 percent of household income. Table D.1 gives the threshholds we selected.

HEPHHI thresholds are intended to be progressive.[4] For instance, households with incomes between $19,349 and $24,999 spend only 2 percent of their own household income on health expenditures before receiving a subsidy, while those making $55,000 and above receive no aid. Responsibility for insurance purchase lies with households themselves, distinguishing the arrangements from purely government-provided universal health plans.

Funds Used to Insure the Uninsured

Funds for insuring the uninsured are from both private payments of the previously uninsured and government subsidies. Government subsidies are funded by the health provider revenue tax, the health insurance provider revenue tax, and the compliance levy.

According to our simulation summarized in Figure D.1, health care providers (including hospitals, clinics, and pharmaceutical companies) will receive a gain in aggregate revenues of $47 billion from newly insured people (or a 3.3 percent increase in total aggregate revenue, MEPS). At the same time, both health care providers and health insurance providers are subject to a tax of 3.3 percent of revenues that will cover the $103 billion in government aid not covered by the sales levy (the sales levy will cover $4 billion of the $107 billion in government aid needed). This allows the government to access cost-shifting dollars in the present system.

---

[4] Methodology was described but is omitted here.

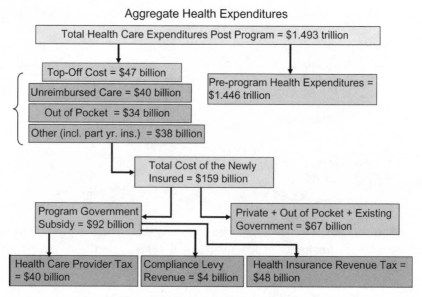

Figure D.1. Sources and Uses of Funds

A person who does not purchase health insurance will pay an additional 8 percent tax on goods and services purchased at retail establishments. He or she will be exempt from the levy by confirming health insurance coverage through the electronic swipe of a credit card, driver's license, or government issued insurance coverage verification card at the retail establishment. If the person forgets all forms of identification, he or she can save the receipt and file for a levy rebate at a later time such as when filing the regular income tax return.

We chose the tax rate to be 8 percent so that the average newly insured person will face the choice of spending either 8 percent or more of his or her annual household consumption net of health care of $38,401 (Bureau of Labor Statistics average household consumption, annual sales levy = $0.08 \times \$38,401 = \$3,046$) versus spending $3,046 annually (average household health care expenditures of the MEPS newly insured group, net of government subsidies) on health insurance. A tax level set near 8 percent is expected to induce the average person in our sample to purchase insurance or seek government aid, because the annual taxes paid in lieu of purchasing insurance, on average, will be higher (BLS, MEPS).

The tax could be set higher if desired, ensuring compliance of almost all of the population. A full assessment of tax inducement behavior was outside the scope of this project.

Also, we considered factors for determining a base plan that people could purchase to avoid the compliance levy.[5]

Those who currently have health insurance (private, government provided employer provided) along with those who become insured can receive a card that will serve as a proof of insurance, or insurance coverage can be confirmed through credit cards and driver's licenses. Cards and insurance coverage verification will be administered by the Center for Medicare and Medicaid Services, which currently administers federal Medicare and Medicaid coverage. When a person purchases insurance, insurance companies, as mandated by a new law, will automatically update the CMS database with basic information (name, birth date, a unique identifier, insurance coverage date of initiation/expiration, and address) that will trigger the verification of this coverage and/or the release of a personalized health insurance card via mail. Electronically, as the Social Security Administration does with Social Security Benefits (SSA Web site), the CMS database will assess whether the person qualifies for the government subsidy via a direct electronic link to his or her IRS records. If the person does qualify, CMS will electronically send the monthly premium bill directly to the insurance company that e-registered the card. Upon termination of the policy, CMS's database system will automatically deactivate the card (so that the person now must pay the sales levy on purchases again) and any government subsidy checks to insurers will terminate.

As a substitute for automatic registration, a separate mechanism can allow people to register on CMS's Web site, or, if they do not have a computer or access to a public library with one, in person at the local Social Security Administration.

Post-Program Expenditures

Post-program total personal health care expenditures for the entire U.S. population will be $1.493 trillion (MEPS). This figure includes a "top-off cost," or the additional personal health care expenditures to the country resulting from universal insurance coverage, of $47 billion. The increase in health care expenditures by the previously uninsured is the "top-off cost."

It is important to note that prior to the universal coverage program, cost shifting, or the level of non-reimbursed care reflected in higher premiums, is covered by the insured population. After the implementation of the health care plan, the added costs related to raising the uninsured from a health care utilization level of 50 percent (Kaiser, MEPS) of what the typical insured

[5] Details omitted in this appendix.

person utilizes to 100 percent results in an increase in total national personal care expenditures.

The total national expenditure of the newly insured is $159 billion, which includes non-reimbursed care of the previously uninsured ($40 billion) added to the top-off costs of $47 billion and the out-of-pocket expenditures of the newly insured (assumed to remain $34 billion). The remaining $38 billion is the insurance coverage for those previously insured for part of the year as well as new private self-pay. Government subsidies to those who cannot afford insurance will total $107 billion, funded by $103 billion in health insurance provider tax revenue and health care provider tax revenue combined, and $4 billion in compliance levy revenue.

Long-Term Effects

As everyone in the population starts to buy his or her own insurance, the number of dollars spent by the insured to subsidize non-payers will decrease. Once the uninsured population joins the program, insurance premium prices will adjust accordingly, and buying insurance will be more affordable for everyone. In the long run, the burden of non-reimbursed care will shrink to covering a much diminished group of non-compliers, people who refuse to purchase insurance on their own or have their purchase subsidized by the program. As noted earlier, the best estimate of a non-compliance rate is that of Switzerland, because the Swiss possess the health care system most similar to the Targeted Intervention Plan (Chapter 9).

The Swiss system mandates that all citizens purchase insurance, and it provides government support to those who qualify for it. If a person remains uninsured, upon seeking medical treatment at a health service provider, he or she is automatically enrolled in a private plan selected by the federal government and is charged a penalty. The Targeted Intervention Plan does not mandate purchase but instead encourages it by an incentive levy.

D.3. Recommendations

The Targeted Intervention Plan can succeed as a universal health care plan if it addresses certain political risks and the research is developed more fully. Politically, leaders must have a working prototype example before taking the political risk of sponsoring a proposal. We suggest running a pilot program for children, giving families the health insurance card proposed (and subsequent tax rebate if they forget their card) if the family insures all of its children.

Also, the revenue gains of health care providers under the Targeted Intervention Plan should be highlighted to mitigate opposition to the provider tax. The purpose of the compliance levy solely as a compliance incentive measure should be stressed.

This plan provides net aggregate benefits for health care providers, the currently insured, insurance companies, and, most importantly, the currently uninsured. The program achieves almost universal coverage with relatively little in government aid, and this aid can be fully funded by the proposed mechanism. If its implications are researched and a working prototype is implemented, the proposal is politically feasible.

D.4. Summary and Evaluative Discussion

The purpose of the project was to improve understanding of the ramifications of plan feasibility and to identify relevant costs from a national perspective. The graduate students also researched the choice of insurance instrument (work not summarized in this appendix) and decided that it should include all benefits that have a premium-lowering or premium-neutral effect, benefits mandated by twenty-five or more states, benefits that every state Medicaid plan includes, plus preventive services as outlined by the U.S. Preventive Services Task Force of the Department of Health and Human Services. They also researched the potential for cost savings from improved choice of financial parameters for health insurance coverage (choice of deductible, co-insurance, and out-of-pocket rates) and concluded that savings were possible. They did not incorporate savings estimates into their estimates of program costs, however, to provide an expanded margin for error. We acted as advisers to the project but did not impose choices. Thus, the aid schedule adopted by the students may have been somewhat more generous and the insurance product coverage somewhat more broad – especially for younger adults – than others might have selected.

Nevertheless, the students' choice of plan parameters was feasible, was self-funding, and could accomplish the objective of inducing nearly all of the American population to purchase high-quality health insurance at a price that did not seem daunting. They found the following:

- "Top-off" costs were $47 billion ($341 per member of the workforce, 0.43 percent of GDP, 5.93 percent of personal income taxes),[6]

---

[6]   The 2003 GDP = $10,960.8, 2003 civilian employment = 137,736 million, personal income taxes = $793.7 billion (*Economic Report of the President*, 2007).

- Needed government aid was $92 billion ($668 per member of the workforce, 0.84 percent of GDP, 11.6 percent of personal income taxes), and
- Total cost of health care for the (currently) uninsured was $159 billion ($1,154 per member of the workforce, 1.5 percent of GDP, 20 percent of personal income taxes).
- The program is self-financing using a 3.3 percent provider revenue tax (plus a small amount expected to derive from the compliance levy) because the base is broad.

Keeping costs close to the (encouraging) numbers described requires careful implementation of features that make the plan elements incentive-compatible to users and payers. Separating income aid (Earned Income Tax Credit) from inducements to purchase insurance (compliance levy), financially engineering the insurance instrument to retain incentives for consumer cost-conscious decision making, and keeping plan coverages only to those features that everyone wants at each age cohort are examples. Rationalizing the health care marketplace and insurance underwriting (Chapters 7 and 8) was outside the scope of the students' work but is equally important.

Appendix E

Market Power Response to Insurance

Sellers with market power respond to insurance by extracting more from their buyers. For example, presume that a monopolist – this could be a pharmaceutical manufacturer with a drug under patent – sells quantity q_0 at price p_0. Next, assume that buyers acquire insurance that specifies their payment to be fraction c of the product's cost. The seller responds by raising the price charged to $\frac{1}{c}p_0$ and adjusts to a different price and quantity only if profits are thereby raised further. A 10 percent co-insurance provision, for example, would magnify the supplier's profits more than a tenfold increase in price at the original output would. In addition to the appearance of abusing an insurance program, the increase in market price makes it harder for those not covered with insurance who buy the same product. Figure E.1 shows the effect on price and quantity for a linear example. Given initial demand curve D, price and quantity are p_0 and q_0 at point a.

Introduction of the prescription drug program causes the effective demand curve to shift to D', where the price at point b is $\frac{1}{c}p_0$. The monopolist is guaranteed to earn at least the additional profits associated with the multiplied price but in fact does better because the change affects marginal revenue and the new profit maximizing choice of output occurs at quantity q_1 associated with point c where post-program marginal revenue equals marginal cost. Thus as already noted, if 10 percent is the assumed co-insurance percentage, the rise in price from a to b is tenfold and profits rise by more than the amount this would sustain.

The same outcome is shown analytically. Let downward sloping demand for the prescription drug be $q = D[p^d]$, where p^d is demand price (the price paid by the buyer) and q is the quantity demanded. If the insurance program subsidizes fraction $(1 - c)$ of the product's cost, the demand price becomes $p^d = cp^s$ where p^s is the price received by the seller. The patentee maximizes post-program profits

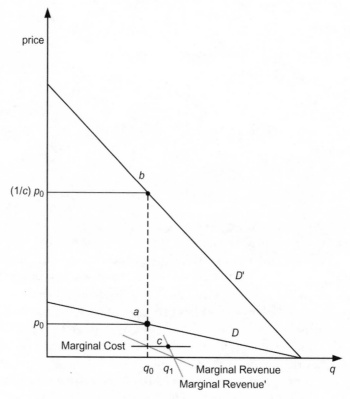

Figure E.1. Monopoly Price Response to Buyer Co-Payment

$$\Pi[p^d, c] = R[p^d, c] - C[q[p^d]] = \frac{1}{c}p^d D[p^d] - C[D[p^d]] \qquad \text{(E.1)}$$

by choice of price p^d where $C[q]$ is total cost of supplying q units of product. By the envelope theorem,

$$\frac{d\Pi}{dc} = \frac{\partial\Pi}{\partial c} = \frac{\partial R}{\partial c} = \frac{d(\frac{1}{c})}{dc} p^d q. \qquad \text{(E.2)}$$

In other words, insurance raises expenditures on the product and the profits of the patent holder in proportion to the amount that the change in subsidy raises the multiplier $\frac{1}{c}$.

Glossary and Definitions

Actuarially fair premiums: The actuarially fair premium for an insurance policy is equal to the expected claims payout on the policy to the insured.

Adverse selection: A feature of insurance markets resulting from asymmetric information whereby an insurer may be unable to predict the risk type, or attract the risk type it desires, for insurance policies it offers. Buyers, who know their risk, self-select into policies (higher/adverse risk individuals tend to choose higher levels of insurance), while the insurer, who may not be able to identify in advance the different risk levels of buyers, may not be able to attract a homogeneous risk type for its policy.

Co-insurance: The fractional portion of a health care claim paid by the insured. See **co-pay**. Some use the terms "co-pay" and "co-insurance" synonymously.

Co-pay: A fixed sum paid by the insured as his or her portion of a health care claim. See **co-insurance**. Some use the terms "co-pay" and "co-insurance" synonymously.

Cost shifting: Cost shifting refers to the practice of charging some customers more than the cost of their good or service and using the surplus to pay for goods or services of other customers who do not pay or who pay less than the cost of providing them the goods and services they receive.

Community (group) rating: The practice of grouping individuals of a given community or group into a common insurance pool and charging them the same premium for insurance, regardless of their different ages, sex, and likelihood that they will have claims of unequal value.

Crowding out: The tendency of public programs to supplant private means that accomplish the same objective. In the case of public health insurance, crowding out implies that individuals with private health insurance drop their private coverage and enroll in the government program because it is publicly supported.

Deadweight loss: See **tax deadweight loss.**

Deductible: A stated dollar amount, usually applying to health care claims over a year's time, which the insured is expected to pay out of pocket.

Experience rating: A method whereby the premium paid for the insurance coverage of an individual is based on the actuarially fair, or expected payout, benefit that applies to that individual from the coverage.

Guaranteed renewability: A guarantee that a buyer of health insurance can buy the base insurance plan for the same premium payment as others of identical age, sex, and location of residence.

High risk: Individuals with expectation of higher than average future health expenditures than others of their age, sex, and residence location.

Incentive: An inducement or encouragement to act in a given way, where the choice to act or not to act remains with the individual. Incentives are usually pecuniary, as in a price advantage or reward.

Indemnity insurance: Insurance that pays a previously determined payout upon the occurrence of a specified risky event. Most health care insurance, in contrast, makes payment according to medical charges incurred in treatment of a medical condition.

Mandate: An authoritative law or command that requires all individuals to act in a given way. See **incentive**.

Major medical insurance: Medical insurance characterized by a deductible amount, a co-insurance rate, and an out-of-pocket limit. Cumulative expenses up to the deductible total are paid 100 percent by the insured. Payments beyond the deductible are paid by the insured at the co-insurance rate, and payments beyond the out-of-pocket limit are paid entirely by the insurer. Provisions usually apply on a yearly basis.

Moral hazard: The phenomenon that the presence of insurance and the nature of the insurance offered cause the need for increased payout for covered events where the payout exceeds the net social value. Insuring one's home for greatly more than it is worth in the event of fire might create the incentive for arson – hence the term "moral" hazard – but moral hazard arises from legal and moral choices of behavior as well. Writing insurance in a way that retains the insurance function but reduces outlays where the expenditure exceeds the social value of what is received is said to reduce moral hazard.

Opportunity cost: The opportunity cost of a choice is the lost benefits of the forgone next best alternative.

Out-of-pocket limit: The dollar amount above which the insurer pays 100 percent of the cost of medical claims for the insured. A $3,000 out-of-pocket limit, for example, guarantees that the insured will pay no more than $3,000 in any given year for health care expenses.

Pre-paid care: Payment made into a health care plan in advance for care that is predictable (not based on the outcome of a risky event).

Private good or service: Good or service characterized by rivalness in consumption; consumption of a private good or service by one individual precludes another individual from consuming the same good or service.

Public good or service: Good or service characterized by non-rivalness in consumption; consumption of a pure public good by one individual does not preclude another individual from consuming the same good. For example, consumption of a radio broadcast by one individual does not prevent other individuals from consuming the same broadcast. See expanded discussion in Section 4.3, "Public Goods."

Ramsey pricing: Choosing taxes across goods and services in such a way that the resulting prices generate the needed tax revenue with minimal loss in well-being of the residents of the taxed economy.

Rate bands: In insurance premium setting, the variation in premiums allowed by state regulations. Rate bands are expressed as a multiple of the average rate. For example, a 10 percent rate band might allow premiums equal to 1.1 times the index or average rate. See **re-insurance**.

Rationalize: To remove unreasonable features from something. With respect to the health care sector, rationalization involves establishing conditions for the functioning of market competition. With respect to health insurance, rationalization involves changing features of insurance itself (such as requiring guaranteed renewability of insurance at standard rates for all policyholders) and removing restrictions on the freedom to underwrite, such as eliminating overly burdensome coverage requirements.

Reclassification risk: The risk that an individual will enter a medical state where permanently higher future medical costs can be expected, compared to those of others of the same description (age, sex, geographic location, and verifiable lifestyle choices affecting health).

Re-insurance: "Insurance for insurance companies," that is, insurance where the buyers and sellers are insurance companies. Re-insurance is usually accomplished by an association of insurance companies that pool their resources to pay high-cost claims. In Chapter 8 a re-insurance mechanism was described whereby individuals in higher-than-average risk class could be re-insured to allow them to transfer insurance from company to company after reclassification events have occurred.

Rent ("economic rent"): Payment to a factor above the amount needed to keep it in its current use. Payment to a factor above its opportunity cost.

Risk pooling: Forming a group or pool into which all members make payments. Outlays made from the common pool go to members of the group who experience insured events. For participants, risk pooling converts their exposure to risky random outlays into a predictable stream of premium payments.

Social insurance: Insurance where beneficiaries pay actuarially fair premiums operated under the auspices of government, such as indemnity insurance issued through government auspices. Premiums are tax payments and all citizens participate under penalty of law. The term "social insurance" is sometimes used loosely by others (but not in this book) to refer to any of various forms of insurance in which a government is an insurer, including programs that contain substantial elements of charity, and hence actuarially unfair premiums.

Tax deadweight loss: The amount by which lost economic well-being to the private sector (lost consumer surplus and firm profits) due to a tax exceeds the amount of tax collected; the extra loss incurred by the private sector, beyond the amount of tax collected.

Top-off costs: Were uninsured individuals to become insured their use of health care resources would rise. Top-off costs are the extra cost to the nation of this increased usage reflecting universal insurance coverage.

Underwriting: The creation of insurance agreements that bind the insurer, in return for a premium payment by the insured, to contribute a sum of money to the insured in case of certain losses specified in the policy. Freedom of underwriting implies the ability of insurance carriers to decide what policies to write, whom to sell to, and what premiums to charge. In the Targeted Intervention Plan, the elements of the plan's base policy only would be determined programmatically to vary by the age and sex of the buyer, and to provide guaranteed renewability.

References

Acton, Lord. Letter to Bishop Manndell Creighton, 1887.

Adams, Scott J."Employer-Sponsored Health Insurance and Job Change," *Contemporary Economic Policy*, 22(3), July 2004, 357–369.

Agha, Ali, and Jonathan Haughton. "Designing VAT Systems: Some Efficiency Considerations," *Review of Economics and Statistics*, May 1996, 303–308.

American Hospital Association. *Hospital Statistics 2005*. Chicago: AHA, October 2005.

American Hospital Association. "A Time for Action: A Unified Health Care Policy for the U.S.," document supplied to the authors by Richard J. Pollack, Executive Vice President, 17 March 2005.

Anderson, Gerard F., Uwe E. Reinhardt, Peter S. Hussey, and Vardhui Petrosyan. "It's the Prices, Stupid: Why the United States Is So Different from Other Countries," *Health Affairs*, 22(3), May/June 2003, 89–105.

Anderson, Greg. "Empowering Patients and Frontline Staff Is the Key to Better Healthcare" (eGov Monitor, 7 November 2005) www.egovmonitor.com/node/3443.

Andrews, L. B. "The Gene Patent Dilemma: Balancing Commercial Incentives with Health Needs," *Houston Journal of Health Law and Policy*, 2, 2002, 65–106.

Arrow, Kenneth. "Uncertainty and the Welfare Economics of Medical Care," *American Economic Review*, December 1963, 941–973.

Arrow, Kenneth. "The Economy of Trust," *Religion & Society*, Acton Institute, 16(3), Summer 2006. http://www.acton.org/publicat/randl/interview.php?id=556.

Ballard, Charles L., John B. Shoven, and John Whalley. "General Equilibrium Computations of the Marginal Welfare Costs of Taxes in the United States," *American Economic Review*, 75, 1985, 128–138.

Barlett, Donald L., and James B. Steele. "Why We Pay So Much for Drugs," *Time Magazine*, 163(5), 2 February 2004, 45–52.

Barton, John H. "TRIPS and the Global Pharmaceutical Market," *Health Affairs*, 23(3), 2004, 146–154.

Bastiat, Frederic. "What Is Seen and What Is Not Seen," reprinted in *Selected Essays on Political Economy*, ed. George B. de Huszar. 1995, http://www.econlib.org/library/Bastiat/basEss1.html.

Bastiat, Frederic. *Economic Harmonies*, trans. W. Hayden Boyers, ed. George B. De Huszar. Irvington-on-Hudson, NY: The Foundation for Economic

Education, 1996. http://www.econlib.org/library/Bastiat/basHar17.html [accessed 23 May 2003].

Baumol, W. J., and D. Bradford. "Optimal Departures from Marginal Cost Pricing," *American Economic Review*, 60(3), 1970, 265–283.

Beck, Konstantin, Stefan Spycher, Alberto Holly, and Lucien Gardiol, "Risk Adjustment in Switzerland," *Health Policy*, 65, 2003, 63–74.

Becker, Gary S. "Are We Hurting or Helping the Disabled?" *Business Week*, 2 August 1999, p. 21.

Bennefield, Robert L. "Dynamics of Economic Well-Being: Health Insurance 1993 to 1995, Who Loses Coverage and for How Long?" U.S. Census Bureau, *Current Population Reports*, P70-64, August 1998, 1–6.

Bennett, William F. "Report: 40 Percent of County's Medi-Cal Births to Illegal Immigrants," NCTimes.com, 8 January 2007. www. nctimes.com/articles/2007/01/07news/top_stories10_40_021_6—07.prt.

Bernhardt, Daniel, and Jan Zabojnik. "Welfare-Harming Competitive Health Insurance When Health Care Is Uncompetitive," University of Illinois, University of Southern California, Working Paper, 2006.

Blendon, Robert J., Kelly Hunt, John M. Benson, Channtal Fleischfresser, and Tami Buhr. "Understanding the American Public's Health Priorities: A 2006 Perspective," *Health Affairs Web Exclusive*, 17 October 2006, 508–515.

Bombardieri, Marcella. "Clinton Eyes Boost to 401(k) Savings," *Boston Globe*, 10 October 2007. http://www.boston.com/news/nation/articles/2007/10/10/clinton_eyes_boost_to_401k_savings/ [accessed 3 December 2007].

Brooks, Arthur C. *Who Really Cares: The Surprising Truth about Compassionate Conservatism*. New York: Basic Books, Perseus Books Group, 2006.

Buchanan, James M. "The Samaritan's Dilemma," in *Freedom in Constitutional Contract*. College Station: Texas A&M University Press, 1977, 169–185.

Buchanan, James M. "Interview with James Buchanan," *The Region*, September 1995. www.minneapolisfed.org/pubs/region/95-09/int959.cfm [accessed 4 August 2006].

Buchmueller, Thomas C. "Does a Fixed-Dollar Premium Contribution Lower Spending?" *Health Affairs*, 17(6), 1998, 228–235.

Bundorf, M. Kate, and Mark V. Pauly. "Is Health Insurance Affordable for the Uninsured?" *Journal of Health Economics*, 25, 2006, 650–673.

Bureau of Labor Statistics. 2003 Consumer Expenditure Data. www.bls.gov.

Burk, D. L., and M. A. Lemley. "Policy Levers in Patent Law," *Virginia Law Review*, 89, 2003, 1575.

Cannon, Michael F., and Michael D. Tanner. *Health Competition: What's Holding Back Health Care and How to Free It*. Washington, DC: Cato Institute, 2005.

Carnegie, Andrew. "Popular Illusions about Trusts," *The Gospel of Wealth and Other Timely Essays*, ed. Edward C. Kirkland. Cambridge, MA: Harvard University Press, 1962.

Carnegie Commission on Higher Education. *Higher Education: Who Pays? Who Benefits? Who Should Pay?* New York: McGraw-Hill Book Company, 1973.

Cato Institute. "It's Your Money: A Citizen's Guide to Social Security Reform." 2005. http://www.socialsecurity.org/daily/05-11-99.html.

Cavers, David. "More Private Health Insurance Is Desirable and Inevitable," in *Ethics in Public and Community Health*, ed. Peter Bradley and Amanda Burls. New York: Routledge, 2000, 151–164.

Census, U.S. 2003 Supplement. www.census.gov.

Center on Budget and Policy Priorities. "The Number of Uninsured Americans Continued to Rise in 2004," 30 August 2005. http://www.cbpp.org/8-30-05health.htm.

Centers for Medicare and Medicaid Services. NHE Web Tables, Data on U.S. Prescription Drug Expenditures, 2004. http://www.cms.hhs.gov/NationalHealthExpendData/downloads/tables.pdf [accessed 4 April 2007].

Chappell, Les. "Senate Wants State Involved in Healthcare IT Partnership" (Wisconsin Technology Network, 2 March 2006), http://wistechnology.com/article.php?id=2741.

Citizens' Council on Health Care. "Distribution, Utilization and Impact of the MinnesotaCare Provider Tax," January 2000. http://www.cchconline.org/publications/providertaxsumm.php3.

Citizens' Council on Health Care. Issues – Provider Tax. www.cchc-mn.org/issues/providertax.php3.

The Citizens' Health Care Working Group. "Group Suggests System Guidelines," reported in *USA Today*, 15 June 2006, 4B.

Cleveland, Grover. *Congressional Record*, 49 Congress, 2d Session, Vol. XVIII, Pt. II, 1887.

Coase, Robert. "The Problem of Social Cost," *Journal of Law and Economics*, 3(1), 1966, 1–44.

Congressional Black Caucus Foundation. "Congressional Budget Office Study Finds 60 Million without Health Care." http://www.cbcfinc.org/Resources/Health_Care03.html.

Congressional Budget Office. "How Many People Lack Health Insurance and For How Long?" Washington, DC: The Congress of the United States, May 2003. http://www.cbo.gov/showdoc.cfm?index=4210&sequence=0

Congressional Budget Office. "Research and Development in the Pharmaceutical Industry." Washington, DC: The Congress of the United States, October 2006, i–vii, 1–46.

Copeland, Craig. "Characteristics of the Nonelderly with Selected Sources of Health Insurance and Lengths of Uninsured Spells," *EBRI Issue Brief* No. 198, June 1998.

Corning, Peter A. *The Evolution of Medicare. . .from Idea to Law*. History contracted by the Social Security Office of Research and Statistics. 1969. http://www.ssa.gov/history/corning.html [accessed 17 July 2007].

The Council for Affordable Health Insurance. "Can Government Force People to Buy Insurance?" March 2004. www.cahi.org/cahi_contents/resources/pdf/n123GovernmentMandate.pdf.

The Council for Affordable Health Insurance. "Health Insurance Mandates in the States 2005," 9 September 2005. www.cahi.org/cahicontents/resources/pdf/MandatePubDec2004.pdf.

Council of Economic Advisers. *Economic Report of the President, 2003*. Washington, DC: U.S. Government Printing Office, 2003, 199. http://www.gpoaccess.gov/usbudget/fy04/pdf/2003_erp.pdf.

Cox, W. Michael, and Richard Alm. *By Our Own Bootstraps: Economic Opportunity and the Dynamics of Income Distribution*. Dallas: Federal Reserve Bank of Dallas, 1995, 8. http://www.dallasfed.org/fed/annual/1999p/ar95.pdf.

Cutler, David M., and Jonathan Gruber. "Does Public Insurance Crowd Out Private Insurance?" *Quarterly Journal of Economics*, 111(2), May 1996, 391–430.

Cutler, David M., and S. J. Reber. "Paying for Health Insurance: The Tradeoff between Competition and Adverse Selection," *Quarterly Journal of Economics*, 113(2), 1998, 433–466.

Cutler, David M. and Richard J. Zeckhauser. "The Anatomy of Health Insurance," in *Handbook of Health Economics*, Vol. 1, ed. A. J. Culyer and J. P. Newhouse. Amsterdam: Elsevier Science, 2000, 563–643.

Danzon, Patricia M. "Price Discrimination for Pharmaceuticals: Welfare Effects in the US and the EU." *International Journal of the Economics of Business*, 4(3), 1997, 301–321.

De Bartolome, Charles A. M. "The Public Provision of Private Goods," Ph.D. Dissertation, University of Pennsylvania, 1985.

Debates in Congress, Publisher, Date Unidentified.

Debreu, Gerard. *Theory of Value: An Axiomatic Analysis of Economic Equilibrium.* New Haven, CT: Yale University Press, 1959.

DeGrazia, David. "Why the United States Should Adopt a Single-Payer System of Health Care Finance," *Kennedy Institute of Ethics Journal,* 5(2), June 1996, 145–160.

Deloitte Center for Health Solutions. "2008 Survey of Health Care Consumers: Executive Summary." Washington, DC: Deloitte Development LLC, 2008.

Derose, Kathryn Pitkin, Jose J. Escarce, and Nicole Lurie. "Immigrants and Health Care: Sources of Vulnerability," *Health Affairs*, 26(5), September/October 2007, 1258–1268.

de Tocqueville, Alexis. "Government of the Democracy in America," Chapter 13 in *Democracy in America.* 1835. http://xroads.virginia.edu/~HYPER/DETOC/toc_indx.html [accessed 27 November 2007].

de Tocqueville, Alexis. *Memoir on Pauperism,* trans. Seymour Drescher. London: Civitas, 1997, 30.

DiMasi, Joseph A., Ronald W. Hansen, and Henry G. Grabowski. "The Price of Innovation: New Estimates on Drug Development Costs," *Journal of Health Economics*, 22(2), 2003, 151–185.

Dixit, Avinash. "Tax Policy in Open Economies," in *Handbook of Public Economics*, Vol. 1, ed. A. J. Auerbach and M. Feldstein. New York: Elsevier Science Publishers, B.V. (North-Holland), 1985, 313–374.

Drexler, Madeline. "The Little Scratch That Almost Killed Him," *Good Housekeeping*, 6 January 2007, 52 ff.

Duncan, Greg J., and James N. Morgan. "An Overview of Family Economic Mobility," in *Years of Poverty/Years of Plenty*, ed. Greg J. Duncan. Ann Arbor: Survey Research Center, Institute for Social Research, University of Michigan, 1984, 13.

Economic Report of the President. Washington, DC: U.S. Government Printing Office, 2008.

Ehrlich, Eva. "The Size Structure of Manufacturing Establishment and Enterprises: An International Comparison," *Journal of Comparative Economics*, 9(3), September 1985, 267–295.

Ellis, Edward S. *The Life of Colonel David Crockett*. Philadelphia: Porter & Coates, 1884.

Ellis, Randall P., Arlene S. Ash, John Z. Ayanian, David W. Bates, Helen Burstin, Lisa I. Iezzoni, and Gregory C. Pope. "Diagnosis-Based Risk Adjustment for Medicare Capitation Payments," *Health Care Financing Review*, 17(3), 1996, 101–128.

Ellis, Randall P., and Thomas G. McGuire. "Provider Behavior under Prospective Reimbursement: Cost Sharing and Supply," *Journal of Health Economics*, 5(2), 1986, 129–152.

Ellis, Randall P., and Thomas G. McGuire. "Optimal Payment Systems for Health Services," *Journal of Health Economics*, 9(4), 1990, 375–396.

Enthoven, Alain C. "Employment-Based Health Insurance Is Failing: Now What?" *Health Affairs*, Web exclusive W3, May 28, 2003, 237–249. http://content. healthaffairs.org/cgi/reprint/hltaff.w3.237v1.

Feldstein, Martin. "Tax Avoidance and the Deadweight Loss of the Income Tax," *The Review of Economics and Statistics*, 81(4), November 1999, 674–680.

Fowles, J. B., J. P. Weiner, D. Knutson, E. Fowler, A. M. Tucker, and M. Ireland. "Taking Health Status into Account When Setting Capitation Rates: A Comparison of Risk-Adjustment Methods," *Journal of the American Medical Association*, 276(16), 1996, 1316–1321.

Frank, Robert. *What Price the High Moral Ground?* Princeton, NJ: Princeton University Press, 2004.

Franklin, Benjamin. "On the Price of Corn, and Management of the Poor," (1766) in *The Works of Benjamin Franklin*, Vol. 2, ed. Jared Sparks. Chicago: Townsend Mac Coun, 1882, 355–360.

The Franklin Institute. http://fi.edu/franklin/statsman/statsman.html [accessed 6 February 2007].

Frech, H. E. and Paul Ginsburg. "Imposed Health Insurance in Monopolistic Markets: A Theoretical Analysis," *Economic Inquiry*, 13(1), 1975, 55–70.

Friedman, Milton. *Capitalism and Freedom*. Chicago: University of Chicago Press, 1962.

Friedman, Milton. "Gammon's Law Points to Health-Care Solution," *Wall Street Journal*, 12 November 1991, A20.

Friedman, Milton. (1998). "The Role of Government in Education." http://www. schoolchoices.org/roo/fried1.htm.

Friedman, Milton. "Speaking the Truth about Social Security Reform," *Cato Institute Briefing Papers*, No. 46, 12 April 1999.

Friedman, Milton. "How to Cure Health Care," *The Public Interest*, Winter 2001, 3–30. http://www.thepublicinterest.com/archives/2001/winter/articlel.html.

Gallup Poll. 9–12, November 2006. http://www.pollingreport.com/health3.htm, [accessed 21 February 2007].

Gauthier, Anne, and Michelle Serber. *A Need to Transform the U.S. Healthcare System: Improving Access, Quality, and Efficiency*. New York: The Commonwealth Fund, 2005. http://www.commonwealthfund.org.

Genetski, Robert. "Our Pensions: Private Social Security," *Wall Street Journal*, 21 May 1993.

Gilmer, Todd, and Richard Kronick. "It's the Premiums, Stupid, Projections of Uninsured through 2013," *Health Affairs*, Web exclusive, W5, 143–151, 5 April 2005. http://content.healthaffairs.org/cgi/reprint/hltaff.w5.143v1.

Glassman, James K. "Here's What's Wrong with Social Security," *Scripps Howard News Service*, 3 January 2005.

Gold, Marsha R., Jessica Mittler, Anna Aizer, Barbara Lyons, and Cathy Schoen. "Health Insurance Expansion through States in a Pluralistic System," *Journal of Health Politics, Policy and Law*, 26(3), 2001, 581–616.

Goodman, John C. "Characteristics of an Ideal Health Care System," Policy Report No. 242, April 2001. http://www.ncpa.org/pub/st/st242/ [accessed 15 May 2006].

Goodman, John C. "What Is Consumer-Directed Health Care?" *Health Affairs* Web Exclusive, 24 October 2006, 540–543. http://content.healthaffairs.org/cgi/reprint/25/6/w540.

Goodman, John C. "Applying the 'Do No Harm'" Principle to Health Policy," *Journal of Legal Medicine*, 28 May 2007, 37–52.

Gottschalk, Peter. "Inequality, Income Growth, and Mobility: The Basic Facts," *Journal of Economic Perspectives*, 11(2), Spring 1997, 37.

Grabowski, Henry, and John Vernon. "Longer Patents for Lower Imitation Barriers: The 1984 Drug Act," *The American Economic Review: Papers and Proceedings*, 76(2), 1986, 195–198.

Grabowski, Henry, John Vernon, and Joseph A. DiMasi. "Returns on Research and Development for the 1990s New Drug Introductions," *PharmacoEconomics*, 20 (suppl 3), 2002, 11–29.

Grinols, Earl L. *Microeconomics*. Boston: Houghton Mifflin, 1994.

Grinols, Earl L. *Gambling In America: Costs and Benefits*. New York: Cambridge University Press, 2004.

Grinols, Earl L. "The Intervention Principle," *Review of International Economics*, 14(2), May 2006, 226–247.

Grinols, Earl L., and H. C. Lin. "Global Patent Protection: Channels of North and South Welfare Gain," *Journal of Economic Dynamics & Control*, 30, 2006, 205–227.

Grinols, Earl L. "Public Provision of Private Health Care," prepared for the July conference at Sydney Sussex College, 2003, Cambridge University, Cambridge, England.

Grinols, Earl L., and James Henderson. "Replace Pharmaceutical Patents Now," *PharmacoEconomics*. 25(5), 2007, 355–365.

Groombridge, Mark. "America's Bittersweet Sugar Policy," Center for Trade Policy Studies, Cato Institute, Trade Briefing Paper No. 13, December 2001, 1–11.

Gruber, Jonathan. "Health Insurance and the Labor Market," in *Handbook of Health Economics*, Vol. 1, ed. A. J. Culyer and J. P. Newhouse. Amsterdam: Elsevier Science, 2000, 645–706.

Gruber, Jonathan, and Emmanuel Saez. "The Elasticity of Taxable Income: Evidence and Implications," *Journal of Public Economics*, 84(1), April 2002, 1–32.

Guell, Robert C., and Marvin Fischbaum. "Toward Allocative Efficiency in the Prescription Drug Industry," *The Milbank Quarterly* 73(2), 1995, 213–229.

Guesnerie, Roger, and Kevin Roberts. "Effective Policy Tools and Quantity Controls," *Econometrica*, 52(1), 1984, 59–86.

Hadley, Jack, and Judith Feder. "Hospital Cost Shifting and Care for the Uninsured," *Health Affairs*, 4(3), Fall 1985, 67–80.

Hadley, Jack, and John Holahan. "How Much Medical Care Do the Uninsured Use, and Who Pays for It?" *Health Affairs*, Web Exclusive, w3, 66–81, 12 February 2003. http://content.healthaffairs.org/cgi/reprint/hltaff.w3.66vl.

Hadley, Jack, and John Holahan. "Covering the Uninsured, How Much Would It Cost?" *Health Affairs*, June 4, 2003.

Hadley, Jack, John Holahan, Teresa Coughlin, and Dawn Miller, "Covering the Uninsured" in "2008: Current Costs, Sources of Payment, and Incremental Costs," *Health Affairs*, 27(5), September/October 2008 w399–w415.

Haislmaier, Edmund F. "The Significance of Massachusetts Health Reform," WebMemo No. 1035. Washington, DC: The Heritage Foundation, 11 April 2006.

Hansmann, Henry. *The Ownership of Enterprise*. Cambridge, MA: Harvard University Press, 1996.

Hayek, Friederich A. "Introduction" in *Bastiat, Frederic, Selected Essays on Political Economy*, trans. Seymour Cain, ed. George B. de Huszar. Irvington-on-Hudson, NY: The Foundation for Economic Education, Library of Economics and Liberty, 1995. www.econlib.org/LIBRARY/Bastiat/basEss0.html [accessed 4 August 2006].

Hellander, Ida. *U.S. Healthcare System: Best in the World or Just the Most Expensive*. The University of Maine, Bureau of Labor Education, Summer 2001.

Heller, M. A., and R. S. Eisenberg. "Can Patents Deter Innovation? The Anticommons in Biomedical Research," *Science*, 280(5364), 1998, 698–701.

Helms, Robert. *Medicare in the 21st Century: Seeking Fair and Efficient Reform*. Washington, DC: American Enterprise Insititute Press, 1999.

Herzlinger, Regina E., and Ramin Parsa-Parsi. "Consumer-Driven Health Care: Lessons from Switzerland," *Journal of the American Medical Association*, 292(10), 8 September 2004, 1213–1220.

Hillary for President, Press Release. "Retirement Security: A 401(k) Plan for All Americans." 9 October 2007. http://www.hillaryclinton.com/news/speech/view/?id=3640; see also http://www.hillary clinton.com/news/release/view/?id=3693 [accessed 28 November 2007].

Himmelfarb, G. "Welfare as a Moral Problem," *Harvard Journal of Law & Public Policy*, 19(3), 1996, 685–694.

Hixson, Jesse S. "Six Questions Everyone Should Ask about Health System Reform: An Application of Basic Economics," Galen Institute Health Policy Reports, March 2002 http://www.galen.org/fileuploads/Six_Questions.pdf.

Hungerford, Thomas L. "U.S. Income Mobility in the Seventies and Eighties," *Review of Income and Wealth*, 39(4), December 1993, 406.

Immerwahr, John. *The Affordability of Higher Education: A Review of Recent Survey Research*, A Report by Public Agenda for the National Center for Public Policy and Higher Education, National Center Report No. 02-4. http:// www. highereducation.org/affordability_pa/affordability_pa1.shtml [accessed 23 May 2003].

Institute of Medicine. *Crossing the Quality Chasm: A New Health System for the 21st Century*, March 2001 http://darwin.nap.edu/html/quality_chasm/reportbrief.pdf; full text of report available at http://www.nap.edu/books/0309072808/html/.

Jaffe, Adam B. "The U.S. Patent System in Transition: Policy Innovation and the Innovation Process," *Research Policy*, 29, 2000, 531–557.

Jewkes, John J. *Ordeal by Planning*. London: Macmillan, 1948.

Jewkes, John J. "Planners as a Species," in *New Ordeal by Planning: The Experience of the Forties and the Sixties*, 2d ed. London: Macmillan, 1968.

Joint Committee on Taxation. "Updated Distribution of Certain Federal Tax Liabilities by Income Class for Calendar Year 2001," JCX-65-01, 2 August 2001. http://www.house.gov/jct/x-65-01.pdf [accessed 7 December 2007].

Joint Economic Committee. "Updated Distribution of Certain Federal Tax Liabilities by Income Class for Calendar Year 2001," JCX-65-01, 2 August 2001.

Kaiser Foundation. "U.S. Healthcare System Should Pay Only for Cost-Effective Treatments," The Kaiser Foundation and The Advisory Board. www. kaisernetwork.org/dailyreports/healthpolicy.

Kaiser Foundation. "State High-Risk Health Insurance Pool Participation, December 31, 2004." http://www.statehealthfacts.kff.org/cgi-bin/healthfacts.cgi?action= compare&category=Managed+Care+%26+Health+Insurance&subcategory=High +Risk+Pools&topic=High+Risk+Pool+Participation.

Kaiser Foundation. "Health Insurance Survey, October 2004." kff.org/insurance/ loader.cfm?url=/commonspot/security/getfile.cfm&PageID = 48503.

Kaplow, Louis. "The Optimal Supply of Public Goods and the Distortionary Cost of Taxation," *National Tax Journal*, 49, 1996, 513–533.

Kaplow, Louis. "A Note on the Optimal Supply of Public Goods and the Distortionary Cost of Taxation," *National Tax Journal*, 51, 1, 1998, 117–125.

Kelly, Greg. "Can Government Force People to Buy Insurance?" The Council for Affordable Health Insurance, No. 123, March 2004. www.cahi.org/cahi_ contents/ resources/issues.asp.

Kindig, D. A. The Health Care System Should Produce Health, Physician Executive, July 1993, PubMed indexed for Medline. http://www.acpe.org/publications/ PEJ/index.aspx?expand=pej.

Kinsley, Michael. "Social Security: From Ponzi Scheme to Shell Game," *Washington Post*, 14 December 1996. http://www.slate.com/id/2405/.

Kling, Arnold. "How to Get What We Want: Better Healthcare," *San Chronicle*, 1 March 2006.

Kling, Arnold. *Crisis of Abundance: Rethinking How We Pay for Health Care*. Washington, DC: Cato Institute, 2006.

Kondracke, Morton. "Mandatory Insurance Could Solve Health Crisis, Aid Politicians," *New America Foundation*, 15 March 2004. http://www.newamerica.net/index.cfm? pg=article &DocID=1835.

Krasilovsky M. W., and S. Shemel. *This Business of Music*, 9th ed. New York: Billboard Books, Watson-Guptill, 2003.v

Kremer, Michael. "Patent Buyouts: A Mechanism for Encouraging Innovation," *The Quarterly Journal of Economics*, 113(4), November 1998, 1137–1167.

Ladd, Everett Carl, and Karlyn Bowman. *Attitudes toward Economic Inequality*. Washington, DC: American Enterprise Institute, 1998, 47–48. http://www.aei.org/ docLib/20040303_book393.pdf.

Lakdawalla, D., and N. Sood. "Insurance and Innovation in Health Care Markets." NBER Working Paper 11602. Cambridge, MA: National Bureau of Economic Research, September 2005. http://www.nber.org/papers/w11602 [accessed 15 August 2006].

Landro, Laura. "The Informed Patient: Preventative Care Falls Short of Target," *The Wall Street Journal*, 27 July 2005. www.prevent.org/newsletters/2005/dec/pdf/TheInformed PatientWSJarticle.pdf.

Leibenstein, Harvey. "Allocative Efficiency and X-Efficiency," *American Economic Review*, 56, 1966, 392–415.

Lemaire, Jean. "The Cost of Firearm Deaths in the United States: Reduced Life Expectancies and Increased Insurance Costs," *Journal of Risk and Insurance*, 72(3), 2005, 359–374.

Levin, Richard C. "A New Look at the Patent System," *The American Economic Review Papers and Proceedings*, 76(2), 1986, 199–202.

The Liberty Fund. "The Collected Works of James M. Buchanan." http://www.econlib.org [accessed 23 March 2008].

Lindahl, Erik. "Just Taxation – a Positive Solution," in *Classics in the Theory of Public Finance*, ed. Richard Musgrave and Alan Peacock. London: Macmillan, 1958, 98–123.

Lohr, Steve. "Government Wants to Bring Health Records into Computer Age," *The New York Times*, 21 July 2004. www.parsintl.com/pdf/8128-NYT.pdf.

Lomasky, Loren. "Medical Progress and National Health Care," *Philosophy and Public Affairs*, Winter 1981.

Lott, John. "An Explanation for Public Provision of Schooling: The Importance of Indoctrination," *Journal of Law and Economics*, 33(1), 1990, 199–231.

Ma, C. A., and Thomas G. McGuire, "Optimal Health Insurance and Provider Payment," *American Economic Review*, 87(4), 1997, 685–704.

Macfarlane, Alan. "Adam Smith and the Making of the Modern World," in *The Riddle of the Modern World; Of Liberty, Wealth and Equality*. New York: Macmillan, 2000. http://www.alanmacfarlane.com/TEXTS/Smith_final.pdf [accessed 5 December 2007].

Mann, Darrell. *Hands on Systematic Innovation*. Belgium: CREAX nv Press, 2002.

Manning, W. G., and M. S. Marquis. "Health Insurance: The Tradeoff between Risk Pooling and Moral Hazard," *Journal of Health Economics*, 15(5), 1996, 609–639.

Marquis, M. Susan, and Stephan H. Long. "The Uninsured Access Gap: Narrowing the Estimates," *Inquiry*, 31(4), Winter 1994/95, 405–414.

Martinez, Barbara. "Drug-Price Surge May Erode Savings from Medicard Card," *The Wall Street Journal*, 24 March 2004, B1.

Martinez, Barbara. "How Quiet Moves by a Publisher Sway Billions in Drug Spending," *The Wall Street Journal*, 6 October 2006, A1.

Mathews, Merrill, and Victoria Bunce Craig. "An Affordable Way to Help the Uninsured," The Council for Affordable Health Insurance, No. 120, November 2003. www.cahi.org/cahi_contents/resources/issues.asp.

Mayo Clinic. "A New U.S. Healthcare System Creating Substantial Reform by 2011," The Mayo Clinic, 2006. www.mayoclinic. org/health-care-reform/.

Mayo Clinic. "Recommendations," and "Recommendations Expanded Version: Universal Insurance Coverage," 2007. www.mayoclinic.org/healthpolicycenter/recommendationslong.html. [accessed 4 December 2007].

McWilliams, Gary, and Barbara Martinez. "Wal-Mart Cuts Prices for Many Generic Drugs to $4," *The Wall Street Journal*, 22 September 2006, B1.

Means, Gardiner C. "The Administered-Price Thesis Reconfirmed," *American Economic Review*, 62, June 1972, 292–306.

MedAdNews. "The Top 500 Drugs by Class of Drugs." *MedAdNews* 19(5), May 2000, 77–82.

MEPS HC-079: 2003 Full Year Data Consolidated File, November 2005. www.meps.ahrq.gov/PUFFiles/H79/H79doc.pdf.

Meredith, James. "A Challenge to Change," *Newsweek*, 6 October 1997, 18.

Mill, John Stuart. "Applications," Chapter V in *On Liberty*, 1896. http://muse.jhu.edu/journals/logos/v006/6.1mill.html [accessed 7 December 2007].

Minnesota Medical Association. Advocacy News, Updated February 2005. www.mmaonline.net/advocacyNews/fullstory.cfm?recNum=1204.

National Academy of Sciences. "Executive Summary" in *Insuring America's Health*, Washington, D.C.: National Academies Press, 2004, 1–14. http:/books.nap.edu/catalog/ 1087.html].

National Center for Policy Analysis. "Is Preventive Medical Care Cost-Effective?" 10 February 2006. www.ncpa.org/ba/ba188.html.

National Governors Association. "A National Healthcare Innovations Program: A Proposal to Increase the Cost-Effectiveness and Quality of the U.S. Health Care System." 10 February 2005. www.nga.org/cda/files/0502 HEALTHCARE.pdf.

National Health Expenditure Accounts Documentation. Center for Medicare and Medicaid Services, Web site. www.cms.hhs.gov.

"National Health Expenditures 2000–2004," in *Health Guide USA*. http://www.healthguideusa.org/health_statistics/national_health_expenditures_2000s.htm [accessed 23 February 2008].

National Partnership for Women and Families. "Compare Your Healthcare: Become an Informed Consumer." www.nationalpartnership.org/portals/p3/library/HealthCareQualityPatients Rights/CignaBrochure.pdf.

NBC News/Wall Street Journal Poll, 17–20 January 2007. http://www.pollingreport.com/health3.htm [accessed 21 February 2007].

Newhouse, Joseph P. "Reimbursing Health Plans and Health Providers: Efficiency in Production versus Selection," *Journal of Economic Literature*, 34, 1996, 1226–1263.

Newhouse, Joseph P. *Pricing the Priceless: A Health Care Conundrum*. Cambridge, MA: The MIT Press, 2002.

Newhouse, Joseph P., and the Insurance Experiment Group. *Free for All? Lessons from the RAND Health Insurance Experiment*. Cambridge, MA: Harvard University Press, 1993.

Nyman, John A. "The Economics of Moral Hazard Revisited," *Journal of Health Economics*, 18, 1999, 811–824.

OECD Health Data 2006. Paris: OECD, 2006.

OECD Health Data 2007. Paris: OECD, 2007.

O'Reilly, William. *Calendar*, 8 May 2002.

Organization for Economic Cooperation and Development (OECD). *Health Data 2006: Statistics and Indicators for 30 Countries*. Paris: OECD, June 2006.

Paine, Thomas. *Common Sense*, 1776. http://www.ushistory.org/paine/commonsense/singlehtml.htm [accessed 5 December 2007].

Passell, Jeffrey S. "Estimates of the Size and Characteristics of the Undocumented Population," Pew Hispanic Center, 2007. http://pewhispanic.org/reports/print.php?ReportID=44.

Passman, D. D. *All You Need to Know about the Music Business*, 5th ed. New York: Free Press, 2000.

Pauly, Mark V. "The Economics of Moral Hazard," *American Economic Review*, 58, 1968, 533–539.

Pauly, Mark V. "The Welfare Economics of Community Rating," *The Journal of Risk and Insurance* 37(3), September 1970, 407–418.

Pauly, Mark V. "Overinsurance and Public Provision of Insurance: The Roles of Moral Hazard and Adverse Selection," *The Quarterly Journal of Economics* 88(1), February 1974, 44–62.

Pauly, Mark V. *Doctors and Their Workshops*. Chicago: University of Chicago Press, 1980.

Pauly, Mark V. "Taxation, Health Insurance, and Market Failure in the Medical Economy, "*Journal of Economic Literature*, 24, 2 June 1986, 629–675.

Pauly, Mark V. "U.S. Health Care Costs: The Untold True Story," *Health Affairs*, 12, 1993, 152–159.

Pauly, Mark V. "Insurance Reimbursement," in *Handbook of Health Economics*, Vol. 1, ed. A. J. Culyer and J. P. Newhouse. Amsterdam: Elsevier Science, 2000, 537–560.

Pauly, Mark V. "Medicare Drug Coverage and Moral Hazard," *Health Affairs*, 23(1), 2004, 113–122.

Pauly, Mark V. "Statement of Mark V. Pauly, PhD, before the Joint Economic Committee." 22 September 2004. http://jec.senate.gov/archive/Documents/Hearings/paulytestimony22sep2004.pdf.

Pauly, Mark V., P. Danzon, P. Feldstein, and J. Hoff. "A Plan for Responsible National Health Insurance," *Health Affairs* 10(1), Spring 1991, 5–15.

Pauly, Mark V., A. Percy, and B. Herring. "Individual versus Job-Based Insurance: Weighing the Pros and Cons," *Health Affairs*, 1999 18(6), 28–44.

Pauly, Mark V., and Brad Herring. *Pooling Health Insurance Risks*. Washington, DC: AEI Press, 1999.

Pauly, Mark V. and John S. Hoff. *Responsible Tax Credits for Health Insurance*. Washington, DC: AEI Press, 2002.

Pear, Robert. "Academy of Sciences Calls for Universal Health Care by 2010." *The New York Times*, 15 January 2004.

Pharmaceutical Research and Manufacturers of America. "Coverage of Prescription Medicines in Private Health Insurance: Lower Level of Coverage for Medicines Than for Other Items," in *PhRMA Two-Pager Plus*, Washington, DC: PhRMA, Winter 2004.

Philipson, Tom, and George Zanjani. "Consumption versus Production of Insurance," NBER Working Paper No. 6225, October 1997.

Pinchot, Gifford. *Breaking New Ground*. Washington, DC: Island Press, 1947.

Polanvyi, M. "Patent Reform," *Review of Economic Studies* 11, 1943, 61–76

Pollock v. Farmers' Loan and Trust Company. No. 893. SUPREME COURT OF THE UNITED STATES. 157 U.S. 429; 15 S. Ct. 673; 39 L. Ed. 759; 1895 U.S. Lexis 2215; 3 A.F.T.R. (P-H) 2557.

Porter, Michael E. and Elizabeth Olmsted Teisberg. "Redefining Competition in Health Care," *Harvard Business Review* June 2004, 65–76.

President's Advisory Panel on Federal Tax Reform. *Simple, Fair, and Pro-Growth: Proposals to Fix America's Tax System: Final Report*, 3 November 2005. http://www.taxreformpanel. gov/final-report.

Rai, A. K. "Engaging Facts and Policy: A Multi-Institutional Approach to Patent System Reform," *Columbia Law Review*, 103(5), 2003, 1035–1135.

Ramsey, Frank. "A Contribution to the Theory of Taxation," *Economic Journal* 37, 1927, 47–61.

RAND Corporation. "Consumer Directed," in *Health Care Plans: Implications for Health Care Quality and Cost*. Santa Monica, CA: RAND, 2005.

Randall, M. *History of The Common School System of the State of New York,* New York: Ivison, Blakeman, Taylor & Co, 1871.

Reagan, Ronald. Speech to the British House of Commons, London, June 8, 1982. http://www.medaloffreedom.com/RonaldReaganBritishHouseofCommons.htm.

Reinhardt, Uwe E. "Resource Allocation in Health Care: The Allocation of Lifestyles to Providers," *Milbank Quarterly*, 65(2), 1987, 153–176.

Reinhardt, Uwe E. "The Swiss Health System: Regulated Competition without Managed Care," *JAMA*, 2004. jama.ama-assn.org/cgi/content/full/292/10/1227.

Reinhardt, Peter S. Hussey, and Gerald F. Anderson. "U.S. Healthcare Spending in an International Context," Health Affairs 23(3) May/June 2004, 10–25.

Reinhardt, Uwe E. "The Pricing of U.S. Hospital Services: Chaos behind a Veil of Secrecy," *Health Affairs*, 25(1), January/February 2006, 57–69.

Rice, Thomas, Katherine Desmond, and Jon Gabel. "The Medicare Catastrophic Coverage Act: A Post-Mortem," *Health Affairs*, 9(3), Fall 1990, 75–87.

Rice, Thomas. *The Economics of Health Reconsidered*. Chicago: Health Administration Press, 1998.

Ryan, Alan. "Do We Really Want Equality?" *The New Statesman*, 25 September 2000. www.newstatesman.com/200009250027.

Schiller, Mark. "From the President: Dancing with the Devil," *Journal of American Physicians and Surgeons*, 9(1), 2004, 5.

Scotchmer, Suzanne. "Standing on the Shoulders of Giants: Cumulative Research and the Patent Law," *The Journal of Economic Perspectives*, 5(1), 1991, 29–41.

Seldon, Thomas M. Ross H. Arnett III, Joel W. Cohen, Katherine R. Levit, David McKusick, John F. Moeller, and Samuel H. Zuvekas. "Reconciling the Medical Expenditure Estimates from the MEPS and NHA, 1996," *Health Care Financing Review*, 23, Fall 2001, 161–178.

Shavell, S., and T. van Ypersele. "Rewards versus Intellectual Property Rights," *Journal of Law & Economics* 44, 2001, 525–547.

Sheils, John, and Randall Haught. "The Cost of Tax-Exempt Health Benefits in 2004," *Health Affairs*, Web exclusive, W4, 25 February 2004, 106–112.

Short, Pamela Farley, and Deborah R. Graefe. "Battery-Powered Health Insurance? Stability in Coverage of the Uninsured," *Health Affairs*, 22(6), November/December 2003, 244–255.

Shortell, Stephen. "Getting the Quality of Care We Pay For," *San Francisco Chronicle,* 8 January 2006. www.sfgate.com/cgi-bin/article.cgi?f=/c/a/2006/01/08/EDG3EGJAG01.DTL&hw=shortell&sn=003&sc=274.

Smith, Adam. "Of Restraints upon the Importation from Foreign Countries of Such Goods as Can be Produced at Home," in Book IV, Chapter II, *An Inquiry Into the Nature and Causes of the Wealth of Nations.* Edinburgh: 1776a. http://www.adamsmith.org/smith/won-intro.htm [accessed 7 December 2007].

Smith, Adam. "Of the Expence of Supporting the Dignity of the Sovereign," *An Inquiry into the Nature and Causes of the Wealth of Nations by Adam Smith* (1776b), in Volume. 2, Chapter 1: PART IV, edited with an Introduction, Notes, Marginal Summary and an Enlarged Index by Edwin Cannan. London: Methuen, 1904. http://oll.libertyfund.org/title/119/39534/930105 [accessed 7 December 2007].

Spence, Michael. "Cost Reduction, Competition, and Industry Performance," *Econometrica* 52(1), 1984, 101–121.

Tanner, Michael. "No Miracle in Massachusetts: Why Governor Romney's Health Care Reform Won't Work," Briefing Papers No. 97. Washington, DC: Cato Institute, June 6, 2006.

Tompkins, Christopher P., Stuart H. Altman, and Efrat Eilat. "The Precarious Pricing System for Hospital Services," *Health Affairs*, 25(1), January/February 2006, 45–56.

TRIZ Journal. http://www.triz-journal.com/ [accessed 9 January 2007].

Tversky, Amos, and Daniel Kahneman. "Advances in Prospect Theory: Cumulative Representation of Uncertainty," *Journal of Risk and Uncertainty*, 5(4), 1992, 297–323.

U.S. Census Bureau. "Transitions in Income and Poverty Status: 1984–85," Series P-70, No. 15-RD-1, August 1989, 20.

U.S. Census Bureau. "Transitions in Income and Poverty Status: 1985–86," Series P-70, No. 18, June 1990, 21.

U.S. Census Bureau. "Transitions in Income and Poverty Status: 1987–88," Series P-70, No. 24, August 1991, 5.

U.S. Census Bureau. "Income, Poverty, and Health Insurance Coverage in the United States: 2005," in *Current Population Reports, Consumer Income*, Washington, DC: USGPO, 2006.

U.S. Census Bureau. "Income, Poverty, and Health Insurance in the United States: 2006," P60-233, Washington, DC, USGPO, August 2007.

USDA, Economic Research Service. "Food CPI, Prices and Expenditures: Food Expenditures by Families and Individuals as a Share of Disposable Personal Money Income," Table 8. http://www.ers.usda.gov/Briefing/CPIFoodAndExpenditures/Data/table8.htm [accessed 28 February 2008].

U.S. Government Accountability Office. "Long-Term Budget Outlook: Deficits Matter–Saving Our Future Requires Tough Choices Today," GAO-07-389T, Statement of David M. Walker, Comptroller General of the United States, Testimony before the Committee on the Budget, House of Representatives, 23 January 2007a.

U.S. Government Accountability Office. "Saving Our Future Requires Tough Choices Today," GAO-07-937CG, David M. Walker, Comptroller General of the United States, University of South Florida, 30 January 2007b.

U.S. Securities and Exchange Commission. "Pyramid Schemes." http://www.sec.gov/answers/pyramid.htm [accessed 7 December 2007].

U.S. Treasury Department, Office of Tax Analysis. "Household Income Mobility during the 1980s: A Statistical Assessment Based on Tax Return Data," *Tax Notes*, special supplement, 55(9) 1 June 1992.

U.S. Treasury Inspector General for Tax Administration. "The Internal Revenue Service Needs a Coordinated National Strategy to Better Address an Estimated $30 Billion Tax Gap Due to Non-filers," November 2005, Reference Number: 2006-30-006.

Verdecchia, Arduino, Silvia Francisci, Hermann Brenner, Gemma Gatta, Andrea Micheli, Lucia Mangone, Ian Kunkler, and the EUROCARE-4 Working Group. "Recent Cancer Survival in Europe: A 2000–02 Period Analysis of EUROCARE-4 Data," *Lancet Oncology*, 8 September 2007, 784–796.

Vernon, John A. "Simulating the Impact of Price Regulation on Pharmaceutical Innovation," *Pharmaceutical Development and Regulation*, 1(1), 2003, 55–65.

Von Neumann, John, and Oskar Morgenstern. *Theory of Games and Economic Behavior*. Princeton, NJ: Princeton University Press, 1944.

Waterson, Michael. "The Economics of Product Patents," *American Economic Review*, 80(4), 1990, 860–869.

Weale, Albert. "Ethical Issues in Social Insurance for Health," in *Health Care, Ethics and Insurance*, ed. Tom Sorell. New York: Routledge, 1998, 137–150.

Wedig, Gerald J. "Ramsey Pricing and Supply Side Incentives in Physician Markets," *Journal of Health Economics*, 12(4), 1993, 365–384.

West, E. G. *Education and the State*. London: The Institute of Economic Affairs, 1965.

West, E. G. "The Political Economy of American Public School Legislation," *Journal of Law and Economics*, 10 October 1967, 101–128.

White, J. *Competing Solutions*. Washington, DC: Brookings Institution, 1995.

White House. "President Bush Discusses Healthcare Initiatives," Office of the Press Secretary, Press Release, 4 April 2006.

WHO Global InfoBase Online (Obesity Rates). http://www.who.int/ncd_surveillance/ infobase/web/InfoBaseCommon [accessed 6 December 2007].

Wilper, Andrew P., Steffie Woolhandler, Karen E. Lasser, Danny McCormick, Sarah L. Cutrona, David H. Bor, and David U. Himmelstein. "Waits to See an Emergency Department Physician: U.S. Trends and Predictors, 1997–2004," *Health Affairs*, Web Exclusive, January 2008, 84–95

Wright, B. D. "The Economics of Invention Incentives: Patents, Prizes, and Research Contracts," *American Economic Review*, 73, 1983, 691–707.

Zweifel, Peter, and Frederich Breyer. *Health Economics*. New York: Oxford University Press, 1997.

Zweifel, Peter, and W. G. Manning. "Moral Hazard and Consumer Incentives in Health Care," in *Handbook of Health Economics*, ed. A. J. Culyer and J. P. Newhouse. New York: Elsevier, 2000, 409–459.

Zycher, Benjamin. "Comparing Public and Private Health Insurance: Would a Single-Payer System Save Enough to Cover the Uninsured?" Manhattan Institute for Policy Research, October 2007. http://www.manhattan-institute.org/html/ mpr_05.htm [accessed 26 February 2008].

Index